Due

THE CONTEMPORARY CONGRESS

THE
CONTEMPORARY
CONGRESS

Burdett Loomis

UNIVERSITY OF KANSAS

ST. MARTIN'S PRESS
NEW YORK

Sponsoring Editor: Beth A. Gillett
Editorial assistant: Kimberly Wurtzel
Manager, publishing services: Emily Berleth
Publishing services associate: Meryl Perrin
Project management: Publication Services
Production supervisor: Dennis Para
Cover design: Rod Hernandez
Cover photo: Jim Finlayson

Library of Congress Catalog Card Number: 94-74767

Manufactured in the United States of America

0   9   8   7   6
f   e   d   c   b   a

For information, write:
St. Martin's Press, Inc.
175 Fifth Avenue
New York, NY 10010

ISBN: 0-312-10399-9 (paperback)
        0-312-12305-1 (hardcover)

For Charlie Tidmarch:
good scholar, good guy,
good friend

Contents ⸙

Preface ❧

Sometimes, less is more. In seeking to write a relatively brief text on congressional politics, I found the very richness of the past thirty years' legislative research to be a serious obstacle to producing a lean, essaylike book that would emphasize the essence of the contemporary Congress. And then, near the very end of the project, Representative Newt Gingrich (R–Georgia) led the Republicans to a historic victory as they captured the House for the first time in forty years.

This book may well sit at the cusp of two eras on Capitol Hill. Our understanding of the post-1954, overwhelmingly Democratic Congress is solidly based in data and theory. The post-1994 Republican Congress may be a brief interlude, but odds are that the changes in partisan control will be much more fundamental and entrenched. Moreover, the high levels of legislative turnover in 1992 and 1994 have propelled a new generation of legislators into the Congress.

At least as important as the Republicans' House and Senate victories in 1994 has been the changing balance of power in Washington politics. Although we will not return to the late-nineteenth-century dominance of congressional leaders over a weakened presidency, we have witnessed a new era in legislative ascendancy in setting the national policy agenda, both in the Contract with America and the push for a balanced budget.

So, with a rich body of legislative research and a set of potentially revolutionary changes on Capitol Hill, I sought to write a brief overview of congressional politics. As my Scandinavian relatives would say, "Ufta." A rough English translation: "Are you kidding?"

In hewing to my original goal, I have kept the book short. In many ways, it is a thematic essay more than a text. My organizing concept remains an interpretation of the Congress as reflecting a continuing set of tensions between decentralization (centrifugal forces) and centralization (centripetal forces). The strengthened Democratic and Republican leaderships in the House have provided clear evidence of the possibilities of centralization, whereas the highly individualistic Senate remains hospitable to atomistic behavior. In addition, many of the key battles within the Congress can be cast in terms of centrifugal–centripetal tensions. Committee autonomy, the existence of informal legislative organizations, and the fights over pet "pork barrel" projects in an era of budgetary restraint exemplify the ongoing decentralization within a Congress that has at the same time become more centralized through enhanced party leadership.

My intellectual debts within the community on congressional scholars are overwhelming and widespread. Perhaps the most important debt, however, is to the American Political Science Association's Congressional Fellowship Program. Twenty years ago I arrived in Washington to spend a year on Capitol Hill. From my first few days in the Longworth Building, in the crowded office of then-freshman Representative Paul Simon, I knew that the Congress would occupy much of my attention for the remainder of my academic career. It has, to my continuing gratification.

This book is a result of conversations with Joanne Daniels, who expressed a reckless confidence in my ability to produce a well-done, brief volume. Don Reisman and Kimberly Wurtzel have been exceptionally patient as I mushed about in completing this project. As always, Michel and Dakota have proved highly supportive in myriad ways. And yes, Michel, I will clean up all the piles of stuff in my office. Right away. As soon as my mountain of "Newt" material begins to erode.

I would like to thank several reviewers whose suggestions led to improvements in the manuscript as it developed: Cary R. Covington, University of Iowa; Hulen Davis, Prairie View A&M University; Marjorie Randon Hershey, Indiana University, Bloomington; G. Calvin Mackenzie, Colby College; Ronald M. Peters, Jr., University of Oklahoma, Norman; Harold W. Stanley, University of Rochester; Randall W. Strahan, Emory University; and Shirley Anne Warshaw, Gettysburg College.

One ✑

MARGOLIES-MEZVINSKY, GINGRICH, AND THE POLITICS OF REPRESENTATION

A ugust 5, 1993. The vote was at hand on the most important proposal of President Bill Clinton's initial year in office—a five-year, $492-billion deficit reduction package. The top House Democratic leaders and the party's extensive whip organization had worked relentlessly to round up every available vote in support of the deficit reduction proposals that had resulted from endless hours of negotiations in House–Senate conference committee meetings. Almost every representative had come to the floor, eager to witness the concluding scene of this extended struggle. For those who remained undecided, there was no place to run, no place to hide.

As the fifteen minutes formally allowed for voting expired, almost all members had cast their ballots, but the electronic tally board showed the result as still in doubt. President Clinton's fellow Democrats would have to provide the margin of victory; no Republican had broken party ranks. Unanimously, the 174 minority-party legislators had voted against the Clinton package, with its combination of spending cuts and tax increases. Four Democratic members remained in the well of the House, waiting to cast their votes. Representative David Minge, a conservative first-term Minnesotan, wanted considerably more in spending cuts. Representative David Thornton, from the president's own state of Arkansas, and Representative Pat Williams, from Montana's wide-open spaces and ordinarily a staunch party loyalist, objected to the 4.3-cent gas tax increase. The president called Williams and pleaded, "I can't win this without you. My presidency is at stake."[1] Williams agreed to support the package, despite his desire to cast a "no" vote that

---

[1]Clifford Krauss, "Whips Use Soft Touch to Succeed," *The New York Times,* August 7, 1993, p. 29.

1

would please his constituents, who often drove long distances across Big Sky Country.

Representatives Thornton and Minge refused to budge, and both voted against the Clinton budget. For Thornton, to oppose his fellow Arkansan was an especially difficult decision. In the end, however, he observed, "My job is to represent the people of the Second Congressional District."[2]

That left the House's verdict on the Clinton budget proposal in the hands of first-term representative Marjorie Margolies-Mezvinsky (D–Pa.), who had previously announced her opposition to the plan and had steadfastly resisted any tax increases. Although Bill Clinton had received 46 percent of the vote—a bit above his average across the nation—in her upscale, suburban Philadelphia district, Margolies-Mezvinsky won her seat, held by Republicans for the previous seventy-six years, with the extremely narrow margin of 1,373 votes out of 254,000 cast. She had triumphed, she argued, because of her stand "on two basic principles: deficit reduction and holding the line on taxes."[3] True to her word, in May, during the initial House consideration of the 1994 budget, she had voted against the Clinton package. But now the president and the Democratic leadership turned up the pressure. Three months earlier, her support had not been needed, and she could cast her ballot in line with her constituents' clear preferences. By August, however, the House's backing for the budget bill had waned, and her vote had become essential for passage. The pressure on Representative Margolies-Mezvinsky was immense.

As she recounted, "The Speaker requested that I come down to the well and cast my vote. . . . The scoreboard showed the vote was 216–216. Pat Williams and I stood in the well, surrounded by our Democratic peers. . . . Barbara Kennelly, one of those encircling us, leaned over and said, 'You can't let the President down.' I stood there for a moment, and then I heard someone whisper in my ear, 'We need your vote.' 'You've got it,' I replied."[4] With that, she joined Representative Williams and signaled her "aye" vote in support of the measure. As she walked down the aisle of the House, "one Democrat after another hugged her, patted her on the back and touched her as if she were Joan of Arc. . . . Her Democratic colleagues cheered as the Republicans jeered 'Goodbye Marjorie.'"[5] Her vote, crucial for her president and her party leadership, had placed her very reelection in jeopardy. Could she explain her actions to her constituents? The question would hang in the air until November 1994.

---

[2]Ibid.

[3]Richard E. Cohen, "Baptism by Fire for House Newcomers," *National Journal*, June 5, 1993, p. 1366.

[4]Marjorie Margolies-Mezvinsky, *A Woman's Place . . .* (New York: Crown, 1994), p. 202.

[5]Krauss, op. cit.

On November 9, 1994, voters across the country rose up to defeat thirty-six congressional incumbents—thirty-four in the House, two in the Senate, and *every one of them a Democrat*. Representative Margolies-Mezvinsky's constituents narrowly chose her Republican challenger in a rematch of the 1992 election. In January 1995, the 104th Congress convened with fifty-two additional Republicans in the House, giving them a majority for the first time in forty years. The nine-seat GOP gain in the Senate meant that Republican majorities would organize both chambers. Representative Newt Gingrich (R–Ga.) and Senator Bob Dole (R–Kans.) became Speaker and majority leader, respectively, their majorities bolstered by seventy-three new Republican representatives and eleven first-term Republican senators. Remarkably, not one sitting Republican lost his or her seat in 1994. In suburban Philadelphia and across the nation, the voters repudiated the Democratic Congress; within five months of election day, as they had promised, Republican leaders had brought to a vote in the House all ten items in their widely publicized Contract with America, and nine of the ten had won approval.

Despite the changes, there was still considerable continuity. The Senate was slow to act on most of the Contract's provisions, and it defeated the balanced budget amendment to the U.S. Constitution. In both houses, most incumbents returned to Capitol Hill after successful reelection bids, even those who had voted in favor of the Clinton budget package. Indeed, a few hours after Margolies-Mezvinsky's highly publicized vote ensured the budget bill's passage in the House, a similar drama unfolded on the other side of the Capitol. Despite a number of misgivings, Senator Bob Kerrey (D–Neb.), who also faced reelection in 1994, finally agreed to support the Clinton budget. Echoing Montana's Representative Williams, Kerrey explained that he "could not and should not cast the vote that brings down [the Clinton] presidency."[6] Senator Kerrey's decision produced a 50–50 Senate deadlock that Vice-President Al Gore, empowered by the Constitution to be the chamber's presiding officer, broke to give the bill a 51–50 victory. By the narrowest of margins, congressional Democrats had supported their president's first major policy initiative—a mix of spending cuts, enhanced fees, and a modest tax increase for those with annual incomes over $140,000. The impact on Senator Kerrey was minimal. He maintained his distance from President Clinton but supported the president in 90 percent of his votes in 1994. In the end, he won his 1994 reelection bid with a healthy, if not overwhelming, 55 percent of the vote.

Given Kerrey's status as an independent-minded senator, a former governor, and a Vietnam war hero, his willingness to support an unpopular presidential position and his ability to survive the Republican sweep are not so surprising. But why would a first-term representative like Marjorie Margolies-Mezvinsky be singled out for intense scrutiny by the press and congressional

---

[6]Richard L. Berke, "A Walk Offstage, Holding Fate of Budget," *The New York Times,* August 7, 1993, p. 1.

Republicans? After all, 217 of her fellow Democrats voted for the Clinton package. For one thing, the very fact that her vote was so visible tells us a good deal about the contemporary Congress. Since 1986, both chambers have received "gavel-to-gavel" television coverage from C-SPAN. This means that hundreds of thousands of regular viewers monitor congressional actions on this cable network, and the audience swells during debates on key policy issues such as the budget or the Gulf War. Representative Margolies-Mezvinsky knew that some of her own constituents were surely in the audience and that many of them were more than happy to see her squirm.

Not only were her constituents watching; so were representatives of many of the interests that helped fund her 1992 campaign to the tune of $559,000. Both she and her supporters were gratified that she had won appointment to the powerful Energy and Commerce Committee, with its extensive jurisdiction over important issues ranging from toxic waste to telecommunications policy to health care. Party leaders, however, do not bestow such appointments by accident. The first-term legislator owed her committee seat to members of the Democrats' Steering and Policy Committee, a body that included the Energy and Commerce chairman, Representative John Dingell (D–Mich.). He and the party leaders did not offer valuable committee seats without expecting something in return.

For Representative Margolies-Mezvinsky, there may have been no way to avoid extensive publicity, but there would be many more opportunities to play to her legions of constituents, supporters, fellow partisans, and prospective opponents. Moreover, her price for voting with the president was his guarantee to appear at a conference on entitlement spending that she would hold in the fall. Clinton did participate in the Philadelphia event, which was nationally televised on C-SPAN, but Margolies-Mezvinsky's constituents were not appeased. She entered the 1994 campaign season badly trailing her prospective Republican opponents.

In the end, the continuing focus on Margolies-Mezvinsky's budget vote was exceptional; the vote was important, to be sure, but it was only one of a thousand or so recorded votes she cast before submitting herself to the electorate in November 1994. Rarely does a single vote spell doom for a legislator, but the visibility of her action made it difficult to overcome, and retribution on the part of the voters is nothing new. In a previous era, for example, Representative Brooks Hays (D–Ark.) cast a highly visible and unpopular vote in favor of a 1957 civil rights bill; he lost the next election despite a national Democratic landslide. Hays' defeat functioned as a beacon of caution for a generation of legislators who wondered if the next vote might be the one that their constituents might react against.

Although the drama of the last-minute voting decisions captured the public's attention, passing the 1993 budget bill, with its tax increases and spending cuts of almost $500 billion over five years, required more than eleventh-hour arm-twisting by Democratic leaders and wrenching decisions by wavering legislators. For months the Clinton Administration and the Democratic legislative leadership had sought to build a coalition that would pass a deficit reduction package. Despite Democratic control of both houses of Congress and the presidency, in contrast to the divided government of the previous twelve years (1981–1993), passage of meaningful legislation remained uncertain. Why this was so speaks volumes about the United States Congress both in contemporary terms and as it has developed as a political institution over the past 200 years.

In November 1992, the American electorate voted into office 56 Democratic senators (of 100) and 258 Democratic House members (of 435), along with a Democratic president. Party loyalty levels in congressional voting stood at modern highs in both chambers, especially in the House.[7] Most members of Congress agreed that reducing the budget deficit was one of the central problems facing the nation. Yet the Clinton Administration and the Democratic leadership in both houses had to pull out all the stops in order to pass a deficit reduction package. Why?

For the Congress, at least, the answer seems deceptively simple. In responding to 50 state electorates, 435 separate House constituencies, and thousands of distinct interests, the institution has organized itself in decentralized ways that impede the building of consistent majorities that can pass coherent legislation on difficult issues. This is not a recent phenomenon. Congress has traditionally been the "slow institution," emphasizing representation of interests rather than rapid, perhaps overly hasty, responses.[8] As recently as 1992, scholars could reach a rough consensus that in reflecting societal strains, the Congress had become "atomistic," even though some countering trends toward centralizing power could also be observed.[9]

Although members of Congress adopt party labels, express their support or opposition to presidential policies, and seek to solve difficult societywide problems, they must ultimately answer to 435 distinct constituencies in the House and 50 separate state electorates in the Senate. For the most part, American legislators are on their own as they seek election and reelection. They must raise the funds to finance their own campaigns, although parties and presidents will offer some assistance. Moreover, they must often survive primary elections within their own party, just to claim the Democratic or Republican label that they will carry into the November general election.[10]

---

[7]See David Rohde, *Parties and Leaders in the Postreform House* (Chicago: University of Chicago Press, 1991).

[8]Richard F. Fenno, Jr., "Strengthening a Congressional Strength," in Norman J. Ornstein, ed., *Congress in Change* (New York: Praeger, 1975).

[9]Allen D. Hertzke and Ronald M. Peters, "Introduction: Interpreting the Atomistic Congress," in Allen D. Hertzke and Ronald M. Peters, eds., *The Atomistic Congress* (Armonk, NY: M.E. Sharpe, 1992), chap. 1.

[10]Louisiana is exceptional in that it holds a blanket primary: If no candidate wins a majority, the top two vote-getters run off, regardless of party.

Coming to Capitol Hill, legislators will seek the help of party leaders and the president, especially if they share a party label, but they will also react to the pressures of interest groups, the pull of the committees to which they have been assigned, pleas of the bureaucracy that provides seemingly limitless information, and, of course, the often-inconsistent communications from their own constituents. They will be—as Representative Margolies-Mezvinsky was—pushed and pulled from all directions. This struggle is both mystifying and off-putting to those who seek to understand congressional politics. However, Congress is not entirely without order as it seeks to represent constituents and make coherent national policies.

REPRESENTATION AND COLLECTIVE CHOICE

The United States Congress is a representative institution comprising two bodies that must make a series of collective, authoritative decisions—laws.[11] Ordinarily, this occurs by majority vote, or, more accurately, a series of majority votes. Representatives and senators, although sporting party labels and owing much to their respective parties within the Congress, are still beholden to their own distinct district and statewide electorates. Political scientists Roger Davidson and Walter Oleszek distinguish between two different, if overlapping, visions of the United States Congress. On one hand, the legislators constitute a "Congress of Ambassadors," who congregate in Washington to pursue the interests of the individual states and districts. On the other hand, they meet together as a single "deliberative assembly" to address issues and reach accords that roughly serve the broad, collective interest of the nation as a whole.[12]

This sounds straightforward, but from its founding, the United States has embraced an independent, powerful legislature that has often been at odds with the two other branches of government, the presidency and the Supreme Court. Without direct, formal ties to the executive (in contrast to a parliamentary system, where cabinet ministers are drawn from the legislature[13]), the individual lawmakers have prospered by representing their own constituents, districts, states, regions, and specific interests, often at the expense of ill-defined or chimerical national interests. Legislative structures and practices have evolved that facilitate this tendency toward representation of particular

---

[11]David Vogler, *The Politics of Congress*, 6th ed. (Madison, WI: Brown and Benchmark, 1993).

[12]Roger Davidson and Walter Oleszek, *Congress and Its Members*, 3rd ed. (Washington, DC: CQ Press, 1990).

[13]In parliamentary systems, the executive (e.g., the prime minister) is often the leader of the majority party (or coalition among parties) *within* the chamber. The distinction between legislature and executive is thus blurred, especially when compared with the United States' separation of powers.

interests, thereby making it difficult to construct majorities. The rules of the Senate, for example, have long protected the rights of minorities, most notably by requiring supermajorities (usually 60 votes, but sometimes two-thirds of the members) to shut off debate on a bill. Indeed, extended debate—the filibuster—may be the single most distinctive feature of the highly individualistic U.S. Senate.

Although protecting the rights of individual legislators has forged the nature of the U.S. Senate, it is the decentralization of the committee system that has historically marked the operation of the House of Representatives. With its large membership, the chamber has used committees to conduct much of its legislative business. Writing in 1885, Woodrow Wilson observed that the entire House "sits, not for serious discussion, but to sanction the conclusions of its committees as rapidly as possible."[14] Even in 1885 this statement was hyperbole, but it does convey the House's organizational tendency toward decentralization through subunits, as opposed to a highly centralized party structure (as, for example, in the British Parliament). Although the relative power of committees has varied since 1789, it is the standing committee system, as much as any other characteristic, that has defined the operation of the House of Representatives.

Representation as Responsiveness

Legislators take representation very seriously. Although one common, negative view of the Congress depicts it as frequently immobilized by its ties to individual constituencies and interests, such a perspective may largely reflect the highly representative nature of the institution. Political theorist Hannah Pitkin has argued that political representation means "acting in the interest of the represented, in a manner responsive to them."[15] But knowing the wishes of one's constituents across a wide range of complex issues is difficult at best, given most citizens' low levels of knowledge and interest in most policy issues. Nonetheless, motivated by their desire to win reelection, members of Congress seek to represent their constituents as best they can, often trying to anticipate their desires.[16] In this context, representation may be best viewed as a set of overlapping attempts to respond to "a number of targets" within a legislator's environment.[17]

---

[14]Woodrow Wilson, *Congressional Government* (Boston: Houghton Mifflin, 1885).

[15]Hannah Pitkin, *The Concept of Representation* (Berkeley: University of California Press, 1967), p. 209.

[16]See Douglas Arnold, *The Logic of Congressional Action* (New Haven, CT: Yale University Press, 1990).

[17]Heinz Eulau and Paul D. Karps, "The Puzzle of Representation: Specifying Components of Responsiveness," *Legislative Studies Quarterly* 2 (August 1977), p. 241. Much of the following relies on the line of argument in this article.

Indeed, Eulau and Karps advance our understanding of representation by specifying it not in terms of mere agreement on policy preferences between legislators and their constituents. Rather, they outline four kinds of responsiveness that, taken together, constitute representation. These are, respectively, service responsiveness, allocation responsiveness, symbolic responsiveness, and policy responsiveness.[18]

Consider the 1993 actions of Representative Glen Poshard, a Democratic legislator from Illinois' southernmost district. He continued to provide the high levels of service (such as retrieving a lost social security check) that had become a hallmark of his representative style since his initial election in 1986. He sought to have flood relief funding allocated to his hard-hit Mississippi River district and made sure that local newspapers reported on his visible, if symbolic, concern for flood victims. Finally, he voted to support broad policy initiatives in the Clinton budget reconciliation package even though many of his downstate Illinois constituents might well have desired more spending cuts and fewer new taxes.

Put in slightly different terms, on some issues Representative Poshard acted as a delegate[19] of his constituents, especially when their interests and preferences were clear—flood relief; conversely, on other issues, such as the budget, he acted more like a trustee, who had to sort through complex policy options and decide what was most "in the interest of the represented," to use Pitkin's language. After making such a policy choice, he then had to explain his action to his constituents. This after-the-fact explanatory behavior is central to representation, in that it allows constituents to assess their legislators' broad policy decisions, which are often made with only a vague sense of district opinion. Members of Congress must anticipate their constituents' reactions and subsequently educate them in terms of the merits of a vote or policy position. If a legislator has acted responsively on the dimensions of service, allocation, and symbolism, he or she may well have more latitude in convincing district constituents to accept the less popular policy choices made on their behalf.[20]

Deliberation

The focus on individual legislators and their attention to their own districts has often obscured the role of the Congress as a deliberative body capable of

---

[18]Ibid.

[19]The trustee–delegate distinction between representative styles has its roots in Edmund Burke's speech to his Bristol parliamentary constituents in the eighteenth century. The modern discussion derives from Warren E. Miller and Donald E. Stokes, "Constituency Influence in Congress," *American Political Science Review* 57 (March, 1963), pp. 45–57.

[20]For more extensive development of this theme, see Richard F. Fenno, Jr., *Home Style* (Boston: Little Brown, 1978); and Douglas Arnold, *The Logic of Congressional Action* (New Haven, CT: Yale University Press, 1990).

engaging in productive debates on policy issues, large and small. Such discussions do not always occur. For example, the extended congressional consideration of health care reform in 1993–1994 produced little reasoned give and take. Rather, deliberation simply disappeared under a deluge of highly publicized claims, counterclaims, and appeals to emotion.[21] More generally, meaningful deliberation is often missing in congressional debates.[22] As David Vogler and Sidney Waldman point out, reaching decisions on difficult issues is more than simply producing a majority that carries the day. They conclude that

> the democratic legitimacy of Congress rests on both the legislative process and the resulting policies. The value of unitary democracy [that emphasizes face-to-face deliberation] is found not simply in widespread agreement or consensus *but in the creative nature of the process itself.*[23]

The potential for creative solutions to difficult problems continues to reside within the Congress, and there is ample opportunity for deliberation, although much more so in committees, within informal task forces, and perhaps in the House gym than on the floor of either chamber. Only rarely can one tune in C-SPAN and observe substantive deliberation among legislators who are seeking to exercise their creative powers. Rather, one is treated to legislative position taking par excellence, in which almost all senators and representatives represent some specific point of view. Effective deliberation, to the extent that it occurs at all, takes place offstage, where legislators need not worry that their constituents and campaign contributors are watching intently.

Ironically, when Congress does rise to the occasion and acts as a deliberative assembly, the normally skeptical, even cynical, public embraces the congressional actions. The Congress that worked with Lyndon Johnson to enact his Great Society programs achieved widespread popularity among the public; twenty-five years later, another Congress won accolades for its cogent deliberations over the merits of the Persian Gulf War. But public support dipped to new lows for the Congress that cobbled together a highly symbolic crime bill in 1994 and found itself unable to engage in much useful debate over health care reform. Unquestionably, individual legislators can act in their *own* interests, but Congress as a collective finds it most difficult to act for the *whole.*

What, then, are we to make of the rush of legislation through the House of Representatives in the first few months of the 104th Congress? The Republicans

---

[21]See, for example, James Fallows, "A Triumph of Misinformation," *The Atlantic* 275:1 (January 1995), pp. 26–37.

[22]See, for example, the arguments put forth by Representative Gerald Soloman (R–N.Y.) and Donald R. Wolfensberger, "The Decline of Deliberative Democracy in the House and Proposals for Change," *Harvard Journal of Legislation* 31 (1993), pp. 320–370.

[23]David J. Vogler and Sidney R. Waldman, *Congress and Democracy* (Washington, DC: CQ Press, 1984), p. 166.

followed their historic electoral sweep with a legislative whirlwind in the House that was without parallel in this century. Speaker Gingrich and the House GOP captured the agenda and brought the ten Contract items to a vote. An initial analysis would give them high marks for responsiveness and, perhaps, representation and low scores for deliberation. By effectively nationalizing the 1994 congressional elections, using the Contract with America as a legislative agenda, and setting up their individual House offices, Republicans demonstrated all four kinds of responsiveness:

1. By refusing to cut back on office staff, they retained the ability to provide high levels of service to their constituents.
2. By supporting a tax cut, they allocated funds back to their constituents.
3. By passing the balanced budget constitutional amendment, they adopted a policy that was backed by the public at large.
4. By voting in favor of a term limits amendment, but by less than the required two-thirds majority, they proved themselves symbolically responsive to a popular public position without endangering their own seats.

More generally, the Contract allowed House Republicans to claim that they were acting in response to an overall mandate from the electorate, even if the Contract was at best a minor element of their triumph.

At the same time, the first few months of Speaker Gingrich's tenure in the House proved almost completely devoid of deliberation. Constitutional amendments were pushed through committees in a few days, as were tax cuts. As the first 100 days came to a close, the Senate found itself with a huge backlog of major policy initiatives that had gone essentially without deliberation in the House. Indeed, many House Republicans assumed, even hoped, that the Senate's slower, deliberative style would temper the energy and partisanship of the House actions on such items as regulatory reform, welfare reform, and the proposed tax cut.

THE CONTEMPORARY CONGRESS

This book will address the tension between the constituency-oriented, individualistic Congress that emphasizes the representation of particular interests and the Congress that can, on occasion, act coherently to pursue some broader representative goals, perhaps achieving this through creative deliberation. Much of this tension is expressed in organizational terms, with overall tendencies toward decentralization and individualism being countered by the centralizing forces of party and presidential leadership. Even the most centrifugal of forces, such as locally oriented congressional elections, sometimes reflect the unifying pull of national trends, as demonstrated by the elections of 1964, 1974, 1980, and, most recently, 1994.

This book provides a series of related pictures of the Congress that builds on the three aspects of legislative life:

1. The strong element of fragmentation, or decentralization, which reflects centrifugal forces on the Congress. These forces result from the pull of district constituencies, congressional committees, reelection campaigns, individual member offices, and the effects of interests outside the institution.

2. The corresponding centralizing (or centripetal) forces, such as the party leadership, the president, and, on occasion, landmark elections, public opinion, national crises, and broad coalitions of interests.

3. The continuing tensions between the ever-present centrifugal and centripetal forces within the Congress. Even in the extremely decentralized, fragmented period of the late 1970s, there were many forces pushing the Congress toward greater centralization. Indeed, far more interesting and important than merely categorizing different elements of the Congress as centrifugal or centripetal is to examine the interplay between these forces, which simply never ends—and which was dramatically illustrated by Representative Margolies-Mezvinsky's wrenching either-or vote choice between the pressures of Democratic leaders and her constituents.

The next chapter traces the evolution of the modern Congress across two centuries of representation. Chapter 3 focuses on the context of Congress, especially the growth of organized interests and the explosion of national policy, which create hundreds upon hundreds of new constituencies for members to represent. Indeed, the growth of government reflects one essential tension in a Congress increasingly made up of relatively young and conservative Republicans who have little stake in many federal programs.

Chapters 4, 5, and 6 emphasize the foundations of congressional decentralization: elections, committees, and the "enterprises" that surround each senator and representative.[24] Individual legislators mount their own campaigns, operate within the specialized environments of committees, and control substantial resources that afford them great flexibility of action. Should we be surprised that they are hard to organize into working majorities?

Chapters 7 and 8 offer insights into the usual channels of coordination and centralization on Capitol Hill, direction from congressional party leaders and the president. Strangely enough, as the House grew more fragmented in the 1970s with the expansion of subcommittees and the sharp increase in individual office

---

[24]Robert Salisbury and Kenneth Shepsle, "The U.S. Congressman as Enterprise," *Legislative Studies Quarterly* 6 (November 1981), pp. 559–576.

resources, party leaders also won substantial powers. By the mid-1980s, House Democratic leaders harnessed many of these procedural and appointive powers, and Speaker Jim Wright (D–Tex.), backed by the Democratic Caucus, was briefly able to wield great influence. Beset by ethics problems and a restive membership, Wright surrendered the Speakership and his House seat, and the Democratic leadership found itself faced with various minor scandals and a general loss of public confidence. The 1992 election of Bill Clinton brought with it the promise of single-party control of the executive and legislative branches for the first time in twelve years, yet President Clinton found it difficult to muster party-based majorities, especially in light of Senate delaying tactics that often required sixty votes to overcome. Then, in 1995, the Speakership of Representative Newt Gingrich demonstrated strikingly how strong a contemporary House leader could become, although the individualistic Senate remained a much less malleable institution.

Chapter 9 focuses on the formal and informal elements of congressional decision making; both formal rules and informal "folkways" contribute to the tensions between centralizing and decentralizing aspects of policy choice on Capitol Hill. Chapter 10 provides two contrasting case studies: health care reform, where particular interests overwhelmed the policy process, and the Contract with America, where a determined, centralized partisan majority worked its will. Assessing what changed between the unraveling of health care reform in 1994 and the adopting of most Contract items in 1995 may tell us a great deal about the nature of contemporary legislative politics. The richness and scope of these issues allow for extended illustrations of almost all of the general arguments made in chapters 3 through 9, as well as some concluding thoughts on the continuing tensions between centrifugal and centripetal forces in congressional politics, tensions that the Framers recognized and incorporated into the Constitution and that continue to define the essence of decision making on Capitol Hill.

Two ❧

CONGRESSIONAL DECENTRALIZATION IN DESIGN AND EVOLUTION

T he Framers of the Constitution faced a dilemma: how to create a strong national government that would not use its powers in arbitrary or antidemocratic ways. Within the republican construct of federalism and a separation of powers, the powers of the Congress were spelled out in far more detail than were those of the executive or judicial branches. The contradictory concerns of how to concentrate power and simultaneously limit it led the Framers to design a potentially powerful Congress that is capable of acting quickly and decisively, but is ordinarily slow and cautious in struggling to represent the disparate interests of its widely varied constituencies. The Framers might have a difficult time recognizing the size and scope of the modern presidency or the policy reach of the Supreme Court (for example, the *Roe v. Wade* abortion decision based on the "right to privacy," which is nowhere detailed in the Constitution), but most would be at home in a contemporary congressional debate such as that on the North America Free Trade Agreement, in which national benefits (increased exports through lower tariffs) were juxtaposed with potential local costs (the loss of jobs to cheaper foreign labor).

THE FRAMERS CONSTRUCT A CONGRESS

Although they recognized the need for a strong, effective central government, the Framers worried greatly over the potential for abuse that comes with any concentration of power. After all, they had fought a revolution to rid themselves of the British monarchy. By providing the Congress with large grants of well-defined authority, most notably the powers to tax and spend, they placed the largest share of national power in legislative hands. At the same time, "the Framers regarded [the Congress as likely] to succeed in deceiving and dominating the people."[1] They thus engineered a number of design features into

---

[1]For an extended discussion, see Martin Diamond, Winston M. Fisk, and Herbert Garfinkel, *The Democratic Republic* (Chicago: Rand McNally, 1966), pp. 75ff.

the Constitution to reduce the possibility of systematic abuse by willful congressional majorities. Its three basic elements were

1. The representation of "a multiplicity of interests" within an "extended republic."[2]
2. The separation of powers at the national level into the legislative, judicial, and executive branches.
3. The creation of a bicameral (two-chamber) legislative body.

These provisions defined a decentralized congressional structure in three distinct ways. First, the representational nature of the legislature would work against the concentration of power. The Framers knew from first-hand experience how difficult it was to build majority positions from the diverse views harbored by legislators with differing district, state, and regional backgrounds. Even so, vigorous representation of various interests and constituencies was scarcely enough to check a determined congressional majority. Curbing the potential for tyranny required permanent structural barriers to legislative dominance. This was accomplished by constructing both external and internal limitations on the congressional majorities—the separation of powers and bicameralism, respectively.

Second, the separation of powers provides both independence for each of the three branches and the capacity for each branch to retain that independence by checking the actions of the others.[3] This elemental decentralizing feature of American government has produced legendary intragovernmental confrontations ranging from the congressional censuring of President Andrew Jackson in 1834 to the Supreme Court's unanimous 1974 decision requiring President Richard Nixon to hand over the Watergate tapes to the Congress.[4] At the same time, interbranch cooperation is crucial, especially between the executive and legislative branches, for the power of the national government to be effectively mustered. Thus, the president must continually act to promote his legislative agenda, while the Congress presses its own oversight of the executive branch and government bureaucracy. In addition, the judicial branch imposes its own constraints on congressional actions, given its powers to rule laws unconstitutional and to interpret their applications. A substantial amount of legislative activity lies in Congress's responses to judicial

---

[2]Ibid.

[3]See Louis Fisher, *The Politics of Shared Power,* 2nd ed. (Washington: CQ Press, 1987), pp. 4ff.

[4]On the Jackson episode, see Senator Robert C. Byrd, "The Senate Censures Andrew Jackson," in his *The Senate 1789–1989: Addresses on the History of the United States Senate* (Washington: U.S. Government Printing Office, 1988), pp. 127–141. Among many sources on Nixon and the White House tapes, see Louis Fisher, *Constitutional Conflicts between Congress and the President* (Princeton, NJ: Princeton University Press, 1985), pp. 213ff.

decisions (for example, abortion policy in the wake of *Roe v. Wade* and subsequent cases).

Third, not content to rely on external checks on the Congress, the Framers created formidable internal restraints as well. Most of these derive from the adoption of a bicameral structure with distinctive bases of power for each legislative chamber. Given the tendency of legislative authority to dominate in a representative government, James Madison concluded that "the remedy for this inconvenience is, to divide the legislature into different branches; and to render them, by different modes of election, and different principles of action, as little connected with each other, as the nature of their common functions and their common dependence on society, will admit."[5]

The Constitutional Convention's fundamental compromise was to create a two-chamber structure in which only members of the lower body, the House of Representatives, would be elected directly by the people. Senators would be selected by state legislatures, and each state would be represented by two senators, regardless of its population.[6] Senate terms would stretch for six years, as opposed to the two years given Representatives. The Senate would be accorded the power to ratify treaties and confirm executive-branch appointments, and the House would be granted the sole authority to originate revenue bills.

Among their myriad accomplishments, the Framers of the Constitution succeeded in laying the groundwork for a strong national government. This potential for centralized power—realized in fits and starts over the past 200 years—was simultaneously checked by representation of diverse interests, the separation of powers, and a bicameralism that roughly balanced the strengths of the two chambers. Even before the first Congress met or before George Washington assumed the presidency, the stage had been set for the tensions between centrifugal and centripetal forces that have characterized American legislative politics since 1789.

What follows is in no way a complete history, even in outline form, of the United States Congress. Rather, the emphasis on a succession of congressional eras offers a series of sketches on how the legislature has developed since its inception and how the initial tensions over representation and structural experiments, such as bicameralism, have shaped the nature of the institution. Indeed, even as Republicans won control of both houses of Congress in 1994 for the first time in forty years, Speaker Gingrich and his unified band of 230 GOP Representatives were forced to contend with a Senate that has been less eager to enact sweeping legislation and a Democratic president who can exercise his constitutional veto powers.

---

[5]From *Federalist* 51, quoted in Ross Baker, *Senate and House* (New York: Norton, 1989), p. 33.

[6]This practice was ended by the 1913 ratification of the Seventeenth Amendment, which provided for the popular election of senators, although such elections had been adopted widely, if informally, in many states.

THE EARLY CONGRESS: ORGANIZATION AND TENSIONS

Despite defining congressional powers more clearly, and at much greater length, than the other national branches of government, the Constitution did little to dictate how the two houses would be organized.[7] No mention is ever made of committees or political parties; only the offices of Speaker, President of the Senate (the vice-president), and the Senate's President Pro Tempore are noted, although without any demarcation of their duties. The larger size of the House (65 members in 1789 and 181 by 1813, in contrast to 26 and 36 senators for the same years, respectively) led to the development of a more complex structure to conduct its business. To take advantage of its numbers, the House soon developed the decentralized standing committee system that remains an organizational hallmark of the body. Concurrently, however, the House's size also fostered the growth of political parties that served to pull together the diverse interests of their members, who had soon begun to feel the centrifugal pull of their committees as well as that of their constituencies.

For the first ten Congresses, most committees operated as ad hoc bodies to "perfect" the work done by the Committee of the Whole House,[8] but gradually—especially after 1825—standing committees, which continued from one Congress to the next, took on the major tasks of writing and revising legislation.[9] Reliance on growing numbers of committees illustrates the increased decentralization of the House. This organizational style benefited the average Representative by allowing each committee to become expert in its own policy area and share that knowledge with the rest of the members.[10] Moreover, by facilitating a division of labor, the House could take advantage of the very condition—its large number of members—that rendered it most unwieldy.

As committees were beginning to develop the specialized expertise essential to address particular issues, the House also needed some way to build consistent majorities. As with committees, congressional leaders turned to a

---

[7] Elaine Swift argues that the Senate, in particular, consumed much of the Framers' attention. See her *The Making of an American Senate* (New York: Cambridge University Press, 1996).

[8] George Galloway, *History of the House of Representatives* (New York: Thomas Crowell, 1961), p. 70. The Committee of the Whole House is the organizational format in which the House conducts almost all of its business. Rules are somewhat more permissive in this circumstance, and the legislative process is expedited. See Walter Oleszek, *Congressional Procedures and the Policy Process,* 3rd ed. (Washington: CQ Press, 1989), pp. 144ff.

[9] Joseph Cooper, perhaps the leading scholar of congressional organization, concludes that a standing committee system was established by Jackson's presidency. See his *Origins of the Standing Committees and the Development of the Modern House* (Houston: Rice University Press, 1970). Galloway (op. cit.) puts the date at 1816, although he notes that "by 1825, with the appointment of their chairmen by the Speaker . . . so far as its organization was concerned the House of Representatives had assumed its present form" (p. 99).

[10] The contribution of committees to both particularism and the beneficial sharing of expertise will be explored at some length in chap. 5.

structural answer. American politicians of the 1790s–1830s gradually invented a new organization designed for a republican form of government—the political party.[11] Although scholars disagree about the extent of partisanship and party organization in the first two decades of constitutional government, there were distinct factions that opposed each other in elections and within the legislature. As early as the Second Congress (1791), even though parties had not become formalized, "common ideas and concerns were fast binding men together, and when Congress met, many individuals in both houses became more or less firmly aligned into two voting groups—Federalists on one side and republican-minded [a Madison–Jefferson faction] on the other."[12]

The central figure in establishing strong parties and leadership in the House was Representative Henry Clay of Kentucky, who energized the Speakership during his three periods of service in that chamber. By 1814, Clay and his colleagues "had succeeded in erecting a new system, based on the party caucus, in which legislative leadership was now the prerogative of a group of prominent men in the House of Representatives."[13]

Party divisions and organizational strength would vary over the next four decades, but by 1825 the beginnings of a stable party system with regular leaders and consistent voting patterns had taken firm hold as a centralizing force within the House. Indeed, by this time, both committees and parties were established to the point that a scholar could write in 1917, "so far as its organization was concerned, the House of Representatives had assumed its present form."[14] This is a significant observation for contemporary legislative politics because the House of both the 1825 and 1917 eras contained both strong committee systems and forceful, coherent party leaderships, much like that of the Democratic House of Speaker Jim Wright (1987–1989) and the Republican chamber under Speaker Gingrich (1995–).

Through the early 1820s the House, with its emerging structure and growing numbers, was accorded more weight than the Senate largely because of the direct election of its members.[15] The Senate, however, was also changing, if more through evolution than through the impatient leadership of a Clay. By 1830, the Senate had moved from being an elitist imitation of the English

---

[11]The scholarship here is extensive. In relation to Congress, see, for example, James S. Young, *The Washington Community: 1800–1828* (New York: Columbia University Press, 1966); Allan G. Bogue and Mark Marlaire, "Of Mess and Men: The Boardinghouse and Congressional Voting, 1821–1842," *American Journal of Political Science* 19 (May 1975), pp. 207–230; and John F. Hoadley, *Origins of American Political Parties* (Lexington: University of Kentucky Press, 1986).

[12]Alvin M. Josephy, Jr., *On the Hill* (New York: Touchstone, 1979), p. 79.

[13]Galloway, *History of the House of Representatives,* p. 99.

[14]Ralph V. Harlow, *The History of Legislative Methods in the Period Before 1825* (New Haven, CT: Yale University Press, 1917), pp. 176–177.

[15]Ross K. Baker, *House and Senate,* 2nd ed. (New York: W. W. Norton, 1995), pp. 37–38.

House of Lords to a strongly American institution—"close to the people, as proactive as the House, and independent of the executive."[16]

SENATE INDIVIDUALISM AND HOUSE FRAGMENTATION: 1830–1860

By the beginning of the Jackson Administration in 1829, the Senate had begun to attract the most formidable leaders of the day, such as Kentucky's Henry Clay. Clay, who had instituted vigorous party leadership in the House before serving as secretary of state, continued his illustrious, meandering career by returning to Congress in 1831 as a Whig senator. There he would join such notables as Daniel Webster (Whig–Mass.), John Calhoun (D–S.C.), and Thomas Hart Benton (D–Mo.) in a chamber composed of the most notable men of the era. The French observer Alexis de Tocqueville contrasted the "vulgarity" he found in the House with the Senate, which he described as being filled with "eloquent advocates, distinguished generals, wise magistrates, and statesmen of note."[17]

Although many senators operated skillfully behind the scenes, this was a time of great individual oratory and sweeping attempts to hold the Union together. Setting the stage for the era's politics was the legendary Webster–Hayne debate of 1829, which defined the slavery issue in terms of the survival of the Union as a whole. Several other subthemes also ran through the Senate of the 1830s, most of them revolving around the roles of the states and the national government, slavery, the populistic aims of Jackson and the Democratic Party, and the sectional split within the Democrats' ranks between New York's Martin Van Buren and John Calhoun.[18] The freedom of individual action within the still-small Senate (forty-eight members in 1831) meant that coalitions could form and reform as these able legislators jockeyed for advantage over a wide range of issues. All the while, they understood that their fundamental division over slavery might destroy the very system of government that allowed them to flourish.

In contrast, the House found it difficult to organize itself coherently in the 1830–1860 period. With a larger, less stable membership than the Senate, the House could not as easily rely on the leadership of strong individual legislators. Nor could it count on its party factions and sectional interests to provide the organizational coherence demanded by the fractious body. Extended, bitter contests for the Speakership became commonplace. In 1849, for example,

---

[16]Swift, *The Making of an American Senate*, chap. 5.

[17]From *Democracy in America*, quoted in *Origins and Development of Congress*, 2nd ed. (Washington: Congressional Quarterly, Inc., 1982), p. 215.

[18]Byrd, *The Senate: 1789–1989*, p. 107.

five major groupings vied for control, and a Speaker was finally elected on the sixty-third ballot after the members agreed that the office could be awarded to the candidate who won a plurality, not a majority, of the votes. In 1855, a mix of Whigs, Republicans (a newly formed party), Democrats, and various minor parties went 133 ballots before selecting (again by plurality) antislavery Representative Nathaniel Banks (Mass.) of the nativist American (Know-Nothing) Party.

Finally, in the 36th Congress (1859–1861), which again harbored no clear party majority, forty-four ballots over three months were required to elect the most unlikely of Speakers: William Pennington (R–N.J.), who was serving his first (and last!) term in the House. His election to this post matched Henry Clay's 1811 victory as a first-term representative, but Clay had won the Speakership because of his strong personality and forceful leadership qualities; conversely, Pennington was the lowest common denominator in a highly fragmented chamber of a nation that was about to burst apart.

THE RISE OF THE MODERN CONGRESS: 1860–1920

Between the Civil War years and the end of World War I, the United States Congress underwent a series of organizational restructurings that culminated in what can be called its modern form by about 1920. The combination of a growing national industrial base and an increasing U.S. role in world affairs required the legislative branch to adapt to a very different environment than that of the pre-1860 United States, in which an agrarian nation had wrestled with the fundamental, highly divisive slavery issue.

Over the 1860–1920 period, the Congress experimented with strong party leadership in both chambers, created and then limited a separate committee for appropriations, first dominated a series of weak presidents and later looked to the president for coherent leadership initiatives, and eventually moved toward the mixture of standing committee decentralization and oligarchy that would characterize the institution until the mid-1960s. Why such a flurry of activity? As a representative body, the Congress adapts to its environment; new members enter the body, new issues come before it, and new party alignments arise. In the course of adapting to broad societal changes (such as industrialization in the late 1800s and early 1900s) the Congress has often restructured itself internally to consolidate power and regularize procedure.[19]

---

[19]See Roger Davidson and Walter Oleszek, "Adaptation and Consolidation: Structured Innovation in the U.S. House of Representatives," *Legislative Studies Quarterly* 1 (1977), pp. 37ff.

The House

For more than a quarter-century after the Civil War, Congress dominated national politics and policy making, but battles raged over the control of both chambers. Standing committees dominated the legislative process, especially after the House stripped the upstart Appropriations Committee (established in 1865) of much of its authority. At the same time, a number of strong Speakers increased the power of their office; in particular the Speaker could appoint all committee members and could aggressively employ his power to recognize members who wished to speak. Still, Davidson and Oleszek conclude that in the 1880s, "despite growth in the Speaker's prerogatives, centrifugal forces in the House remained strong, even dominant."[20] Although committees contributed to this dominance, even more significant was the almost total inability of House majorities to work their will, largely because of delaying tactics that allowed any member to slow actions of the chamber to a crawl.

Enter Speaker Thomas Brackett Reed (R–Maine), elected to lead the House in 1889. In his first three months as Speaker he rewrote the House rules from his position as chair of the Rules Committee and—on the House floor—revised the rules for recognition of a quorum (a majority of all members). Since the 1830s the House had operated under the odd, but powerful, precedent of not recognizing the presence of those who sat mute in the chamber, refusing to answer a quorum call.[21] As Representative Benjamin Butterworth (R–Ohio) put it, a member may, "while present, arise in his place and assert that he is absent, and we must take his word for it. What an absurdity on the face of it. . . . It is the weapon of anarchy."[22] A unanimous, if slender, Republican majority upheld Reed's decision that all members physically present would be counted as present in constituting a quorum. This ruling was reconfirmed by the Democrats when they took control of the House in the early 1890s.

Reed's quorum ruling and other rules that consolidated organizational power opened the way for twenty years of great centralization in the House. Speakers Reed, Charles Crisp (D–Ga.), and, most notably, Joseph Cannon (R–Ill.) increasingly employed the formidable weapons that the position had accumulated. From 1903 to 1909, "Uncle Joe" Cannon steadily became more

---

[20]Ibid., p. 23.

[21]Davidson and Oleszek note that the "disappearing quorum appears to have originated with [former President] John Quincy Adams, . . . who served with distinction in the House after leaving the White House." Adams refused to vote on a proslavery measure in 1832, and enough fellow members joined him so that a quorum was not present. The House could not conduct business absent a quorum (a majority of its members). "Armed with this precedent, obstructionist minorities for more than fifty years could bring the work of the House to a halt." *Congress Against Itself* (Bloomington: University of Indiana Press, 1977), p. 23.

[22]Quoted in Samuel W. McCall, *The Life of Thomas Brackett Reed* (Boston: Houghton Mifflin, 1914), p. 170.

dictatorial (the word is not too strong) in his command of the House.[23] Finally, a coalition of minority Democrats and insurgent Republican reformers (many from the Midwest) broke the Speaker's hold over the combination of power levers that permitted him to dominate the process and outcomes of House decision making. As we shall see later in more detail, Cannon had lost the majority that allowed him to function as an autocrat. The support of his fellow Republicans, which was crucial to his dominance, had crumbled. Cannon remained as Speaker for the rest of the term, but both his personal power and that of the office were greatly diminished.

For a few years, the Democratic party caucus and the presidential leadership of Woodrow Wilson combined to retain some relatively strong centripetal momentum in the House, but this dissipated with increasing disagreement over international policies surrounding World War I. By 1920, strong party leadership had given way to a decentralized committee system as the principal means of organizing the House—a condition not to change for more than half a century.

The Senate

In his classic account of the nineteenth-century Senate, historian David Rothman concludes that

> the Senate of 1869 was very much like its predecessors; by 1901 it had come to resemble its successors. . . . Senators in the 1870s . . . were free to go about their business more or less as they pleased. By 1900 all this had changed. The party caucus and its chieftains determined who would sit on which committees and looked after the business calendar in detail. Members were forced to seek their favors or remain without influence in the chamber. At the same time, both organizations imposed unprecedented discipline on roll calls.[24]

Though the House could consolidate power around the constitutional office of the Speaker, the Senate had no similar touchstone. Ironically, strong political parties at the state and local levels formed the context from which centripetal forces flowed into the Senate, where party ties rose in importance through the 1880s and 1890s. Most members of this then-sizeable body (ninety lawmakers in 1901) functioned as party loyalists, who provided the votes for the policy positions endorsed by the leadership-dominated party caucus.[25]

---

[23]A compact summary of Cannon's actions can be found in Davidson and Oleszek, *Congress Against Itself,* pp. 25ff.

[24]David J. Rothman, *Politics and Power* (New York: Atheneum, 1969), p. 4. Some of the arguments in the following paragraphs are drawn from Rothman's work.

[25]Over the years Republicans have often called their caucus the Republican Conference. The term *caucus* is used here as a generic description of all the members of one party in one legislative chamber.

Occupying the central positions within the Republican caucus of the 1890s were the chair, Iowa's William Allison, and New York's Nelson Aldrich, perhaps the most talented and influential member of the chamber. They dominated Senate policy making through a combination of formal and informal linkages. The Allison–Aldrich faction gained control of overlapping party committees and standing committee positions to dominate the chamber's agenda and its policy outcomes. For example, controlling the Republican Steering Committee "confirmed the power of the Allison Aldrich faction over the Senate business. Arranging the legislative schedule in detail, week by week, the committee extended the party leaders' authority unimpaired from the caucus to the chamber. Senators knew they had to consult the committee before attempting to raise even minor matters."[26]

Remnants of the traditional Senate individualism remained, but those Republicans who refused to cooperate with the Allison–Aldrich group found themselves without influence. As Rothman notes, "Anyone could use the chamber as a forum and address the nation. Senators willing to abandon the opportunity to increase their own authority could act freely, following their own inclinations. . . . But barring a take-over of the party offices, they could hardly affect the exercise of power. The country might honor their names but the Senate barely felt their presence."[27]

Given the underlying differences among senators, based on region, party, interests, and ideology, the Senate's centralization could not hold for long, and the Republican caucus' domination eroded over the 1901–1912 period. The individualistic, centrifugal forces of the chamber came to the fore in caucus challenges to Aldrich, the growing strength of Progressive senators (often supported by President Theodore Roosevelt), and the election of a Democratic Senate to complement the presidential victory of Democrat Woodrow Wilson in the 1912 election. In addition to the partisan turnover of 1912 came the 1913 adoption of the Seventeenth Amendment to the Constitution, which provided for the direct election of senators. No longer would state legislatures and state party machines formally dominate the selection process, although by the time of the amendment's ratification, most states already selected Senate candidates through the primary election process.[28]

Finally, the Senate did change one further fundamental element of its procedure. From its inception, the Senate had allowed unlimited debate on any subject; the filibuster—or its threat—had proved a powerful tool for many Senate giants of the past. This was one of the strongest decentralizing ele-

---

[26]Rothman, *Politics and Power,* pp. 58–9.

[27]Ibid., p. 60.

[28]Congressional Quarterly's *Origins and Development of Congress,* 2nd ed., cites congressional scholar George Galloway, who notes "that more than half [the senators] chosen by legislative caucuses [in the states] were subsequently approved [through reelection to their office] by the people."

ments within the entire legislative process. An individual senator (or, more likely, a band of legislators with similar, intense feelings) could indefinitely delay consideration of a crucial bill. This occurred in 1917, when, in President Wilson's words, "a little group of willful men" blocked his armed neutrality bill, which had the public support of seventy-five of ninety-six senators.[29]

In the aftermath of this inability to act, the Senate adopted cloture, the first measure that provided a mechanism to shut off debate; cloture could be imposed by a two-thirds vote of those present and voting. Although this procedure was employed in 1919 to end a filibuster on ratification of the Versailles Treaty, until the late 1970s the Senate rarely approved cloture, save in extraordinary cases such as the 1964 Civil Rights Bill. The filibuster remained a potent weapon, both in its occasional implementation and in its frequent use as threat.

The Drift toward Decentralization

Allied with the Republican presidency of William McKinley (1897–1901), the House's strong Speakership, and the Senate's dominant Allison–Aldrich faction, legislative power was highly concentrated in the congressional parties at the turn of the century. The ability of legislative party leaders to set the nation's policy agenda became increasingly important, in that the industrializing U.S. society was placing rising numbers of demands upon government.[30] In the 40th Congress (1867–1869), lawmakers introduced a total of 3,003 bills; by the 52nd Congress (1891–1893) that number had grown to 14,518, and the 60th Congress (1907–1909) witnessed the introduction of almost 38,000 bills, more than a twelve-fold increase in forty years.[31] This volume of legislation eventually benefited those restive representatives and senators who desired to reduce the power of their party leaders.

Absent dominant leaders, some mechanism was needed to handle this immense flow of prospective legislation. The committee system offered the most obvious alternative. In fact, the number of standing committees had proliferated in both chambers, to the point that in 1918 the House had sixty such units and the Senate a staggering seventy-four. The very number of committees might imply the development of a highly decentralized Congress, but through 1910 party leaders combined their leadership roles with those of key committees to produce strongly centralized operations in both chambers.[32] With Speaker Cannon's defeat, the subsequent waning of Democratic caucus

---

[29]Ibid., p. 244.

[30]See Stephen Skowronek, *Building the New American State* (New York: Cambridge University Press, 1982).

[31]Roger Davidson and Walter Oleszek, *Congress and Its Members,* 3rd ed. (Washington: CQ Press, 1990), p. 30.

[32]Steven S. Smith and Christopher J. Deering, *Committees in Congress,* 2nd ed. (Washington: CQ Press, 1990), p. 34.

unity in the House after 1914, and the Senate's growing fragmentation in the period from 1901 to 1919, congressional party organizations could no longer move bills through the legislative process in a predictable, timely manner. Relying on committees would be essential for the sake of coherence and dictated that both chambers reform their committee systems, which they did in 1919 and again, more meaningfully, in 1946.

THE DEVELOPMENT AND DECLINE OF THE TEXTBOOK CONGRESS: 1920-1970

Although Woodrow Wilson could celebrate the work of congressional committees in the 1880s, their great ascendancy did not come until fifty years later and lasted well into the 1960s. Gradually, over the 1920s, 1930s, and 1940s, committee strength grew, and members almost universally advanced on the basis of their seniority—the length of their consecutive tenure on a given committee. The 1946 Legislative Reorganization Act sharply reduced the number of committees in both chambers and thus sharply increased the value of the remaining standing committee chairmanships—nineteen in the House, fifteen in the Senate.

The committee-dominated Congress of the 1950s coincided with the first systematic analysis of the Congress by political scientists trained in behavioral methods.[33] Scholars and students received a much fuller picture of the Congress of the period from the late 1950s to 1970 than of any previous era. The Congress of this time was relatively stable, which allowed for well-documented, detailed analyses to capture the essence of an increasingly complex institution. There is no question that this generation of congressional scholars "got it right." The strength of their analyses was so great that the cumulative picture, circa 1970, was so clear and detailed that it dominated conventional views of the Congress long after the institution changed profoundly in the 1970s and 1980s. In fact, as these scholars put the finishing touches on their work in the late 1960s, the Congress began to restructure itself in ways that would demonstrate the time-bound limitations of their insights.

With his term "the textbook Congress," political scientist Kenneth Shepsle has captured the extent to which the studies made up a received wisdom that still shapes our view of legislative politics.[34] In representing their constituencies and making national policy, legislators confront tensions that "derive from

---

[33]Although many careful scholars had described and analyzed the Congress before the 1950s, never before was there such a systematic examination of the institution. The American Political Science Association's Study of Congress project sponsored much of the work by such scholars as Richard F. Fenno, Jr., Robert Peabody, John Manley, and Charles Jones.

[34]Kenneth A. Shepsle, "The Changing Textbook Congress," in John E. Chubb and Paul E. Peterson, eds., *Can the Government Govern?* (Washington: Brookings, 1989), pp. 238–266.

three competing imperatives—geographical, jurisdictional, and partisan. . . . Congress is [thus] an arena for constituencies, committees, and [party-based] coalitions. The textbook Congress of the 1950s represented an equilibrium among these imperatives involving an institutional bargain that gave prominence to committees."[35] Although legendary party leaders such as Speaker Sam Rayburn (D–Tex.) and Senate Majority Leader Lyndon Johnson (D–Tex.) wielded substantial personal power in the 1950s, the Congress of these years emphasized the work of autonomous committees as directed by a set of senior chairmen.[36] The textbook Congress was both decentralized and oligarchic: decentralized in that committee chairs dominated their own policy domains; oligarchic in that top party leaders, committee chairs (and chairs of the thirteen Appropriations Committee subcommittees) all benefited from their joint control of the domestic policy agenda. Although the House relied more heavily on committee work than did the Senate, the same general committee-based equilibrium existed in both chambers.

The organizationally stable Congress of the 1950s did not bend easily to the winds of change. Popular pressure for more educational spending fell victim to procedural wrangling. In the face of filibusters and a hostile bloc of Southern senators, civil rights legislation proceeded slowly in the aftermath of the Supreme Court's 1954 *Brown v. Board of Education* school desegregation ruling. Nor was medical care for the elderly allowed to wend its way through the legislative process. The committee-dominated system proved superb at slowing the pace of policy change in a narrowly Democratic Congress that faced the moderate-to-conservative Republican presidency of Dwight Eisenhower.[37] Indeed, the title of Robert Bendiner's study of educational policy making, *Obstacle Course on Capitol Hill,* would have been equally apt in describing the limited progress of many other policy initiatives.[38]

The congressional equilibrium began to change with the Democratic landslide in the 1958 congressional elections, which greatly increased the size of the party's majorities in both chambers. More important, many of the newly elected legislators were relatively liberal and committed to policy changes. Six years later another surge of Democratic legislators ascended Capitol Hill, brought there in part by Lyndon Johnson's sweeping presidential victory over

---

[35]Ibid., p. 239.

[36]In the 1950s, with the exception of Representative Leonor Sullivan (D–Mo.), chair of the Merchant Marine and Fisheries Committee, committee chairs were men, and Congress was a bastion of white, middle-aged (and older) men. On Johnson, among many others, see Ralph Huitt, "Democratic Party Leadership in the Senate," *American Political Science Review* 60 (1961), pp. 331–344; on Rayburn, see D. B. Hardeman and Donald C. Bacon, *Rayburn* (Lanham, MD: Madison Books, 1987).

[37]James Sundquist's *Politics and Policy* (Washington: Brookings, 1968) provides an excellent guide to the obstructionism of the 1950s as well as the policy changes of the 1960s.

[38]Robert Bendiner, *Obstacle Course on Capitol Hill* (New York: McGraw-Hill, 1964).

Senator Barry Goldwater (R–Ariz.). Despite coming in disproportionate numbers from Republican districts, these rank-and-file Democratic legislators proved crucial to the passage of several of Johnson's ambitious domestic programs.[39] Liberal voting records denied many first-termers a chance for reelection; those who survived, however, felt entitled to a real voice within the legislative process. The major outlet for this voice came in positions taken by the Democratic Study Group, a body of progressive Democrat House members formed after the 1958 elections.[40] This unofficial, but well-organized, group consistently pressed for a reform agenda, which included reducing the power of committee chairmen.

The standing committee oligarchy was thus ripe for challenge by the late 1960s. Party leaders had begun to chip away at the chairs' powers, while reformist junior members hungered for responsibility within the committee structure. Both leaders and backbenchers stood to gain from reining in the chairs; change was inevitable, but with it came great disruption that lasted for a decade.

REFORMING THE CONGRESS: THE 1970s

It is the members who run Congress. And we will get pretty much the kind of Congress they want. We shall get a different kind of Congress when we elect different kinds of congressmen.

Richard F. Fenno, Jr.

Beginning in 1958, continuing through the 1960s, and culminating in the 1974 and 1976 elections for Democrats and the 1978 and 1980 elections for Republicans, we did get different kinds of new members. Subsequently, we got a different kind of Congress. Fenno's deceptively simple statement[41] captures the essential ability of lawmakers to determine the nature of their institution. More indirectly, voters can roughly determine the direction and extent of change, even if they are unaware of the specific mechanics.

In general, the newly elected legislators were impatient, eager to use their expertise, and unconcerned if they ruffled some senior members' feathers.[42] In the House, subcommittees gained a measure of independent authority; members sought and received many more resources for their offices; most

---

[39]See, in particular, Jeff Fishel, *Party and Opposition* (New York: David McKay, 1973), pp. 161ff.

[40]Arthur G. Stevens, Jr., Arthur H. Miller, and Thomas E. Mann, "Mobilization of Liberal Strength in the House, 1955–1970: The Democratic Study Group," *American Political Science Review* 68 (1974), pp. 667–681.

[41]Richard F. Fenno, Jr., "If, as Ralph Nader Says, Congress Is the 'Broken Branch,' How Come We Love Our Congressmen So Much?" in Norman J. Ornstein, ed., *Congress in Change* (New York: Praeger, 1975), p. 287.

[42]See Burdett Loomis, *The New American Politician* (New York: Basic, 1988), chap. 1.

votes on the floor were recorded and thus open to public scrutiny; and the Democratic Caucus provided enhanced powers for the Speaker and the top party leaders. Shepsle summarizes: "The revolt of the 1970s thus strengthened four power centers. It liberated members and subcommittees, restored to the Speakership an authority it had not known since the days of Joe Cannon, and invigorated the party caucus. Some of the reforms had a decentralizing effect, some a recentralizing effect. Standing committees and their chairs were caught in the middle. Geography and party benefited; the division-of-labor jurisdictions were its victims."[43] The relatively brief reform era of the 1970s produced a highly unstable political environment on Capitol Hill, especially in the House. Even though they held the presidency under Jimmy Carter and enjoyed comfortable numerical advantages over the Republicans in both chambers, Democrats in Congress could not generate consistent majorities to pass major policy initiatives. Leaders and backbenchers alike struggled to understand what their reforms had wrought.[44]

THE POSTREFORM CONGRESS: THE 1980s AND BEYOND

Many analyses of the Congress of the late 1970s emphasized, with good reason, the proliferation of subcommittees, the growth of individual members' resources, and the apparent weakness of both the Carter presidency and the Democratic legislative leadership. In 1980 Republicans ran a pointed national campaign advertisement that depicted Democratic Speaker Tip O'Neill as unresponsive and woefully out of touch on important, pressing issues.[45] Building on substantial public dissatisfaction, Republican candidates ran strongly in 1980, capturing the Senate and narrowing the Democrats' majority in the House to the point that President Reagan's initial tax and budget proposals won speedy congressional approval as conservative Democrats joined with Republicans to provide majority support.

Speaker O'Neill and his fellow House Democrats were not quite dead, however. Their rejuvenation over the next few years derived in part from the Speaker's winning personality; by the time he retired from the House in 1986, he could claim that his popularity levels had surpassed those of Ronald Reagan. O'Neill, a great listener, could find grounds to bring together

---

[43]Shepsle, "The Changing Textbook Congress," p. 256.

[44]A good collection of papers by leading scholars that captures the difficulties of the reform era can be found in Frank Mackaman, ed., *Understanding Congressional Leadership* (Washington: CQ Press, 1981).

[45]The commercial portrayed O'Neill as driving a car and ignoring the pleas of a young aide, who warned him that they were running out of gas. Although effective, the ad focused great attention on the Speaker, increased his stature as a national figure, and encouraged him to take a more aggressive stance toward the Reagan programs in 1981 and beyond.

the different strands of the legislative party. Equally important, however, were the aggressive use of party-strengthening reforms adopted in the 1970s and the consistent reduction of ideological disagreements among House Democrats.[46] Thus, the personally popular O'Neill could lead an increasingly homogeneous group of partisans with a combination of carrots, such as including many members within the leadership, and sticks, such as controlling the process of appointing members to committee seats.

If the reforms of the House produced large-scale changes in the 1970s and 1980s, with fragmentation giving way to Speaker Jim Wright's consolidation of leadership powers in 1987–1988, the Senate of the same period underwent a less striking, more evolutionary transformation.[47] By 1989 both Senate parties had strong, partisan floor leaders in place (Senators Bob Dole [R–Kans.] and George Mitchell [D–Maine]), but the chamber continued to respect the almost sacred status of the individual member. A lone senator could often tie the institution in knots, as the whole deferred to the "rights" of a single willful legislator. Senators like Jesse Helms (R–N.C.) and Howard Metzenbaum (D–Ohio) gained notoriety and power as they proved willing, time and again, to bring the business of the Senate to a halt if their desires were not accommodated.[48] Senators chose not to limit their colleagues' excesses, and the chamber has become steadily less collegial since the 1960s. Indeed, when compared with the sharp partisanship of the House in the 1980s and 1990s, complete with competing visions of the role of government, the contemporary Senate has often seemed less focused and less sure of its step. This may be an "identity crisis" of a highly individualistic body, but it may also reflect the traditional Senate role of addressing issues in a leisurely and frustratingly repetitive manner.[49]

Finally, the development of the postreform Congress coincided with an era of divided government. From 1969 to 1993, the same party controlled both houses of Congress and the presidency for only four years (1977–1981). Until the onset of the Clinton Administration, the Democrat-dominated postreform legislature had functioned only with Republican presidents. Despite the constitutional need to cooperate, the interbranch relationship was often adversarial. In 1993–1994, despite the eagerness of many Democratic legislators to

---

[46]These issues will be considered at greater length later in the book (in chap. 7, especially). A minimal list of key sources includes David Rohde, *Parties and Leaders in the Postreform House* (Chicago: University of Chicago Press, 1991); Barbara Sinclair, *Majority Leadership in the U.S. House* (Baltimore: Johns Hopkins University Press, 1983); and Roger H. Davidson, ed., *The Postreform Congress* (New York: St. Martin's, 1992).

[47]See, especially, Barbara Sinclair, *The Transformation of the U.S. Senate* (Baltimore: Johns Hopkins University Press, 1989).

[48]Why this is so requires some detailed untangling; see chap. 9.

[49]See Norman J. Ornstein, Robert L. Peabody, and David W. Rohde, "The U.S. Senate in an Era of Change," in Lawrence Dodd and Bruce I. Oppenheimer, eds., *Congress Reconsidered,* 5th ed. (Washington: CQ Press, 1993), pp. 13–40.

serve with a Democratic president, single-party control of the national government scarcely eliminated interbranch wrangling.[50]

With the election of 1994, all bets were off. Divided government returned with the Republican victories in the House and Senate. Given the evolutionary nature of change in the Senate, and Republican control of that body between 1981 and 1987, Senator Bob Dole moved easily into his majority leadership role. The Gingrich-led House has proven to be a different story, as Republicans embarked on systematically addressing the most ambitious policy agenda since Franklin Roosevelt's first 100 days as president in 1933. Speaker Gingrich has exercised an extraordinary amount of power in a House where power has been steadily, if unevenly, centralized since the late 1960s by the ruling Democrats. Speakers O'Neill and Wright demonstrated the great opportunities offered leaders who could command the allegiance of their fellow partisans; more than any Speaker since Joseph Cannon, Gingrich has done exactly that. We need to go back to Speakers like Clay, Reed, and Cannon to adequately place Gingrich and the House Republicans in context.

More generally, the postreform Congress has evolved from the constitutional and organizational elements that have shaped the institution in previous eras. It remains highly responsive to constituency interests, even as it addresses national issues such as health care and welfare reform. The separation of powers continues to affect its operations. Committees and party leaders are still central to congressional organization. Henry Clay and John C. Calhoun would recognize the ins and outs of politics on Capitol Hill 150 years after their salad days.

At the same time there have been great changes, both within the Congress and in its relations with its environment. This chapter has traced some continuities and changes on Capitol Hill. Before considering these in more detail, we will examine some external forces that affect the capacity of Congress to act. In particular, we will look at the growth of special interests and organized groups and the related expansion in the role of government. Clay and Calhoun may have faced the slavery question, the single most divisive issue in the American experience, but they did not have to parcel out a $1.6 trillion annual budget and respond to tens of thousands of special interests and lobbyists seeking to influence thousands of separate federal programs. In many ways, the seeds of fragmentation and individualism on Capitol Hill are sown by interests from across the country (and beyond) whose lobbyists congregate in committee rooms and whose fax messages pile high on 535 legislators' desks. The politics of Congress remains a politics of representation.

---

[50]President Clinton compiled a strong overall success record in 1993–1994 as he won on more than 86 percent of the votes on which he took a position. On major issues, however, especially health care, he was much less effective.

Three ✑♪

THE CHANGING
ENVIRONMENT OF
CONGRESSIONAL POLITICS

Many of the centrifugal forces affecting Congress originate outside the institution. Indeed, as a representative body, Congress was designed to offer easy access to those interests and individuals who sought to influence policy. To a greater or lesser extent, it has always fulfilled this goal. Until the mid-twentieth century, save in extraordinary circumstances (war, the Depression), Congress met for about half the year. From July through January, members would live at home, among their constituents. With the New Deal, World War II, and the growth of government, to say nothing of the widespread installation of air conditioning in Washington, congressional sessions have come to run virtually year-round. At the same time, air travel has allowed almost all members the possibility of living in their districts and joining the "Tuesday through Thursday" club of those spending three days a week in Washington. Although many recently elected legislators have made this choice, the observation of members of the California delegation stumbling into committee hearings after returning on the Tuesday morning "red-eye" flight scarcely offers much encouragement for coherent lawmaking. In addition, large increases in staff allotments, the growth of district offices, and advances in communication mean that almost all members are well informed about their districts, regardless of their formal place of residence.

CONGRESS: THE PERMEABLE BRANCH

In Washington, members of Congress can almost always carve a few minutes from their busy schedules to chat with visitors from their districts. Moreover, responding to constituents' mail receives priority attention from legislative offices. After all, it is the home folks who have sent the representatives to Capitol Hill. However, access to Congress is scarcely limited to members' constituents. Traditionally, interest groups have found lawmakers hospitable to their requests for time and attention. The ease of obtaining a legislative audience contrasts markedly with the lengthy process of obtaining a hearing in the judiciary or the difficulty of gaining an audience with top-level executive-branch officials. In its 1993–1994 session, for example, the Supreme Court issued fewer than 100 signed opinions from among the thousands of appeals filed before it. Likewise, the presidency and the top rungs of the bureaucracy are highly insulated from most citizens (electronic mail and town hall–style meetings notwithstanding). Conversely, the Congress—especially the House—has always opened its doors to complaints and requests from citizens and organized interests. Over the years, as the national government has grown larger and made increasingly important decisions, the demands on Congress have risen in number and intensity, but even before the policy explosions of the New Deal and the Great Society there were many instances of intense, sophisticated, and frequently successful lobbying efforts by organized interests.

As industry expanded and flourished in the 1870s, interests swarmed around the Congress, often directly and corruptly influencing individual legislators. For example, in the years following World War I, the farm lobby, led by the American Farm Bureau Federation (AFBF) demonstrated its worth—in terms of information and support—for dozens of legislators, who repaid the agriculture interests with increasing access to the process of lawmaking.[1] More subtle than most interests from the pre-1900 era, the farm lobby often worked through farmers back in the legislators' home districts. The political and policy information provided to members of Congress by the farm groups gave them good reason to listen to these organizations. Legislators face great uncertainties in understanding both the policy and political effects of their actions; well-informed groups such as the AFBF could offer information that would make members a bit less uncertain, especially in terms of their constituents' opinions and the positions of the farm community. Providing regular access to the Farm Bureau thus benefited both the lawmakers and the interest group.

The "textbook Congress" that emerged by the 1950s dictated a committee orientation for interests in search of access. In the 1950s many committees served as one corner of close-knit triangular relationships, variously labeled "cozy" or "iron" triangles that linked them to key outside interests and, as the third corner, to particular agencies within the federal bureaucracy.[2] For example, sugar interests worked with the appropriate Agriculture Committee subcommittees in the House and Senate and the relevant USDA officials to maintain domestic sugar prices that were consistently several times higher than those in world markets. By the 1960s, various interests began to challenge the tidy, profitable sugar subsystem. Consumer and environmental

---

[1]See John Mark Hansen, *Gaining Access* (Chicago: University of Chicago Press, 1991), pp. 57–58.

[2]There is a very large literature here. For a contemporary summary, see James A. Thurber, "Dynamics of Policy Subsystems in American Politics," in Allan Cigler and Burdett Loomis, eds., *Interest Group Politics,* 3rd ed. (Washington: CQ Press, 1991), pp. 319–344.

groups, among others, began to influence agriculture policies. In 1974 the sugar triangle broke apart, as the subcommittee could not maintain control over the price support policies.[3] Subsequently, however, sugar interests succeeded in lobbying a broad mix of legislators to reconstruct a similar marketing system that continues to fix U.S. prices at a considerably higher level than elsewhere in the world.

More generally, while the Congress changed greatly from 1960 into the 1980s, so too did its environment. In parallel, related developments, more interests became politically active and more governmental policies prompted them to action.[4] Environmental groups, for example, possessed almost no political clout in the 1950s; either they emphasized traditional conservation issues or they remained outside the policy debate. By 1970 both traditional and newly formed environmental organizations had become major players in policy making on issues that ranged from pesticide levels to air quality standards to toxic waste disposal. As a result, many old policy assumptions, such as maximizing returns for domestic sugar producers, were open to question.[5]

Not only did interest groups serve as effective advocates on behalf of specific programs, but new policies engendered new agencies, even whole new departments (for example, Energy and Education), each with its own turf to protect.[6] As the federal budget rose from $100 billion in 1969 to $1.6 trillion in 1996, many interests had become entrenched within government as well as outside it. Legislative consideration of issues thus has proceeded within a complicated, dense environment of complex policies and numerous organized interests.

Equally important, in the 1960s presidents like John F. Kennedy and Lyndon Johnson could promise new programs for particular constituencies, such as the poor and the elderly, that would simply distribute new benefits.[7] Indeed, the impulse to distribute benefits to specific constituents and interests operates as a key centrifugal force within the Congress.[8] Lawmakers seek to deliver concentrated benefits (such as a dam or farm support payments) paid for by widely dispersed costs (a few cents of every tax dollar). But as both

---

[3]The "three pillars" of the sugar program include loans for the sugar industry, import restrictions, and regulations, at times, of domestic sugar allotments for planting. See David Hosansley, "Florida Sugar Growers Edgy as Farm Bill Nears," *CQ Weekly Report,* May 13, 1995. pp. 1311–1315.

[4]Kay Lehman Schlozman and John T. Tierney, *Organized Interests and American Democracy* (New York: Harper & Row, 1986).

[5]David Vogel, *Fluctuating Fortunes* (New York: Basic, 1989).

[6]Lawrence Brown, *New Policies, New Politics* (Washington: Brookings, 1983).

[7]James Sundquist, *Politics and Policies* (Washington: Brookings, 1968).

[8]Congressional scholars differ as to how effective legislators are in distributing their largesse to their geographic constituencies. In *Congress and the Bureaucracy* (New Haven, CT: Yale University Press, 1979) Douglas Arnold, summarizing several works, sees as too simplistic just addressing the variations in programs and policies as they affect members' districts (pp. 15–16).

federal programs and budget deficits have grown, distributive politics has proven an increasingly difficult game to play.

In the 1990s, for every policy winner there are often many policy losers. Given huge budget deficits, new programs must compete against established policies. Entitlement programs such as Medicaid or farm price support payments often require increased funding; the expenditures must increase the deficit or come from someplace else. But where? Such redistributive questions continually bedevil members of Congress, who cannot endlessly distribute benefits when the government consistently spends more than it takes in. Redistributive policies—which reallocate funds from one sector of society to another, as in welfare—ordinarily produce sharp conflicts on Capitol Hill.[9] The tremendous partisan battles over budgets in the 1980s and 1990s have done little to increase public confidence in the Congress, largely because individual legislators have continued to provide benefits to their constituencies and their favored interests.

This chapter will explore four major changes in the congressional environment: the advocacy explosion, as the number and specialization of interests have grown steadily since the 1960s; the policy explosion and the impact of sixty years of an activist federal government; the overwhelming attention given to budgetary considerations since the early 1980s—the so-called fiscalization of policy making; and the declining respect for Congress. The growing numbers of interests and policies have exerted significant decentralizing pressures on the Congress, whereas the fiscalization of policy has operated to centralize congressional actions, as budgetary concerns dominate decision making. And the low public standing of Congress may make it all the more difficult for its members to address divisive, and potentially unpopular, policies.

Related to these developments, several other external changes also have occurred; these range from the gradual weakening of political parties to the growing political sophistication of business interests to major transformations in the media and in information technology. In short, the Congress of the 1950s did its work in a very different context than did the Congress of the 1980s and 1990s. Over all, the contemporary Congress has grown both highly responsive to particular interests and remarkably insular within the hothouse environment of Washington policy making and Capitol Hill politics.

The Advocacy Explosion

In the early 1960s political scientists, if not journalists, often discounted the impact of interest groups on most policy making. Lobbyists plied their trade, of course, but many interests lacked the resources and sophistication to wield

---

[9]Randall B. Ripley and Grace A. Franklin, *Congress, the Bureaucracy, and Public Policy,* 5th ed. (Pacific Grove, CA: Brooks Cole, 1991).

much influence.[10] Between 1960 and 1990, the number of active organized interests and their use of a wide range of techniques for influencing policy makers rose sharply. Simply put, more lobbyists have been working for more interests and have been employing more tactics to affect policy outcomes. Although much popular attention has been directed toward the tremendous post-1974 growth of political action committees (from 608 PACs in 1974 to 4,009 in 1984, with a modest rise to 4,729 in 1992),[11] organized interests have expanded their actions across the board. The number of Washington-based interest representatives grew from 4,000 in 1977 to more than 14,500 in 1991; registered lobbyists rose in numbers from around 1,000 in the 1960s to almost 6,000 in 1981 and an astonishing 23,000 in 1989; trade associations relocated their offices in Washington in great numbers during the 1980s; and between 1973 and 1983, the District of Columbia Bar increased its membership from around 11,000 lawyers to more than 37,000.[12] As of 1994, the best estimate of the number of individuals who earn their living from Washington-based attempts to influence policies stood at an astounding 91,000.[13]

The advocacy explosion has not affected all sectors of the Washington community with equal force. Most notable, perhaps, have been the declining role of labor unions, the growing presence of corporate and professional interests, and the increasing importance of large-scale citizens groups, ranging from Common Cause to the Sierra Club to the American Association of Retired Persons and its 33 million members.[14] In addition, American states, cities, and other governmental units came to Washington in droves during the 1970s era of revenue sharing, stayed to press their cases during the leaner years of the Reagan Administration, and have remained to lobby against unfunded federal

---

[10]See Raymond A. Bauer, Ithiel de sola Pool, and Lewis Anthony Dexter, *American Business and Public Policy* (Chicago: Aldine, 1963); and Lester Milbrath, *The Washington Lobbyists* (Chicago: Rand McNally, 1963).

[11]Indeed, the number of active PACs has always been less than the total. As of 1992, there were 1,677 inactive PACs that made no contributions, of which 910 were defunct as organizations. See Paul Herrnson, *Congressional Elections* (Washington: CQ Press, 1994), p. 109.

[12]The preceding figures are cited in Mark Petracca, "The Rediscovery of Interest Group Politics," Mark Petracca, ed., *The Politics of Interests* (Boulder, CO: Westview, 1992), pp. 14–15.

[13]Kevin Phillips, *Arrogant Capital* (Boston: Little Brown, 1994), cites James Thurber on the above figure.

[14]Schlozman and Tierney present data that demonstrate the rise of individual corporate representation, the decline of trade groups (as a percentage of all groups), and the decline of the percentage of citizens groups. At the same time, the overall number of groups with Washington representation had shot up, so that even labor unions, whose presence had decreased from 11% of all interests in 1960 to 2–3% in 1980, still increased in absolute numbers, from about 55 groups in 1960 to more than 100 in 1980. Individual corporate representation, in contrast, rose from about 80 firms in 1960 to approximately 3,000 in 1980. Given differences among data, these comparisons may be a little loose, but the overall trends are clear. See Schlozman and Tierney, *Organized Interests and American Democracy,* p. 77.

mandates.[15] In addition, foreign governments and private interests, often acting through sophisticated Washington lobbying and public relations firms, have become important players in the complex politics of trade, foreign aid, and international business.[16]

From the 1960s through the early 1990s the thousands of interests actively seeking to influence congressional decisions multiplied several times over. Equally important, however, has been the wide variety of strategies and tactics that organized interests have employed in their efforts to gain advantage. By the end of the 1980s a majority of Washington-based organizations reported using more than twenty different techniques for exercising influence; these ranged from testifying at legislative hearings to joining coalitions to mounting grassroots lobbying efforts.[17] At the same time, these groups have used most of these techniques considerably more often than they had in the past. For example, two-thirds of the organizations noted that they paid increased attention to press relations, worked harder at building coalitions, and spent more time contacting governmental officials.[18]

In the end, the advocacy explosion encompasses at least three distinct elements. First, there are more groups and interests in the fray. Second, there are many new techniques available to all interests; computers and enhanced communication capacities allow groups to serve as linking agents between the public—or specific sectors of the public—and legislators. Third, both well-established groups and new entries are employing a more extensive range of techniques to influence policy decisions.[19] As a result, more messages from more interests than ever before are aimed at legislators. Whether they hear those messages remains an open question.

The 1993–1994 struggles over U.S. trade policy illustrate how this new interest group environment can affect congressional actions (see also chapter 10 for an extensive discussion of similar pressures in the politics of health care reform). The Congress was faced with implementing the North American Free Trade Agreement (NAFTA) and ratifying the General Agreement on Tariffs and Trade (GATT). Given that both agreements were supported strongly by Presidents Reagan, Bush, and Clinton, the Congress represented the logical venue for opponents to mount their attacks, which emphasized the loss of

---

[15]See, in particular, Donald Haider's *When Governments Come to Washington: Governors, Mayors, and Intergovernmental Lobbying* (New York: Free Press, 1974) for the 1970s era and Beverly Cigler's "Not Just Another Special Interest: Intergovernmental Representation," in Allan Cigler and Burdett Loomis, eds., *Interest Group Politics*, 4th ed. (Washington: CQ Press, 1995), pp. 131–153) for a perspective on the 1980s and 1990s.

[16]Eric Uslaner, "All Politics Is Global," in Cigler and Loomis, *Interest Group Politics*, 4th ed.

[17]Schlozman and Tierney, *Organized Interests and American Democracy*, p. 180.

[18]Ibid., p. 155.

[19]Ibid., p. 169.

American jobs (with NAFTA) and sovereignty (with GATT), in that international tribunals could rule against some practices of U.S. businesses.

Opponents of NAFTA included an unlikely coalition of organized labor; consumer advocates (particularly Ralph Nader); some environmental groups; and, perhaps most importantly, 1992 independent presidential candidate Ross Perot. Perot brought both his own constituents and his highly public tactics to the battle. Indeed, Nader, the environmentalists, and Perot combined to produce an effective outside attack on the trade accord; they could direct their own supporters to lobby hundreds of members of Congress while they simultaneously advertised extensively against the pact. Only late in the day did NAFTA backers, often prompted by President Clinton, counter the public arguments of Perot, Nader, and their allies.

NAFTA opponents did not have to rely solely on sophisticated grassroots lobbying techniques, clever public relations, and considerable paid advertising; they enjoyed the support of key Democratic legislators near the core of the party leadership. House Democratic Whip David Bonoir (D–Mich.) proved inexhaustible in his coordination of opposing forces within the House. Less public, to reduce the embarrassment of his own party's president, was the firm opposition of House Majority Leader Richard Gephardt (D–Mo.). As a highly representative body (both Bonoir's and Gephardt's districts included large numbers of union members), the House encourages interests to seek out powerful champions to provide inside leadership on key issues. NAFTA foes could have scarcely done better than to enlist two of the three top leaders in the House. Only after the Clinton White House made some eleventh-hour pleas, agreed to a few modest concessions, and issued some specific policy clarifications did NAFTA win House approval. The opponents had set the terms of the debate, mounted impressive grassroots campaigns by constituents, and benefited from advertising purchased by Perot and others.

Many of the same interests came together to oppose GATT's approval in late 1994. Obscured by the debate over health care reform, GATT provides a somewhat different illustration of the ways in which organized groups and the Congress can serve each other's needs. Although some business interests opposed NAFTA, virtually all major corporate bodies expressed strong support for the lower tariffs promised by GATT.[20] GATT induced considerably less public opposition than did NAFTA. Nonetheless, congressional consideration of the treaty offered an attractive opportunity for foes of the trade pact. Under the rules of the Senate, Senator Ernest Hollings (D–S.C.), whose state's textile industry desired protection from the competition of cheap foreign labor, was able to hold up a vote on GATT for forty-five days—from early October until after the 1994 congressional elections. Given the delay, opponents hoped to mount a vigorous and public challenge to GATT, with Ross Perot again playing a major role.

---

[20]Keith Bradsher, "Foes Set for Battle on GATT," *The New York Times,* October 3, 1994.

The Senate's individualism, like the House's sensitivity to district concerns, provided an opening for groups to delay or defeat trade legislation.

Helped by generally supportive Republican leaders, the Clinton Administration won approval for the treaty, but only after vigorous debate; given a design that usually discourages speedy or efficient decision making, Congress offered organized interests, with their increased numbers and capacities to mobilize key constituents, an inviting opportunity to take advantage of the very openness that defines the institution.[21]

The Policy Explosion

Tied directly to the growth of interests is the great increase in the volume of national policy established since the 1930s, especially since the 1960s. In 1930 the reach of the federal government did not extend very far in terms of expenditures, taxation, or regulation. Congressional committee chairs may have been gaining independent power at this time, but they had very little to control.

Political analyst Michael Barone writes that "macroeconomic fiscal policy, redistribution of wealth, and government spending programs were not major issues [because] the federal government neither raised nor spent . . . much money in the late 1920s."[22] Most federal spending went to pay for the military, either in the form of current expenses, interest on the national debt incurred by borrowing to pay for past wars, or veterans' benefits. Of the $3.3 billion budget for 1930, less than $1 billion went to fund all other governmental activities.[23]

Even after the increased spending commitments of the New Deal, domestic expenditures stood at just $7.8 billion in 1940 and $12.6 billion in 1946, the first post–World War II year. As late as 1954, domestic spending amounted to only $21.6 billion, a figure that almost doubled by 1960, the last year of the Eisenhower Administration. Defense costs averaged $47 billion between 1952 and 1960; by 1960, the year of John F. Kennedy's election, total federal spending totaled $92 billion—a substantial increase since 1930, to be sure, but a figure that did not provide for much in the way of ambitious social programs.

The pent-up demand for more federal domestic intervention (such as Medicare) and more regulation (for example, the Environmental Protection Agency), along with continued requirements for high levels of Cold War defense spending (including Vietnam), produced great increases in both domestic and military spending during the 1960s (see Table 3–1). Still, the major story told in Table 3–1 is that of the great escalation in governmental expenditures during the 1970s and 1980s, when Republicans controlled the presidency for all but Jimmy Carter's 1977–1981 term.

---

[21]In *Home Style* (Boston: Little Brown, 1978), Richard F. Fenno concludes that the representativeness of the Congress makes it, at least most of the time, "the slow institution"—a description that should not be taken as criticism.

[22]Michael Barone, *Our Country* (New York: Free Press, 1990), p. 31.

[23]Ibid., p. 31.

TABLE 3-1
Federal Spending, 1940-1990 (in billions, not adjusted for inflation)

Year	National Defense	Nondefense	Total (including interest on debt)
1940	$ 1.7	$ 7.8	$ 9.5
1950	13.7	28.8	42.6
1960	48.1	44.1	92.2
1970	81.7	114.0	195.6
1980	134.0	456.9	590.9
1990	299.0	848.9	1,151.8
1995	271.0	1,034.7	1,518.9

Sources: Harold W. Stanley and Richard G. Niemi, eds., *Vital Statistics on American Politics,* 2nd ed. (Washington: CQ Press, 1990), pp. 385–386; and Allen Schick, *The Federal Budget: Politics, Policy, Process* (Washington: Brookings, 1995), pp. 8, 33; *CQ Weekly Report,* February 11, 1995, p. 429.

No single explanation adequately accounts for burgeoning federal budgets, but the very existence of new programs in the 1960s and 1970s helped to create great pressures, both inside and outside the government, to increase spending levels. For example, the adoption of Medicare in 1965 produced a continuing rise in federal health-related costs over the next decade—from $9.9 billion in 1965 to $41.5 billion in 1975. More important than the mere cost, however, was the fundamental redefinition of health care as an issue in American politics. As one scholar notes, "By nationalizing a large portion of the bill, Medicare made health care inflation a public-sector problem and placed it on the policy agenda."[24]

Although the new policy commitments of the 1960s and 1970s often required more spending in such areas as health, education, and nutrition (in the form of food stamps), the reach of federal regulatory programs was at least as long. As shown in Table 3–2, from 1940 to 1980 the length of one year's body of regulations, printed in the *Federal Register,* grew almost twenty-fold, although the 1980 figure is artificially high; the Reagan Administration cut

TABLE 3-2
The Growth of Federal Regulation

Year	Number of Pages in *Federal Register*
1940	5,307
1950	9,562
1960	14,479
1970	20,032
1980	87,012
1990	53,618

Sources: Harold W. Stanley and Richard G. Niemi, *Vital Statistics on American Politics,* 2nd ed. (Washington: CQ Press, 1990), p. 248; Ornstein et al., *Vital Statistics on Congress, 1993–1994,* p. 158.

---

[24]James A. Morone, *The Democratic Wish* (New York: Basic, 1990), p. 266.

back substantially on regulations but still managed to average 54,000 pages of *Federal Register* material per year. More importantly, most regulations stayed on the books, thus producing an overwhelmingly dense policy environment by the 1980s.

Even before the Reagan era, Theodore Lowi had described a national government that had fundamentally changed the nature of American political life. He saw the results as a "two-part model" of highly institutionalized politics, in which

▶ "The national government by some formal action monopolizes a given area of private activity." This may be accomplished through spending, regulation, or other means.

▶ "Following that, a program is authorized and an administrative agency is put into operation to work without legal guidelines through an elaborate, sponsored bargaining process [between governmental agencies and specific interests]."[25]

In the end, tens of thousands of governmental units and interests have large stakes in countless discretionary decisions made within the bureaucracy, inside the presidency, by the judiciary, and on Capitol Hill. Lowi argues that there is virtually no accountability for most decisions; instead of clear policy and well-defined procedure, there is only process.[26]

This "process" has become the heart and soul of relations between organized interests, the bureaucracy, and the Congress. Robert Salisbury observes that much activity by groups and other interests emphasizes the monitoring of capital information sources: "Washington is, after all, the main source of what governmental officials are doing or planning to do. To get that information in a timely way, a continuous and alert presence . . . is vital."[27] Moreover, it is accurate information on political contingencies, not on policy alternatives, that is often most at a premium. Given its size and diversity, the Congress is ideally suited to provide such knowledge. Individual members and their staffs are well positioned to convey valuable political information to particular interests; in turn, these interests will have good reason to support their reelection bids. Through the 1980s, ideology played little role in the game. Rather, majority House Democrats became the vehicles for many business interests that wanted to "invest" in careerist legislators who would, it seemed, control the

[25]Theodore Lowi, *The End of Liberalism,* 2nd ed. (New York: Norton, 1979), p.278.

[26]Ibid., p. 63.

[27]Robert H. Salisbury, "The Paradox of Interest Groups in Washington—More Groups, Less Clout," in Anthony King, ed., *The New American Political System,* rev. ed. (Washington: American Enterprise Institute, 1990), p. 203.

Congress, and especially the House, for the foreseeable future.[28] Of course, once Republicans won a majority of the House seats in 1994, such an arrangement lost much of its luster for many corporate and professional interests, whose support for the GOP increased dramatically.

The Budget as an 800-Pound Gorilla

The growth of organized interests and the extended reach of national policies are developments that have reinforced each other. For the most part, both trends reflect an increased fragmentation of the decision-making context. Historically, the way the Congress appropriated funds also contributed to this decentralization. After the president proposed a unified budget, the Congress, through the appropriations committees in both House and Senate, would break up the spending proposals into thirteen separate pieces, each initially considered by one House appropriations subcommittee. Only at the end of the legislative process, with the passage of thirteen distinct bills, would the Congress and the president know how much had actually been appropriated. This decentralized format worked reasonably well into the 1960s,[29] but by the early 1970s pressures began to mount for a more coherent congressional approach to the entire budget.

Legislators began to face major budgetary problems as a result of enacting numerous policies and having many groups capable of competing to influence them; policies cost money (obtained from taxes) in addition to conferring benefits. During the 1950s and 1960s, the appropriations committees could maintain a check on overall spending by the Congress, but by the early 1970s, this informal constraint had weakened substantially.[30] In the 1970s, the Congress provided itself with the staff and committee structure to increase its role in constructing annual budgets, which had been almost totally the province of the president and the well-staffed Office of Management and

---

[28]The key figure for congressional Democrats was Representative Tony Coelho, first in his role as chair of the Democratic Congressional Campaign Committee and then as Democratic Whip. Coelho brought Democratic House members and various business interests together to their mutual benefit. In 1989, Coelho resigned from the House after reports surfaced of his favored treatment in the purchase of bonds, although no charges were ever brought against him. In the 1990s, Coehlo, as a managing partner of a New York investment firm, maintained contacts with the Democrats and emerged as a key adviser to President Clinton. See Brooks Jackson, *Honest Graft*, rev. ed. (Washington: Farragut, 1990), and Ruth Shalit, "The Undertaker," *The New Republic*, January 2, 1995, pp. 17–25.

[29]In his 1966 book, *The Power of the Purse* (Boston: Little Brown), Richard F. Fenno, Jr., could characterize the appropriations process in the Congress as a system. Within a few years, that system had broken down in terms of controlling expenditures and priorities, and Congress was unable to limit presidential intervention in the form of impounding funds.

[30]See various works by Allen Schick and later editions of Aaron Wildavsky's *The Politics of the Budgetary Process* (Boston: Little Brown).

Budget.[31] After 1974, when Senate and House Budget Committees and the Congressional Budget Office were established, members of Congress could fight their "budget wars" with the executive branch on roughly equal footing.[32] This legislative capacity became especially important during the Reagan Administration, when 1981 tax cuts meant that every succeeding budget would include a large deficit and result in great pressures on existing levels of spending.

Over the 1980s, a centralizing change that was implicit in the new budget arrangements modified the nature of congressional actions: the fiscalization of the policy process. In short, fiscalization simply means that the question of paying for services and programs has become the proverbial "800-pound gorilla," a beast that can sit wherever it wants. Within the contemporary Congress, this budgetary ape camps out in almost every committee room and leadership meeting. Controlling spending levels and the funding (or killing) of continuing programs have become the central issues of the postreform Congress. In sum, the budget has ceased to be an "empowering process," at least for federal initiatives. Rather, the contemporary budget "often appears to be a limiting process . . . [and it] crowds out genuine choice; it forces tomorrow's programs to give way to yesterday's decisions."[33]

With little ability to fund new programs, legislators sought to control the spending commitments that had already been enacted into law. The large annual deficits through the 1980s and into the 1990s demonstrate the difficulty of reducing expenditures; nonetheless, the post-1981 period has been dominated by budgetary politics. In several highly centralized budget summits from 1982 to 1993, congressional leaders negotiated with top executive-branch officials to arrive at acceptable spending and deficit levels. Thurber and Durst conclude that this will continue, in that "budget and party leaders will continue to build coalitions to formulate the budget and to negotiate with the president about spending priorities. [Current practices produce] a tighter zero-sum budget game with more control and with top-down, centralized budgeting by the congressional party leadership."[34]

This party-based, centralized process is what came crashing down on Democratic first-term Representative Margaret Margolies-Mezvinsky, as she came under intense pressures from the party leadership and the Clinton

---

[31]There is a vast literature here. A good starting place is Allen Schick's *Congress and Money* (Washington: The Urban Institute, 1980).

[32]Allen Schick introduces the term *budget war* in reference to the 1966–1974 period, but there has scarcely been a peace after the adoption of the Budget Reform Act. See Schick, *Congress and Money.*

[33]Allen Schick, *The Federal Budget* (Washington: Brookings, 1995), p. 2.

[34]James A. Thurber and Samantha L. Durst, "The 1990 Budget Enforcement Act: The Decline of Congressional Accountability," in Lawrence C. Dodd and Bruce I. Oppenheimer, eds., *Congress Reconsidered,* 5th ed. (Washington: CQ Press, 1993), p. 391.

Administration to vote in favor of the 1993 budget agreement, whose taxation provisions she had consistently opposed. The context for such pressures is a budget process that regularly produces high-visibility votes on the entire set of spending and taxing commitments for an entire year. Every increase in funding for one program must be taken out of the spending for some other governmental activity. Debate over policies thus turns more and more on fiscal considerations. Put bluntly, how much will each program cost? In such an environment, it is those who can survey the entire budget—members of the budget and appropriations committees and the party leadership—who have the most leverage in determining outcomes. The very nature of redistributive, or zero-sum, decision making is to empower those whose reach facilitates negotiations and whose power can enforce agreements, as long as they can convince even a bare majority of members to agree. Short of voting against the entire budget agreement, rank-and-file members of both parties can exercise little influence over the budgets that their leaders construct.

Congressional backing for a balanced budget amendment, described by many legislators as "a bad idea whose time has come,"[35] reflects the difficulty that deficits have caused for the Congress. Moreover, the public, seeing the legislature wrestle unsuccessfully, and even dishonestly, with deficits, has provided less and less support for the Congress as an institution.

Can't Get No Respect: The Unpopular Congress

Let there be no mistake about congressional popularity: The legislative branch, despite its putative ties to "the people," has never won great adulation from the public at large. Nor from editorial pages.[36] Historically, the Congress has been savaged by editorialists, much as it has been in more recent times. Most individual legislators do not help the situation, as they often engage in the practice of running for reelection by running vigorously against the institution.[37]

The percentage of the population viewing the Congress in favorable terms has remained a minority since the mid-1960s; on average, during this period

---

[35]Senator Nancy Kassebaum (R–Kans.), among others.

[36]In the author's classes on Congress, he has a standing wager that no one will be able to bring in a post-1970 cartoon that depicts the institution in an unambiguously positive light. In more than ten years, no student has yet collected; the 104th Congress may well break this streak.

[37]Of the many key findings in Fenno's *Home Style,* none was more important or more surprising than his conclusion that campaigning against the Congress was a ubiquitous strategy (p. 168). This contradicted the notion that members of Congress felt a strong sense of "institutional loyalty" to their body. Although this norm of loyalty may have had some continuing impact in Washington, it had virtually no impact on members' behavior back in their home districts.

one in three adults has had a favorable image of the Congress at the time.[38] Adding insult to injury, evaluations of the president and the Supreme Court have been consistently more positive than those of the legislative branch.[39]

More importantly, the denigration of Congress as an institution has contrasted sharply with the highly positive evaluations given individual legislators by their constituencies, as witnessed both by polling data (see Table 3–3) and the overwhelming proportion of incumbents who win reelection. Individual legislators can usually present themselves in positive terms, whereas the Congress as a whole depends on the characterizations of others, especially those of the executive and the media. Although there are always interbranch tensions, the prevalence of divided government in the 1969–1993 era encouraged Republican presidents to issue regular attacks on an allegedly obstructionist and partisan Democratic Congress.

More than partisan interbranch bickering, however, declining support for Congress may result from the nature of congressional press coverage in the post-Watergate era. "Over the years," concludes one recent study, "press coverage has moved from healthy skepticism to outright cynicism. . . . To believe the modern reporter or editor, legislators are egregiously overpaid, indulged,

TABLE 3–3
High Approval for Members; Low Approval for Congress

Individual Members	Congress as an Institution
Serve constituents (usually done effectively).	Resolves national issues only with difficulty or not at all.
Run against Congress.	Has few defenders.
Emphasize personal style and outreach to constituents.	Operates as collegial body, difficult to understand.
Are reported on by local media in generally positive terms.	Is often reported on negatively by national media (scandals, etc.).
Respond quickly to most constituent needs/inquiries.	Moves slowly; cumbersome procedures limit rapid responses.
Are able to highlight personal goals and accomplishments.	Has many voices, but none can speak clearly for the Congress as a whole.

Source: Adapted from Davidson and Oleszek, 4th ed., p. 444.

[38]Among others, see Glenn Parker, *Characteristics of Congress* (Englewood Cliffs, NJ: Prentice Hall, 1989), chap. 3; and Roger H. Davidson and Walter J. Oleszek, *Congress and Its Members,* 4th ed. (Washington: CQ Press, 1994).

[39]In 1993, the following percentage of respondents expressed a "great deal of confidence" in the three branches of government: the Supreme Court, 31 percent; the executive branch, 12 percent; and the Congress, 7 percent. In 1973, the Congress had received a 24 percent confidence rating in a similar survey. (*Source:* National Opinion Research Center surveys, cited in Karlyn Bowman and Everett Ladd, "Public Opinion toward Congress," in *Congress, The Press, and The Public* [Washington: AEI/Brookings, 1994], p.54.)

and indifferent to the problems of constituents who lack six-figure incomes and fantastic job perquisites."[40]

The press' relationship with Congress has become more complex over the years. In sheer numbers, the Washington press corps has grown steadily since about 1960, when it comprised fewer than 1,000 reporters predominantly representing newspapers and periodicals. By 1990, more than 3,000 reporters were at work in the capital, with a slight but growing edge to those from television and radio.[41]

However significant the growth of the press corps and the rising importance of the electronic media, other developments have been equally telling. First, the nature of political reporting has changed since Watergate (c. 1972); the historically cozy relationships between Washington politicians and reporters, although not disappearing, became more contentious, even adversarial—especially at the national level. Second, technical advances such as satellite linkages allowed many members of Congress to communicate directly with their constituents, often through local television outlets that are far less critical than are the national media.[42]

At the same time, the steady growth of cable television, which carries C-SPAN and its intense, unfiltered coverage of the Congress, and the popularity of talk-show radio, with its ability to generate thousands of letters and phone calls, have increased constituent pressures on members of Congress. Media sources are simply more varied and less subject to the control of any one voice, be it the president's or a legislative leader's. And many of the voices, most notably those on talk radio, take a relentlessly negative approach to what they see as the needlessly complex and insular context of Capitol Hill politics. The capacity of talk shows to affect the Congress became clear in 1993. Then-Representative James Inhofe (R–Okla.), an obscure minority-party congressman,[43] relentlessly traveled the talk-show circuit, pushing his proposal to open up the process of prying a bill out of committee through the use of a discharge petition, which, to succeed, requires a majority of members' signatures. His campaign turned on the highly technical point that members who signed the petition should have their names made public. The House leadership wanted to retain the cloak of anonymity on signees; such a

---

[40]Mark J. Rozell, "Press Coverage of Congress," in Thomas E. Mann and Norman J. Ornstein, eds., *Congress, The Press, and the Public* (Washington: AEI/Brookings, 1994), pp. 109–110.

[41]Harold W. Stanley and Richard G. Niemi, *Vital Statistics on American Politics*, 2nd ed. (Washington: CQ Press, 1990), p. 52.

[42]See Timothy Cook, *Making Laws and Making News* (Washington: Brookings, 1989), and his "PR on the Hill: The Evolution of Congressional Press Operations," In Christopher Deering, ed., *Congressional Politics* (Chicago: Dorsey, 1988), pp. 62–89.

[43]In something of an upset, Representative Inhofe won a Senate seat in 1994, but the Republican sweep was probably more responsible than any credit that he could claim from his discharge petition triumph.

practice allowed them privately to urge members not to sign, whereas public disclosure would increase pressures from outside interests to discharge a bill (and thus upset the leadership's control of legislative business). In a clever move, Inhofe constructed his own discharge petition to bring to the floor a bill that would open up the discharge process. Despite intense leadership opposition, this tactic succeeded, and the bill moved to floor debate and eventual approval.

Only within the legislative branch would such public intervention into an arcane intra-institutional conflict be easily available as a tactic. Representative Inhofe and his supporters could defeat the Democratic leadership by campaigning vigorously through radio talk shows against the way the Congress conducts its own business. Despite the occasional airing of divisions within the executive and judicial branches, only the highly permeable Congress would change its internal rules because of public pressures orchestrated through the media from within the institution itself.

CONGRESS IN CONTEXT

As a representative body, Congress necessarily responds to changes in its context, and we can best understand it within its contemporaneous environment. The strong parties of the early 1900s helped produce well-disciplined legislative parties and the most powerful congressional leaders in the American experience (see chapter 7). On regular occasions the electorate has modified its partisan preferences and thus changed the nature of Congress.[44] In such circumstances the usual condition of congressional elections as local contests is overwhelmed by national forces; the 1994 congressional elections reflect such an instance, even though the forty-year period of Republican minorities in the House does represent a historically unprecedented duration of such status.

Although the 1994 elections may indicate the commencement of a new congressional alignment, the 1970s and 1980s produced a legislative context that does not lead to broad, party-based change. Rather, the growth—even explosion—of both organized interests and public policies during this period has created a context that has encouraged decentralization. In this postreform era, incumbents relied on political action committee funds to win reelection in record numbers (see chapter 4), subcommittees proliferated (see chapter 5), informal caucuses of members became commonplace (see chapter 6), and individual members' enterprises evolved to enhance their representative capacities (also chapter 6). With the growth in the number and complexity of

---

[44]David Brady, *Critical Elections and Congressional Policy Making* (Stanford, CA: Stanford University Press, 1988).

public policies, Congress has positioned itself centrally for access to ongoing programs and those who administer them.[45] Even so, in cooperating with thousands upon thousands of groups and tens of thousands of lobbyists, Congress has also contributed to an interest-dominated context that allows for much responsiveness to individual concerns but little capacity to respond to major issues as articulated by the president and party leaders.[46]

Ironically, the very responsiveness of individual members of Congress to specific constituencies may have rendered the Congress as an institution unresponsive to major societal concerns such as budget deficits, health care costs, crime, and welfare. Members of Congress know best how to serve constituents and groups with particular interests, even though they may desire to make large-scale changes to address broad societal problems. Given continuing deficits (see chapter 8) and great restraints in either shaping new programs or eliminating old ones, legislators have contributed to a context that breeds distrust and invites cynicism, a combination that makes coherent policy making all the more difficult.

---

[45]Morris Fiorina, *Congress: Keystone of the Washington Establishment,* 2nd ed. (New Haven, CT: Yale University Press, 1989).

[46]Among others, see Phillips, *Arrogant Capital;* Jonathan Rauch, *Demosclerosis* (New York: Times Books, 1994); and Theodore Lowi, *End of Liberalism,* 2nd ed. (New York: Norton, 1979).

Four ✒

CONGRESSIONAL ELECTIONS: ROOTS OF THE CENTRIFUGAL CONGRESS

I n 1992, tremendous change rocked the U.S. House of Representatives. Extensive redistricting in the wake of the 1990 census and widespread abuse of check-cashing privileges at the House Bank had induced members to retire, led to nineteen primary election defeats and twenty-four general election losses by incumbents, and resulted in the largest turnover since 1948—110 newcomers (sixty-three Democrats and forty-seven Republicans), more than a quarter of the chamber's 435 Representatives. Republicans did gain House seats, but, much to their dismay, Democrats continued to hold substantial majorities in both House and Senate.

Two years later, however, Republicans picked up fifty-two additional seats in the House and eight seats in the Senate to gain control of both bodies for the first time in forty years.[1] If the number of 110 new House members represented the most important aspect of the 1992 elections, in 1994 the central result was that all Republican incumbents in both houses waged successful bids for reelection (among Democrats, however, thirty-four Representatives and two senators were defeated[2]).

In sum, the 1992 and 1994 elections shook up much of the conventional wisdom about congressional elections in the postreform era, a conventional wisdom that emphasized stability, incumbency, and the insularity of sitting legislators from effective challenges. Moreover, few scholars or political professionals had viewed the Democratic House as vulnerable to a Republican takeover. Nonetheless, on January 3, 1995, Republican Newt Gingrich was sworn in as the presiding officer of the House—a House in which more than half the members had served for four years or less.

---

[1]A ninth Senate seat came to the Republicans through the November 1994 party switch of Alabama Democrat Richard Shelby. They added a tenth seat with Senator Ben Nighthorse Campbell's (Colo.) switch in March 1995.

[2]Beyond the thirty-four Democratic incumbents who lost in the general election, two more lost in Democratic primary contests.

Even with this dramatic change, though, at a time when public support for Congress had reached historic lows, when an internal House Bank scandal scarred literally hundreds of members, when congressional gridlock and term limits were continuing topics for editorial writers and pundits, in 1992 and 1994 more than nine of every ten incumbents who sought reelection were successful in their quests.[3] To an extent, the more things changed, the more they remained the same. Even with large-scale changes in membership and party alignment, the Congress remained a reasonably congenial place for incumbent legislators.

This chapter explores a fundamental building block of the centrifugal Congress—the politics of congressional elections. In the postreform era, this has meant the politics of reelection, given that the vast majority of successful candidates are sitting Representatives and senators. Indeed, the very success of these legislators represents part of a perplexing problem. Writing before the 1992 and 1994 elections, scholar Gary Jacobson observed that "political incapacity and stalemate are encouraged by a peculiar shortcoming of contemporary congressional election processes. They give us representatives and senators who are individually responsive but collectively irresponsible."[4]

Jacobson may have been correct, but the Congress does change—both in its membership and in its attitudes toward policies. Although most congressional results are determined by local issues and candidates, national trends also influence the electorate. The 1992 elections generated new concerns about the deficit, and legislators began to make efforts to reduce crime through enhanced funding for police and modest gun control policies. More definitively, the 1994 Republican triumph resulted from strong national forces that increased the vulnerability of many sitting House Democrats. Ironically, although "voters know little about their representatives and only a little more about their senators," the electorate as a whole tends to elect "a more representative Congress than [it] seems to deserve."[5]

Why this is so will be examined in this chapter. We will explore how local and national elements combine to forge a new Congress every two years. Local forces often seem to dominate congressional decision making, as lawmakers protect their constituents' particular interests, ranging from grazing

---

[3]Setting aside those incumbents who ran against other incumbents in redrawn districts, the success rate of challengers to incumbents in the general election was just 5.5%. See John Hibbing, "The 1992 House Elections and Congressional Careers," *Extension of Remarks, Legislative Studies Section Newsletter,* June 1993, p. 2. Put another way, of 349 incumbents who ran in the general election, 325 (93%) won reelection. The 88% figure used below is thus a generous assessment of the 1992 results, in terms of the vulnerability of incumbents.

[4]Gary Jacobson, *The Politics of Congressional Elections,* 3rd ed. (New York: HarperCollins, 1992), p. 2.

[5]Robert S. Erickson and Gerald C. Wright, "Voters, Candidates, and Issues in Congressional Elections," in Lawrence Dodd and Bruce I. Oppenheimer, eds., *Congress Reconsidered,* 5th ed. (Washington: CQ Press, 1993), p. 113.

rights for cattle to ship building to the aerospace industry. At times, however, these centrifugal forces are offset by national issues and by increasingly heterogeneous congressional districts, where one or a few interests cannot dominate. Sometimes (most often after a high-visibility presidential election) the legislative and executive branches respond to the electorate by moving significant policy initiatives through the complex and slow legislative process. This occurred dramatically with the results of the election of 1994 and the initial months of the 104th Congress. Not only did Republicans win majorities, they proved themselves capable—at least in the House—of passing an impressive array of legislation, much of it drawn from a single campaign document, the Contract with America.

This chapter will first examine the forces of fragmentation—localism, incumbency, and campaign finance—that have grown increasingly important in congressional elections since the 1970s. Then, more general forces will be explored to see how much a Congress might reflect a "national verdict"[6] on hotly contested issues. If a national message is clear, congressional leaders and the president may well be able to overcome, or at least balance, the tendencies of members to look homeward in developing their policy positions.

LOCAL ELECTIONS FOR A NATIONAL OFFICE

All politics is local.

Former Speaker Thomas P. (Tip) O'Neill

Much of the fragmentation on Capitol Hill lies in the profoundly local nature of congressional elections, especially for Representatives, whose districts remain relatively homogeneous (even as they have become less dominated by a few interests over time). To be sure, a few constituencies cover immense areas such as the whole of Alaska, Montana, and Wyoming, each with a single representative. Other districts reflect highly diverse populations, such as those metropolitan seats that include substantial numbers of the urban poor, various racial and ethnic groups, small business owners, and wealthy suburbanites. Nonetheless, when compared with a presidential campaign or those for a few large-state U.S. Senate seats, most congressional races are fought within a well-defined local context.

Members of Congress continually talk of their constituents, as if they knew exactly who these individuals are. In fact, all legislators relate to several different, overlapping constituencies. Richard Fenno finds that "each member of Congress perceives four concentric constituencies: geographic, reelection, primary, and personal."[7] Roughly speaking, the geographic constituency reflects

---

[6]Ibid., p. 91.
[7]Richard F. Fenno, *Home Style* (Boston: Little Brown, 1978), p. 27.

the physical boundaries of the district; the reelection constituency comprises the number of voters, and their preferences, that have provided (and will provide) electoral success; the primary constituency is that group that "each congressman believes would provide his last line of electoral defense in a primary;"[8] and the personal constituency consists of those long-time intimates whom the legislator can trust to offer unvarnished advice and accurate political information.

Geographic Constituencies

In the wake of a series of key Supreme Court decisions and voting rights legislation in the 1960s, all congressional districts have had roughly equal populations;[9] post-1990 districts average about 570,000 as a result of the regular decennial apportionment, which allocated seats to states in accord with their populations. Thus, California's House delegation grew from forty-five in the 1980s to fifty-two in the 1990s, and each district has a total population of a little more than 571,000. In that congressional seats are awarded to states through a mathematical formula and districts cannot cross state lines, population variations from state to state can be much more substantial. For example, in 1991 the state of Montana filed an unsuccessful suit over the loss of one of its two congressional districts in the 1992 reapportionment process, which left the state with a single constituency of almost 800,000. Conversely, Oklahoma districts consist of about 524,000 residents, about 8 percent less than the national average.

Members of the House all represent roughly the same number of constituents with roughly the same resources (see chapter 6 on congressional enterprises). This ensures a substantial fragmentation within the House, given the great differences in culture, race, ethnicity, age, wealth, and so forth, across the nation, but recent judicial interpretations of the 1965 Voting Rights Act (and its 1982 extension) have greatly increased the importance of racial representation.

The 1982 legislation mandated that redistricting—the actual redrawing of congressional districts, usually by state legislatures after reapportionment— not dilute minority voting strength. Minorities were explicitly defined as African Americans and Hispanics. Congressional redistricting in 1991–1992 thus produced a slew of "minority-majority" districts that elected fifty-eight

---

[8]Ibid., p. 18.

[9]The Constitution mandates the reapportionment of House seats among the states every ten years, after the decennial census. Each state must then redraw its district lines to comply with equal representation requirements. For a good contemporary overview of redistricting and reapportionment, see David Butler and Bruce Cain, *Congressional Redistricting* (New York: Macmillan, 1992).

minority Representatives in 1992, up from thirty-eight in 1990.[10] Minority populations were concentrated in districts by legal gerrymandering; that is, many odd-shaped seats were created specifically so that minority legislators would be elected. These expectations were fulfilled, in that "sixteen new black elected officials joined the 1992 Congress, each from a majority black district."[11]

In many ways, the emphasis on the racial composition of districts has turned the notion of gerrymandering on its head. Although gerrymandering—drawing political boundaries to benefit one candidate, party, or population grouping—has a long history in the United States, it has always been considered unethical.[12] The Voting Rights Act of 1965 and a series of important Supreme Court decisions in the mid-1960s established a "one-person, one-vote" rule that opened up the electoral system to minorities, but the impact of minority voters often appeared diluted. For example, in North Carolina, African Americans made up 22 percent of the population in 1990, but the state had elected no minority member to Congress in this century. The state's 1992 redistricting produced two districts designed to send an African American to Washington. Gerrymandering to concentrate minority voting strength had become an officially sanctioned policy.[13]

In fact, the most remarkable example of racial gerrymandering came in North Carolina's "I-85 district," so labeled "because it consists of a series of urban black areas, many of them poor, partially connected by a line sometimes no wider than I-85, splitting adjacent districts in two"[14] (see Figure 4–1). The government-sanctioned gerrymander worked; African American candidates, both Democrats, won the seats that had been carved out for them.

The long-term impact of more minority-majority districts is unclear, especially as the Supreme Court rules on their constitutionality.[15] Unsurprisingly, they have elected Democrats in overwhelming numbers. In the 1992 congressional elections, only one Republican, from a heavily Cuban area of Miami, emerged victorious in such a district. At the same time, these heavy concentrations of Democratic votes have produced a large number of winnable seats for Republicans, especially in 1994. Whereas the 1992 elections resulted in

---

[10]See Jon Meacham, "Voting Wrongs," *The Washington Monthly* (March 1993), p. 28. Of the fifty-eight minority House members, fifty-two came from minority-majority districts.

[11]Lani Guinier, "Don't Scapegoat the Gerrymander," *New York Times Magazine*, January 8, 1995, pp. 36–37.

[12]See Butler and Cain, op. cit., pp. 1ff.

[13]Several legal cases have challenged this policy; the Supreme Court heard arguments on a Louisiana case in 1995.

[14]Michael Barone and Grant Ujifusa, *The Almanac of American Politics 1994* (Washington: National Journal, 1993), p. 969.

[15]See, among others, Carol M. Swain, "The Future of Black Representation," *The American Prospect* (Fall 1995), pp. 78–85.

FIGURE 4-1
North Carolina's 12th District

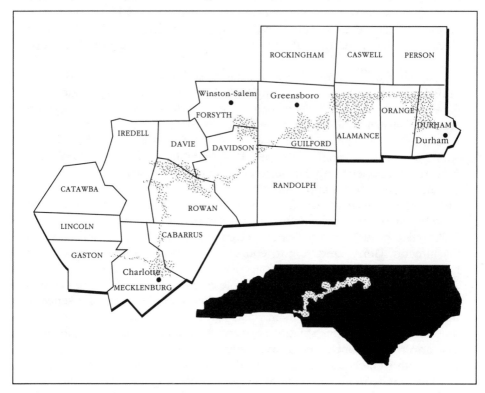

Source: *Congressional Quarterly Weekly Reports* (April 25, 1992), p. 1086.

only a modest swing toward the GOP, the 1994 results reflected exactly what Republican strategists had anticipated: a loss of sixteen Democratic seats in the eleven states of the old Confederacy. Moreover, these seats will probably remain Republican for some time to come, given their racial composition and the strong tendency of white males to vote for GOP candidates.

In addition, the larger numbers of minority Democrats from "safe" districts and of Southern Republicans may increase the ideological distance between the two parties in the House, reinforcing a trend of the past thirty years and leading to a pair of more combative, unified sets of partisans (see chapter 7). Conversely, the growing strength of minority caucuses renders them important independent sources of power; Democratic leaders often must accommodate the wishes of the thirty-six-member Congressional Black Caucus, for example, or face the possibility of defection of African American legislators on key votes.

More generally, the drawing of district lines to maximize racial representation and population equality necessarily reduces other representational
emphases. Thus, save for single-seat states such as Delaware or Wyoming,
congressional districts do not reflect other governmental units (for example,
cities and counties) or broad, nonracial community patterns (such as a large
concentration of Italian-Americans).

The Other Constituencies: Behavior and Perception

If the geographic constituency is unambiguous in its boundaries, the other
constituencies identified by Fenno are more subjective. Even in the same district, no two incumbents would put together the same reelection constituency.
Nor would we expect their primary supporters or their personal backers to be
the same. In particular, personal constituencies are unique; Fenno recalls sitting in the living room of one member's top district staffer and best friend,

> watching an NFL game with the congressman, the district aide, the state
> assemblyman from the congressman's home county, and the district attor-
> ney of the same county. The last three were among the five people with
> whom the congressman had held his first strategy meeting four years ear-
> lier. . . . Between plays and at halftime, over beer and pretzels, the four
> discussed every aspect of the congressman's campaign. . . . Ostensibly
> they were watching the football game. Actually, the congressman was
> exchanging political advice, information, and perspectives with three of
> his oldest and closest political associates.[16]

Examining the evolution of constituencies within a single congressional
district demonstrates both how the geographic boundaries can change
through redistricting and how a series of incumbents construct their own
unique bases of support. From 1972 through 1995, for example, Kansas's
Second Congressional District has changed its representative stripes as much
as any seat in the country; five different individuals have held the seat in that
period. Not only was the district redrawn in 1972, in 1982, and in 1992, but
each of the incumbents developed his or her own set of personal, primary,
and reelection constituencies (see Table 4–1).

Over this twenty-five-year period, the population size of the Second
District grew dramatically—from a low of 454,000 in the 1970s to well over
600,000 in the 1990s (Kansas lost one of its five House seats after the 1990
census)—and its geographic configuration changed as much. Historically, it
had encompassed a varied but relatively compact area in northeast Kansas; in
1992, however, it spread from the Nebraska border on the north to the
Oklahoma line on the south.

---

[16]Fenno, op. cit., p. 25.

TABLE 4-1

Changing Constituencies in a Single Congressional District: The Kansas Second, 1971-1995

Member, Term	Constituency Type			
	Geographic	Reelection	Primary	Personal
Bill Roy (D), 1971–1975	479K, NE 1/4 of KS, rural/urban	Democrats/ Independents/ Moderate Republicans	Kansas City, KS, Democrats; federal/state employees	State legislators' support, medical doctors
Martha Keys (D), 1975–1979	454K, NE 1/4 of KS, rural/urban	Democrats/ Independents/ Moderate Republicans	McGovern Democrats	Antiwar Democrats, 1972 campaign
Jim Jefferies (R), 1979–1983	454K, NE 1/4 of KS, rural/urban	Republicans/ Conservatives	Conservative Republicans	Reagan backers in 1976
Jim Slattery (D), 1983–1995	472K, NE 1/4 of KS, rural/urban	Democrats/ Independents/ Moderate Republicans	Topeka and moderate Democrats	Loyalists from state legislature days
Sam Brownback (R) 1995–	619K, east 1/3 of KS, save suburban Kansas City	Republicans/ Perot supporters/ Reagan Democrats	Traditional Republicans	Agricultural community, Kansas State University, family media base

Source: *Almanac of American Politics,* various editions.

Even more significant have been the changes in the reelection, primary, and personal constituencies represented by the five incumbents. A district with roughly the same geographic boundaries elected two fairly liberal Democrats, a moderate-to-conservative Democrat, a conservative Republican, and an extremely conservative Republican—each with his or her own set of personal supporters and winning reelection coalition. Because their constituencies differed, so too did the ways in which they viewed the district. In addition, communication patterns from constituents changed; for example, many liberals considered conservative Representative Jim Jefferies a lost cause, and many Republicans viewed Representative Martha Keys, a liberal Democrat, unsympathetic to their concerns.

Incumbents also develop their own funding constituencies, often bringing in hundreds of thousands of dollars from *outside* the confines of their physical districts. With a seat on the powerful Energy and Commerce Committee, Representative Jim Slattery proved especially adept at obtaining substantial PAC funding from groups with little direct interest in Kansas's Second District. In his last two campaigns (1990 and 1992) he spent a total of $1,169,000, with $767,000 (or 66 percent) coming from PACs.

Careful cultivation of Fenno's four concentric constituencies—geographic, reelection, primary, personal—as well as maintaining a strong funding base allows incumbents considerable latitude in deciding how to represent their districts, especially if they are skilled at explaining their positions. Nevertheless, there are real limits to this flexibility. As Democratic House members discovered in 1992 and 1994, incumbents can face problems as a result of unpopular votes, well-funded opponents, strong national trends, scandals of their own making, or some combination of the above. However successful members are at playing to their constituencies, they remain uncertain over their abilities to win reelection.[17] This uncertainty, in turn, represents a shaky base for building an extended congressional career.

ELECTIONS IN A CAREERIST CONGRESS

If a group of planners sat down and tried to design a pair of American electoral assemblies with the goal of serving members' electoral needs year in and year out, they would be hard pressed to improve on what exists.

David Mayhew, *Congress: The Electoral Connection*

Over the course of the past 100 years, the Congress has developed into an institution that fosters long careers. In the 1990s this may be changing, as formal and informal pressures for term limits affect legislators' choices, but over the course of the twentieth century, extended careers have become the norm. Between 1911 and 1971, the number of "careerists" (legislators serving ten or more terms) rose steadily, from 2.8 percent to 20 percent. After substantial turnover in the 1970s, the percentage of careerists has stabilized at about 15 percent of the House, and the average number of terms served by all members has held at slightly more than five. Senate tenure is similar, averaging about 11 years.[18]

Careerist legislators want to remain in office; every two (or six) years they must thus win reelection. Unsurprisingly, with the careerist, professional Congress have come both increased incentives to run for reelection and enhanced capacities for incumbents to emerge victorious. Since 1950, 90 percent of House incumbents ordinarily run for reelection and well over 90 percent of them win.[19] Incumbency success rates rose to historic highs in the

---

[17]This is not new. For an earlier analysis of electoral uncertainty among House members, see Thomas Mann, *Unsafe at Any Margin* (Washington: American Enterprise Institute, 1978).

[18]Charles S. Bullock III, "House Careerists: Changing Patterns of Longevity and Attrition," *American Political Science Review* 66 (1972), pp. 1295–1305. See also Donald Matthews, "Legislative Recruitment and Legislative Careers," in Gerhard Loewenberg, Samuel C. Patterson, and Malcolm E. Jewell, eds., *Handbook of Legislative Research* (Cambridge, MA: Harvard University Press, 1985), pp. 17–56.

[19]Jacobson, op. cit., pp. 26–18.

1984–1990 period, when House members won a staggering 97 percent of their bids for reelection. Even in 1992, with anti-incumbency sentiment running at a fever pitch and the House Bank scandal in full bloom, almost nine in ten (88 percent) of those seeking reelection were returned to office. Sitting senators are more vulnerable than House incumbents, with the 1952–1992 period producing an overall reelection rate of 79 percent. From 1982 on, however, Senate incumbents have won more than 85 percent of their races, indicating a trend toward a greater safety that roughly mirrors that in the House.

Why are incumbents so difficult to unseat? And what difference does it make that they remain relatively safe? The answers to both these questions are central to understanding the fragmentation, or atomization, of the United States Congress. Most of our attention will be directed at House elections, given the greater safety of House members and the extensive research that has focused on these contests.

House Incumbents and the Structure of Competition

Although House members have consistently won reelection at high rates, there have been major changes in how this has occurred in the past forty years, especially since the early 1970s. First, incumbents' margins rose substantially over this period; second, freshman members, who were historically more vulnerable than their more experienced colleagues, improved their success rates to match those of the chamber as a whole. Congressional campaigns have also changed tremendously in terms of their spending levels and funding patterns since the mid-1970s, and, as we shall see in chapter 6, individual members voted themselves consistently higher levels of office resources in the 1960s and 1970s. With large numbers of staff and substantial travel budgets, Representatives could wage a "permanent campaign" if they so chose.[20] Many did, even when no opponent emerged. For example, incumbents who ran unopposed in 1990 added to their safety by spending an average of more than $250,000 of campaign money for political purposes during the 1989–1990 period.[21]

Increasing Margins and the "Sophomore Surge"

In the 1960s and 1970s, fewer and fewer congressional races were won by narrow margins. By historical standards the "marginals," or closely contested seats in which the winning candidate receives no more than 55 or 60 percent of the vote, were vanishing.[22] This stark observation, illustrated in Figure 4–2, set off a scramble to find a "smoking gun" explanation for this phenomenon.

---

[20]This term was popularized by Sidney Blumenthal's book *The Permanent Campaign* (New York: Touchstone, 1982).

[21]Sara Fritz and Dwight Morris, *Gold-Plated Politics* (Washington: CQ Press, 1992), pp. 14–15.

[22]David R. Mayhew, "Congressional Elections: The Case of the Vanishing Marginals," *Polity* 6 (1974), pp. 295–317.

FIGURE 4-2
House Vote in Districts with Incumbents Running, 1948 and 1972

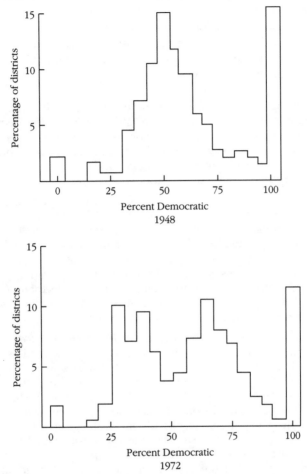

Source: Morris P. Fiorina, "The Decline of Collective
Responsibility in American Politics," reprinted by permission of
Daedalus, Journal of the American Academy of Arts and
Sciences, from the issue entitled, "The End of Consensus?,"
Summer 1980, Volume 109, Number 3.

Political scientist Morris Fiorina concluded in 1977 that "the bureaucracy
did it," as legislators created a series of programs to which they could subsequently control access (thus winning credit for their assistance in providing
benefits).[23] Over the next decade, numerous scholars weighed in with their
own assessments of the growing margins, as they looked at congressional

---

[23]Morris P. Fiorina, "The Case of the Vanishing Marginals: The Bureaucracy Did It," *American
Political Science Review* 71 (1977), pp. 177–181.

redistricting, the growth of the congressional enterprise and its resources (such as staff, franking, and trips home), levels of casework, and patterns of campaign funding.[24]

This welter of research found no single cause for the sharply reduced number of marginal seats, but a rough consensus has formed to explain the trend toward reduced levels of congressional competition in the 1970–1990 era.[25] Findings include the following:

▶ *Redistricting has had no systematic effect.* Although some incumbents may have been protected, redrawing district lines after decennial censuses is not the cause of increasing margins.[26] The exception to this conclusion is the 1992 redistricting, which produced both heavily Democratic minority-majority districts and many new seats in which Republicans could and did compete effectively.

▶ *The "personal vote" has grown.* That is, while broad partisan and national trend bases for voting in congressional elections have declined or remained minimal, the "personal" component has steadily increased.[27] Incumbency represents a large component of the personal vote, even without considering campaign spending or constituency service; incumbents are almost always better known than challengers. In campaigns during the 1980s, for example, almost half the electorate (47 percent) recalled the name of their sitting member of Congress, but only one in five (19 percent) recalled the challenger's name.[28]

▶ *Constituency service is important, but there are 435 ways to do it.* In reviewing research on constituency service, various studies have found no relationship between electoral results and casework, federal spending in the district, travel back to the district, or size of staff. "The latest academic research," Fiorina incredulously wrote in 1989, "appears to show that members of Congress can close up their district offices, dismiss their staffs, spend weekends in Washington with their families, quit doing case work, abandon their quest for federal funds, discontinue their newsletters . . . and *nothing will happen to them.*"[29] This is patently absurd, but the variety among districts, individual members' home styles, and the required levels of effort in safe and potentially

---

[24]Among an avalanche of studies, see the summary presented in Bruce Cain, John Ferejohn, and Morris Fiorina, *The Personal Vote* (Cambridge, MA: Harvard University Press, 1987), pp. 121ff.

[25]The best brief summary here can be found in Morris Fiorina, *Congress: Keystone of the Washington Establishment,* 2nd ed. (New Haven, CT: Yale University Press, 1989).

[26]Among others, see John Ferejohn, "On the Decline of Competition in Congressional Elections," *American Political Science Review* 71 (March 1977), pp. 166–176.

[27]See Cain, Ferejohn, and Fiorina, op. cit.

[28]Jacobson, op. cit., p. 118. The same tendency holds for name recognition: 92% for House incumbents; 54% for challengers.

[29]Fiorina, op. cit., pp. 94–95.

marginal districts combine to deny incumbents any sure-fire formula to improve their percentage of the vote.

▶ *Campaign spending is important, but mainly for challengers.*[30] If a challenger can spend enough money to gain substantial recognition, the chances of a close race rise sharply. Over the 1974–1992 period, challengers to incumbents have been sorely underfunded. In the 1980s, a challenger needed about $400,000 simply to have a one-in-five chance of defeating an incumbent.[31]

▶ *The incumbent's most effective electoral strategy is to discourage serious opposition.*[32] So-called high-quality challengers—state senators, mayors, previous losers who did reasonably well—start out with substantial name recognition and may well be able to raise funds more easily than a neophyte. Incumbents thus seek to maximize their victory margins, raise substantial sums of campaign funds, and provide excellent service at home in hopes of discouraging strong potential candidates from making what could prove to be a serious challenge.

▶ *Almost all of the rise in incumbents' margins can be accounted for by the "sophomore surge,"*[33] the enhanced performance of first-term House members running in their first reelection contest. Prior to the early 1970s, freshman Representatives provided the best opportunities for opposing candidates to capture a House seat, especially when the seat had changed parties in the previous election. For example, first-term Democrats from the large congressional class of 1964 accounted for most of the thirty-nine seats that changed to Republican control with the 1966 elections. But in 1976, of the forty-nine Democrats who had won a Republican-controlled seat in 1974, only one lost; this pattern was repeated with fairly large batches of freshmen in 1978, 1980, and 1984, as well as the smaller classes of the late 1980s. First-term representatives had learned how to use their large enterprises and raise substantial funds, to the point that their performance roughly equaled that of experienced legislators.[34]

Margins began to increase sharply in the late 1960s and even more so through the 1970s, but incumbents did not become much less likely to lose until the 1980s. By this time, only the occasional scandal provided a likely

---

[30]Jacobson, op. cit., p. 50. For a differing view, see Donald P. Green and Jonathan S. Krasno, "Salvation for the Spendthrift Incumbents," *American Journal of Political Science* 32 (1988), pp. 844–907.

[31]Jacobson, op. cit., p. 50.

[32]Ibid., p. 55.

[33]Albert D. Cover and David R. Mayhew, "Congressional Dynamics and the Decline of Competitive Congressional Elections," in Lawrence Dodd and Bruce Oppenheimer, eds., *Congress Reconsidered* (New York: Praeger, 1977), pp. 54–74.

[34]In fact, experienced House members with long careers have become a bit more vulnerable. See Jacobson, op. cit., p. 29, on the "retirement slump."

avenue for challenger success.[35] Incumbents continued to worry about their survival, however, as almost every election provided a vivid example of some seemingly safe member going down to an unexpected defeat.[36] Survey data demonstrated that increasing numbers of voters held their own representative, and not just the Congress as a whole, responsible for the ills of society, such as large budget deficits and high crime rates. For Democratic legislators, this posed a serious—and often insurmountable—challenge in the elections of 1992 and, especially, 1994. Before examining these contests, let us first look at the patterns of campaign funding that grew up around the incumbent-dominated system of the 1980s.

POLITICAL ACTION COMMITTEES, CAMPAIGN COSTS, AND INCUMBENCY

Along with the increasing official resources available to sitting members and the rising number of federal programs to which members could provide access and ombudsman services, the structure of campaign financing helped increase the margins and safety of House incumbents in the wake of 1974 campaign reform legislation. The 1974 amendments to the Federal Election Campaign Act, which had limited individual donations to $1,000 per campaign, and a 1976 Supreme Court decision (*Buckley v. Valeo*) that struck down limits on campaign spending combined to encourage the proliferation of political action committees (PACs), which could give congressional candidates up to $5,000 for each separate election (for example, a primary in August followed by the general election in November). Although labor unions and a few other groups had long given money to candidates through PACs, the 1974 legislation opened the door to businesses (such as oil companies[37]); trade associations (for example, realtors); and cause groups labeled nonconnected PACs[38] by the Federal Election Commission (such as the National Conservative Political Action Committee) to raise funds and make contributions to congressional campaigns.

In this context, two major changes have taken place in congressional campaign finance since 1974: (1) Campaigns have grown much more expensive,

---

[35]Ibid.

[36]See especially Mann, op. cit.

[37]In particular, the Supreme Court ruled in 1976 that Sun Oil Company could absorb the administrative costs of its political action committee, thus freeing virtually all the funds it raised to be distributed to candidates. This decision encouraged many corporations and trade associations to establish PACs. For a good overview of the first ten years of PAC activity, see Larry Sabato, *PAC Power* (New York: Norton, 1984).

[38]*Nonconnected* means literally not connected to any parent group such as a corporation or a trade association, for example, the American Medical Association or the American Trucking Association.

and (2) increasing percentages of incumbents' funds, especially in the House, have come from PACs. Although these broad trends encompass many specific decisions, they operated, at least until the sobering elections of 1994, to serve admirably the interests of incumbents, especially the majority-party House Democrats.

Rising Costs

Even with inflation pushing up campaign expenses in the post-1974 period, the growth in campaign expenditures has been striking. In 1976, the average House candidate spent $73,000 on his or her campaign; by 1982 that figure had tripled, to $228,000, and it almost doubled again in the next ten years, to $410,000 in 1992.[39] Looking at average expenditures is misleading, however, in that spending by incumbents has increased much more sharply than has that by challengers. To take the same three benchmark years, incumbents averaged $79,000 in 1976, $265,000 in 1982, and a whopping $595,000 in 1992. Challengers, on the other hand, struggled, as their mean expenditure rose from $51,000 in 1976 to $152,000 in 1982 to a relatively paltry $168,000 in 1992.[40] Between 1976 and 1982, challengers' total spending amounted to about 65 percent of what incumbents spent; by the 1988–1992 period, this proportion had decreased to just over 31 percent. Of all the obstacles facing a potential challenger, raising the roughly half-million dollars needed to compete effectively is perhaps the most daunting. Conversely, virtually every incumbent has the capacity to raise such a sum—and often much more.

Although a few candidates—usually challengers such as California's Michael Huffington—personally finance their campaigns, most must solicit funds from friends, acquaintances, like-minded individuals, their party, and, especially, organized interests (through PACs). Incumbents and challengers alike need immense amounts of money, and such a requirement makes almost all serious candidates highly attentive to, if not beholden to, their contributors. In effect, these individuals and groups compose another constituency for a candidate, beyond those within his or her district. Much funding reinforces the local forces that shape representation (such as a tobacco PAC's funding of a North Carolina legislator), but many contributions come from interests far beyond the district's confines, as with the health care industry's $100,000-plus gifts to Representative Pete Stark (D–Calif.), the former health care subcommittee chair on the Ways and Means Committee. As campaigns have grown

---

[39]Norman Ornstein, Thomas Mann, and Michael Malbin, eds., *Vital Statistics on Congress, 1993–1994* (Washington: CQ Press, 1993), p. 75. All other figures and tables in this chapter come from the same source, pp. 75ff., save as noted.

[40]There is a seeming inconsistency here, which can be accounted for by taking open-seat campaigns into account. Thus, the average cost of all 1976 campaigns was $73,000, and incumbents and challengers spent $79,000 and $51,000, respectively. Open-seat candidates, however, averaged more than $124,000.

more expensive, members have turned to PACs as sources of campaign funds. On balance, this trend increases congressional fragmentation by creating a new set of influential constituents whose interests must be taken into account. In a study of campaign funding and its revolutionary practitioner Representative Tony Coelho (D–Calif.), who served as chairman of the Democratic Congressional Campaign Committee (DCCC) during the 1980s, journalist Brooks Jackson concluded that

> increasingly . . . House Members were acting as ombudsmen not only for their constituents but also for their donors. Those who gave money came to be [another] constituency, one not envisioned by the drafters of the Constitution. Coelho interceded for a donor from another state as naturally as he would have for a businessman from Modesto, in his district. One was entitled to help by virtue of residence, the other by virtue of his currency.[41]

Campaign Contributions and the Rise of PACs

In 1972 PACs contributed a bit more than $8.5 million to congressional candidates, about 17 percent of all House campaign spending in that year. Twenty years later, PACs gave more than $127 million to House candidates, a fifteenfold increase; PAC funds amounted to 38 percent of all campaign spending.[42] As dramatic as these changes appear, they mask even more significant patterns in PAC funding of congressional campaigns.

In the post-1974 era of campaign financing, PACs have always given disproportionately to incumbents and to Democrats, and in the 1980s these patterns became more pronounced. As many businesses and trade associations organized PACs in the 1970s, Republicans increased their reliance on PAC funds from 10 percent in 1974 to 30 percent in 1984, but the tendency of these groups to back incumbents has held overall Republican support from PACs to approximately the 30 percent level. Democrats, on the other hand, moved from 22 percent PAC support in 1974 (mostly from long-standing labor groups) to an average of 45 percent in 1990–1992. Indeed, House Democrats have proven the prime beneficiaries of PAC financing in the contemporary era of congressional electoral politics. Such a pattern may well change, however, in a post-1994 era of Republican majorities.

---

[41]Brooks Jackson, *Honest Graft* (Washington: Farragut, 1990), p. 107.

[42]These figures include general election candidates' spending in both the primary and the general elections. Defeated primary candidates are not included. These figures and others in this section are from Ornstein, Mann, and Malbin, op. cit., chap. 3.

A Decade of Change: PAC Support Patterns in 1980 and 1990

In 1980, although incumbents received the lion's share (69 percent) of all PAC contributions, Republican challengers could realistically hope for some significant support from this source. Aside from labor groups, which funded only Democratic challengers, PACs provided substantial funds to the most viable Republican challengers and open-seat candidates (those with no incumbent to challenge). A decade later things had changed dramatically, as Table 4–2 illustrates. Total PAC contributions had tripled and 80 percent went to incumbents. A meager 6 percent of all funds went to challengers (in what was allegedly an anti-incumbent year), and only 2 percent found its way into the coffers of GOP challengers. Republican challengers had garnered $5.25 million in PAC contributions in 1980, compared with $2.17 million ten years later. Open-seat patterns witnessed a similar reversal, although it was not so dramatic. What happened in the 1980s?

TABLE 4–2
Political Action Committee Contributions to House Candidates, 1980 and 1990

Committee Type	Amount Contributed (dollars)	Incumbent		Challenger		Open-Seat	
		D	R	D	R	D	R
1980							
Labor	8,883,834	69	4	16	0	10	0
Corporate	11,662,361	36	32	1	20	1	9
Nonconnected	2,831,209	21	15	5	41	4	12
Trade/membership/ health	11,215,269	39	32	2	17	3	8
Cooperative	985,177	59	26	2	3	3	7
Corporation without stock	387,740	47	30	2	11	2	7
Total	35,965,590	45	24	5	15	4	7
1990							
Labor	27,609,222	66	6	11	0	16	0
Corporate	35,437,851	49	38	1	3	3	6
Nonconnected	8,517,244	44	21	7	6	14	8
Trade/membership/ health	32,539,403	52	33	2	2	6	6
Cooperative	2,252,312	60	29	2	2	4	4
Corporation without stock	2,166,162	61	25	1	3	4	5
Total	108,522,194	54	26	4	2	8	5

Source: Norman J. Ornstein, Thomas E. Mann, and Michael J. Malbin, eds., *Vital Statistics on Congress, 1993–1994* (Washington: CQ Press, 1993).

Part of the explanation is idiosyncratic to the time: Republican challengers were generally seen as enjoying excellent prospects in 1980, given an unpopular Democratic presidential candidate (Carter) and a record of success in the 1978 elections. In 1990, however, Republicans ran with an incumbent president of their own party, which placed them in a more defensive position. Much more was at work, though, as PACs increasingly "invested" their funds with Democratic incumbents who had controlled the House since 1955. In particular, Representative Coelho and the DCCC succeeded in changing the contribution patterns of all nonlabor PACs.

The hard-driving, politically savvy Coelho became chair of the DCCC in 1981, after the Democrats had suffered serious losses in the congressional elections of 1978 and 1980.[43] Coelho not only possessed a gift for prying funds from contributors, he rapidly increased donations from PACs representing businesses and trade associations—the Republicans' natural allies. Coelho's job was to convince the business and trade PACs of two things: that Democrats would control the House for the foreseeable future and that business and trade interests could work effectively with Democratic party and committee leaders. Coelho and his lieutenants worked hard to reassure key PAC managers that his party would help them, while holding in reserve the real threat that House Democrats might well look unkindly toward interests that did not contribute.

Up to and including the election of 1992, the strategy of Coelho and his successors at the DCCC proved successful in retaining Democratic House majorities, weathering the Reagan–Bush period of Republican presidents, and maintaining expectations that the Democrats would control the House for years to come. Despite some indications that incumbents had grown increasingly vulnerable in 1990 and 1992, Democrats emerged from the 1992 elections with a seemingly healthy 258–176 margin in the House of Representatives.[44] Even so, Democrats looked ahead to the 1994 congressional elections with some trepidation for the following reasons:

▶ Given control of the presidency, their party could be held responsible for the actions of the national government.

▶ President Bill Clinton received only 43 percent of the 1992 vote, while independent Ross Perot's antigovernment rhetoric helped him garner 19 percent.

▶ The president's party generally loses seats at midterm elections, and Democrats had lost ten seats in 1992.

---

[43]For a fascinating account of Coelho and the DCCC, see Jackson, op. cit.

[44]This margin was later trimmed, through special elections to fill vacant seats, to 256–178, with one independent.

▶ As November 1994 approached, less than 40 percent of the electorate expressed the opinion that President Clinton was doing either an "excellent" or "good" job.

THE ELECTORAL EARTHQUAKE OF 1994

Assessing the 1994 congressional elections, in which Republicans captured control of the Congress by gaining fifty-two House and eight Senate seats, various analysts reached for metaphors to communicate the breadth and depth of the change on Capitol Hill. One Washington editor likened the Republicans' victory to a "meteorite striking the American political landscape,"[45] and another editor, a Californian, viewed it as a "political earthquake that will send aftershocks rumbling through national politics for years to come."[46] The earthquake image seems much the more convincing, in that it reflects the electoral tensions that have grown in an era of divided government and of heightened frustration within the electorate. Moreover, the notion of aftershocks captures the political and policy implications of the Republicans' capture of the House for the first time in forty years.

Although the Republicans' Senate triumph, which produced a fifty-three–forty-seven-seat margin (gaining eight seats in the election and adding the partisan defection of Alabama Democrat Richard Shelby), was noteworthy, it was not a great surprise, in that Senate elections have proven much more competitive than House contests and the Republicans had controlled the upper chamber as recently as January 1987.[47] All observers predicted some gains for House Republicans, but almost none, save for GOP partisans, foresaw the Democrats losing their majority.[48] The House Republicans needed to win forty seats to gain control; their fifty-two-seat swing represented the largest shift since 1946, when Democrats suffered a fifty-five-seat loss. The Republicans' 1994 triumph was all the more significant because it came in an era of enhanced incumbent safety (despite some decline in 1990 and 1992) and it swept Democrats out of office all across the country. In 1994, at least, all politics was not local (see Figure 4–3).

---

[45]Robert W. Merry, "Voters' Demand for Change Puts Clinton on Defensive," *CQ Weekly Report,* November 12, 1994, p. 3207.

[46]Gary C. Jacobson, "The 1994 Midterm: Why the Models Missed It," *Extension of Remarks, Legislative Studies Section Newsletter,* Winter 1995, p. 2.

[47]The GOP lost control of the Senate in the 1986 elections, but they did not formally hand over the reins of power until January 3, 1987. In reality, Democratic control began in the wake of the 1986 elections, as did Republican control in 1994 after the final adjournment of the Senate in early December.

[48]Two weeks before the 1994 election, then-Minority Leader Gingrich put the odds at two to one that Republicans would win the House. Katharine Q. Seelye, "With Fiery Words, Gingrich Builds His Kingdom," *The New York Times,* October 27, 1994, p. A1.

FIGURE 4-3
Partisan Change in the 1994 Congressional Election

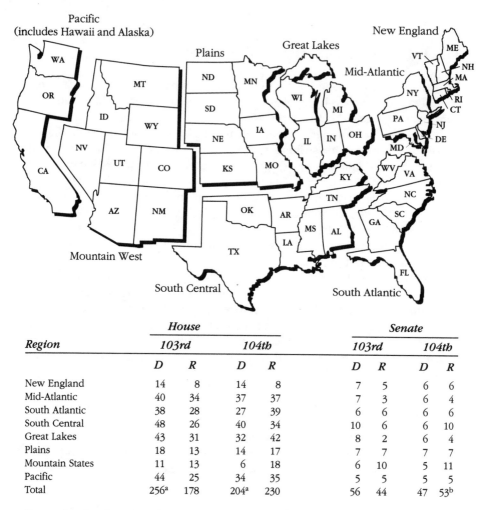

Region	House				Senate			
	103rd		104th		103rd		104th	
	D	R	D	R	D	R	D	R
New England	14	8	14	8	7	5	6	6
Mid-Atlantic	40	34	37	37	7	3	6	4
South Atlantic	38	28	27	39	6	6	6	6
South Central	48	26	40	34	10	6	6	10
Great Lakes	43	31	32	42	8	2	6	4
Plains	18	13	14	17	7	7	7	7
Mountain States	11	13	6	18	6	10	5	11
Pacific	44	25	34	35	5	5	5	5
Total	256[a]	178	204[a]	230	56	44	47	53[b]

[a]One member elected as independent; three Democrats subsequently switch party affiliation in the 104th
Congress.

[b]One Democratic senator subsequently switches party affiliation in the 104th Congress.

Source: Adapted from *National Journal,* November 12, 1994, pp. 2628–2629.

The nationalization of the 1994 election was no random event. Rather, congressional Republicans—above all, Representative Newt Gingrich—made it a
national election. Most obviously, in conjunction with political consultant and
pollster Frank Luntz, Gingrich announced early in the year that on September 27,
1994, Republican House candidates would gather in Washington to offer their

support for a ten-item "Contract with America," which would explicitly lay out the changes they would propose in the first 100 days of the new Congress. Even though most voters had little understanding of the Contract's specifics, Gingrich's use of the document nationalized the voting decision to an extent and offered him, as Speaker, a useful vehicle to push a series of reforms. Most voters neither knew nor cared what was in the Contract; indeed, as the election grew near and Republican hopes soared, even Gingrich moved to distance himself from the Contract. In the end, however, all but three freshman Republicans signed the document, which took on a life of its own.

Beyond the Contract, Gingrich and his allies had other help in nationalizing the election, given that neither President Clinton nor the Democratic Congress enjoyed great popularity; the millions of voters who supported Ross Perot for president in 1992 saw little to like in the 103rd Congress (of 1993–1994). In two Tennessee races, Perot voters had "broke[n] for [the victorious] Republican Senate candidates by a margin of about 75 percent to 20 percent," and in California and Pennsylvania they had chosen Republicans for the Senate by two-to-one margins.[49]

Supplementing strong national trends, Gingrich, other top leaders, the Republican National Congressional Committee (RNCC), and like-minded PACs worked on behalf of Republican candidates on a district-by-district basis. Indeed, Gingrich helped recruit many members of the Republican majority, instructed them on key issues, campaigned for most of them, and raised money for their campaigns. Through GOPAC, a Gingrich-directed group, funds and campaign assistance flowed to Republican candidates, and the RNCC could guarantee the maximum allowable contribution of $25,000 to any seriously competitive candidate. From the perspective of many Republicans, their capture of the House came one district at a time, with each individual new member owing a great deal to the assistance provided by then-Minority Whip Gingrich. In the end, both the national themes and the leaders' expertise, funding, and energy contributed to a great unity among first-term members in particular and the entire Republican majority in general. It is no wonder that grateful GOP legislators have allowed Newt Gingrich to exercise greater power than any leader since Representative Joseph Cannon's (R–Ill.) dictatorial days came to an end in 1910.

LOCAL CAMPAIGNS FOR NATIONAL OFFICE: THE MIX OF FORCES

Buoyed both by Tip O'Neill's homey advice that "all politics is local" and by dozens of academic studies that explain or assume the power of incumbency, a strong conventional wisdom about the reduced competition in congressional

---

[49]Merry, "Voters' Demand for Change Puts Clinton on Defensive," p. 3208.

elections emerged during the early 1970s and held sway for more than twenty years.[50] Bolstered by PAC funds and the contributions of interests and individuals who wanted to invest with the majority party, Democrats succeeded in sheltering their House members and, to a lesser extent, their senators from the winds of national politics that filled the sails of Republican presidential candidates in five of six elections between 1968 and 1988.[51]

As marginal seats vanished, less opportunity existed for powerful national forces to sweep large numbers of new members into office.[52] In part, however, this resistance to change had its foundation in the assumption of a continuing Democratic majority in the House of Representatives. As of 1994, however, that assumption no longer holds, and the underlying structure of competition has changed substantially. In particular, Republican majorities may well generate shifts in candidate recruitment and PAC contributions, which could make the GOP dominant in congressional elections. For example, 233 House Republicans raised $13.3 million in PAC funds during the first six months of the 104th Congress (January through June 1995). This compares with $11.7 million raised by 258 House Democrats in the comparable period of the 103rd Congress.[53]

Despite the recent changes, the value of incumbency has scarcely evaporated; in 1994, 92 percent of House incumbents won their general election contests, and all sitting Republican Representatives and senators succeeded in returning to the 104th Congress. However, voters have begun to align their judgments on congressional candidates with their presidential choices.[54] This cannot be good news for Democrats, whose presidential candidates have failed to attract more than half the vote in any contest since 1964. Congressional elections remain a series of locally focused contests, but through the development of themes and the provision of resources, Republicans have added a substantial national element, thus fundamentally changing the nature of politics on Capitol Hill.

---

[50]See the list in the previous section on the "sophomore surge."

[51]Some voters may well have chosen to balance a Republican president with a Democratic Congress, and many have grown comfortable with it, but to see divided government as an explicit choice of rational voters may push the interpretation a bit too far. For a coherent discussion, see Gary Jacobson, *The Electoral Origins of Divided Government* (Boulder, CO: Westview Press, 1990), especially pp. 119–120.

[52]For a useful summary of the relative import of national and local forces, see James Campbell, *The Presidential Pulse of Congressional Elections* (Lexington: University Press of Kentucky, 1993).

[53]Eric Moses, "To the Victors Go PAC Spoils," *National Journal,* September 16, 1995, p. 2295.

[54]Jacobson, "The 1994 Midterm," p. 14.

Five ❧

CONGRESSIONAL COMMITTEES

More than a century ago, a young political scientist named Woodrow Wilson wrote,

> The House sits, not for serious discussion, but to sanction the conclusions of its Committees as rapidly as possible. It legislates in its committee-rooms; not by the determination of majorities, but by the resolutions of its specially-commissioned minorities [the committees]; so that it is not far from the truth to say that Congress in session is Congress on public exhibition, whilst Congress in its committee-rooms is Congress at work.[1]

Wilson's words, especially those of the last two lines, have been quoted ad infinitum, and like Tip O'Neill's dictum that "all politics is local," Wilson's phrase has become a cliché, yet its essence remains true; the Congress, especially the House, performs the vast majority of its work within the confines of its committee rooms. Despite the enhanced powers of contemporary party leaders and the independence of individual members, committee decisions and committee leadership dictate much of the pace and content of congressional legislation.

Committees remain important and powerful because their existence makes such good sense, both for individual legislators and for the Congress as a whole. Acting on their own, 435 House members or 100 senators cannot reasonably be expected to hammer out coherent legislation across the entire spectrum of issues on each year's congressional agenda. Like most large organizations, the Congress has profited from a division of labor among smaller work groups. Committees specialize in particular policy areas ranging from those taken up by the broadly inclusive Commerce Committee to the relatively narrow focus of the Small Business Committee. Committees are designed to serve their parent

---

[1]Woodrow Wilson, *Congressional Government* (Baltimore: Johns Hopkins University Press, 1981 [original publication date, 1885]), p. 69.

chambers, which has meant continuing changes over the years in the number, membership levels, and jurisdictions of the units. In 1995, for example, the House's Republican majority endorsed its leadership's proposal to eliminate three committees, to alter the jurisdiction of others, and to limit the number of subcommittees to five per committee. In the 104th Congress the District of Columbia, the Post Office and Civil Service, and the Merchant Marine and Fisheries Committees all ceased to exist, and their responsibilities were farmed out to other panels (see Table 5–1). In the Senate, on the other hand, the new Republican majority proposed no major changes.

Viewing committees as efficient sharers of information allows one to see how decentralization can benefit the Congress as a whole.[2] Given a $1.6 trillion annual budget and a federal government that regulates everything from trucking to toxic waste, congressional decentralization through the committee system allows lawmakers to specialize and make informed decisions on a wide range of complex, often conflicting policies. In fact, by sharing information across committees, Congress may produce a relatively coherent, consistent set of policies.

Nevertheless, a fragmented committee system can and does serve more individualistic ends. Members often seek committee seats to serve their constituents' interests. Thus, most Merchant Marine and Fisheries members traditionally came from coastal areas, whereas the Public Lands and Resources Committee, which controls federal lands, has usually been dominated by legislators who represent districts west of the Mississippi River. Historically, the House Agriculture Committee's members have rural constituencies.[3]

Most notably, perhaps, the Agriculture subcommittee responsible for tobacco policy has fought (and won) to retain favored treatment for its crop in the face of a constant stream of attacks since the mid-1960s. And no wonder, given the subcommittee's membership over the past thirty years (see Table 5–2). Despite the growing number of subcommittee members and the expansion of their jurisdiction, the number of legislators from tobacco-growing states sitting on the subcommittee is far out of proportion to their overall numbers in the Congress. In 1973, with a single minority-party exception, all subcommittee members came from the South or border states. Ten years later, there was a bit more variation, but this region continued to dominate. By 1993, after some committee reshuffling,[4] the subcommittee on tobacco had ceased to exist as a

[2] Keith Krehbiel, *Information and Legislative Organization* (Ann Arbor: University of Michigan Press, 1990).

[3] Theodore J. Lowi, "How the Farmers Get What They Want," *The Reporter,* September 14, 1964, pp. 34–37; William Browne, *Cultivating Constituents* (Lawrence: University Press of Kansas, 1995); John Mark Hansen, *Gaining Access* (Chicago: University of Chicago Press, 1991).

[4] As of the 103rd Congress (1993–1994), committees were limited to six subcommittees. The Agriculture Committee chose to eliminate all crop-specific committees, replacing them with three umbrella panels that dealt with general farm commodities, livestock, and specialty crops, respectively.

TABLE 5-1
Standing Committees, 103rd and 104th Congresses

House of Representatives

103rd Congress (1993–1994) (22 Committees)	104th Congress (1995–1996) (19 Committees)
Agriculture (27D/19R members)	Agriculture (26R/21D)
Appropriations (37D/23R)	Appropriations (31R/21D)
Armed Services (33D/22R)	National Security (27R/23D)
Banking, Finance, and Urban Affairs (31D/20R)	Banking and Financial Services (27R/23D)
Budget (26D/17R)	Budget (24R/16D)
District of Columbia (7D/5R)	——
Education and Labor (24D/15R)	Economic Opportunity (19R/16D)
Energy and Commerce (27D/17R)	Commerce (24R/16D)
Foreign Affairs (26D/15R)	International Relations (21R/18D)
Government Operations (26D/16R)	Government Reform and Oversight (21R/17D)
House Administration (12D/7R)	House Oversight (5R/3D)
Judiciary (21D/14R)	Judiciary (20R/15D)
Merchant Marine and Fisheries (29D/19R)	——
Natural Resources (33D/22R)	Public Lands and Resources (19R/16D)
Post Office and Civil Service (14D/10R)	——
Public Works and Transportation (38D/25R)	Transportation and Infrastructure (31R/27D)
Rules (9D/4R)	Rules (9R/4D)
Science, Space, and Technology (33D/22R)	Technology and Competitiveness (27R/23D)
Small Business (27D/18R)	Small Business (19R/16D)
Standards of Official Conduct (7D/7R)	Standards of Official Conduct (7R/7D)
Veterans' Affairs (21D/14R)	Veterans' Affairs (17R/14D)
Ways and Means (24D/14R)	Ways and Means (21R/14D)

Senate (17 Committees)

	103rd Congress	104th Congress
Agriculture, Nutrition, and Forestry	10D/8R	9R/8D
Appropriations	16D/13R	15R/13D
Armed Services	12D/10R	11R/10D
Banking, Housing, and Urban Affairs	11D/8R	9R/7D
Budget	12D/9R	12R/10D
Commerce, Science, and Transportation	11D/9R	10R/9D
Energy and Natural Resources	11D/9R	11R/7D
Environment and Public Works	10D/7R	9R/7D
Finance	11D/9R	11R/9D
Foreign Relations	11D/9R	10R/8D
Governmental Affairs	8D/6R	8R/7D
Indian Affairs	10D/8R	10R/7D
Judiciary	10D/8R	10R/8D
Labor and Human Relations	10D/7R	9R/7D
Rules and Administration	9D/7R	9R/7D
Small Business	12D/10R	10R/9D
Veterans' Affairs	7D/5R	8R/4D

Sources: *Politics in America, 1994* and *1996*.

TABLE 5-2
Membership on House Agriculture Committee Subcommittee Dealing with Tobacco
Issues (chairman in boldface)

Subcommittee on Tobacco, 1973	Subcommittee on Tobacco and Peanuts, 1983	Subcommittee on Specialty Crops and Natural Resources, 1993
Stubblefield, D–Ky.	**Rose, D–N.C.**	**Rose, D–N.C.**
Jones, D–N.C.	Jones, D–N.C.	Baesler, D–Ky.
Mathis, D–Ga.	Hatcher, D–Ga.	Bishop, D–Ga.
Rose, D–N.C.	Thomas, D–Ga.	Brown, D–Calif.
Litton, D–Mo.	Whitley, D–N.C.	Condit, D–Calif.
Mizell, R–N.C.	Tallon, D–S.C.	Clayton, D–N.C.
Wampler, R–Va.	English, D–Okla.	Thurman, D–Fla.
Madigan, R–Ill.	Stenholm, D–Tex.	Minge, D–Minn.
Young, R–S.C.	Hopkins, R–Ky.	Inslee, D–Wash.
	Roberts, R–Kans.	Pomeroy, D–N.D.
	Skeen, R–N.M.	English, D–Okla.
	Franklin, R–Miss.	Stenholm, D–Tex.
		Peterson, D–Minn.
		Lewis, R–Fla.
		Emerson, R–Mo.
		Doolittle, R–Calif.
		Kingston, R–Ga.
		Goodlatte, R–Va.
		Dickey, R–Ark.
		Pombo, R–Calif.

Sources: *Almanac of American Politics, 1974; Politics in America, 1984* and *1994.*

separate entity, but the Specialty Crops subcommittee that handled tobacco policies was chaired by North Carolina's Representative Charlie Rose and remained firmly under the control of legislators from the leading tobacco-producing states. With the Republican takeover in 1995, tobacco interests remained well protected, in that Virginia's Representative Thomas Bliley, an ardent defender of the crop and its related industry, became chairman of tobacco's chief nemesis, the Commerce Committee.

In short, committees and subcommittees can and do serve the Congress as a whole by providing specialized information to the chamber at large. At the same time, though, the very decentralization of the committee system allows for particular interests to be well represented on very specific subjects where the stakes are high (and the visibility of committee actions is low). This dispersion of power and information serves both the whole Congress and its individual members, especially in the House of Representatives, where committee-based decentralization shapes how most bills advance and what comes out of legislative process.

Richard Fenno's simple statement that "we get the kind of Congress that the members give us,"[5] meshes seamlessly with his equally straightforward assertion that committees differ, one from another.[6] Their environments (including the range of their interests and the scope of their policies) differ, as do the motivations of their members. Not only do they differ from one another at any given time, but they have changed over time as the institution has adapted to its context in various political eras.[7] For example, between the mid-1980s and the mid-1990s, telecommunications policy has commanded increasing attention of the House Commerce Committee, whose members have responded to a mind-numbing onslaught of technological advances and intense competition between major players such as AT&T, the cable television industry, and the regional phone companies, among others.[8] Members construct the kind of committee system they want, and they seek positions on these committees based on their districts' interests (such as agriculture), their own policy aims (such as those concerning science and technology), or a desire for power within the institution (such as a seat on the powerful Appropriations Committee). In addition, some committee slots reflect a willingness to serve the Congress as a whole, but there are few, if any, volunteers for the Standards of Official Conduct panel, whose members must sit in judgment of their own colleagues.

COMMITTEES OVER TIME

From the first days of the Republic, both the House and the Senate have used committees to process and draft legislation. Early on, most of these were ad hoc bodies that reported back to their chambers on specific bills. By 1810, however, the 142-member House had organized ten standing committees, including familiar panels such as those on Interstate and Foreign Commerce and Ways and Means. Increasingly, legislation began its journey toward passage within committees, rather than following from an initial floor discussion, in which the House would constitute itself into the committee of the whole and conduct less formal consideration of the issue at hand.[9] In addition, the

---

[5]Richard F. Fenno, Jr., "If, As Ralph Nader Says, Congress Is the 'Broken Branch,' How Come We Love Our Congressmen So Much?" in Norman Ornstein, ed., *Congress in Change* (New York: Praeger, 1975), p. 287.

[6]Richard F. Fenno, Jr., *Congressmen in Committees* (Boston: Little Brown, 1973).

[7]See Steven S. Smith and Christopher Deering, *Committees in Congress*, 2nd ed., (Washington: CQ Press, 1990), p. 18.

[8]See *The Information Arena*, a special issue of *CQ Weekly Report*, May 14, 1994.

[9]Ibid., p. 26. The House ordinarily dissolves into the committee of the whole to conduct its legislative business under lenient rules that allow for the more efficient conduct of business. Decisions made in the committee of the whole are formalized in subsequent passage through the House.

existence of standing committees produced greater continuity from one congress to the next, both in terms of organizational stability and members' ability to gain expertise on particular subject matters over time.

Between the early 1800s and the onset of the Civil War, committees slowly became integral to the legislative process, even though most key decisions were made on the floor. The number of standing committees grew steadily (see Figure 5–1), but their memberships changed substantially from congress to congress.

Ironically, the expanding numbers of congressional committees in the era between 1862 and 1919 did *not* lead to increased fragmentation. Rather, committees most often served the purposes of both chambers' party leaders, who controlled appointments and the capacity to move legislation on the floor. Nonetheless, committees became increasingly important elements of the legislative process, and their memberships grew more stable as lawmakers constructed careers inside the Congress—careers that were often based on the expertise they accumulated in specialized committees and subcommittees. In

FIGURE 5-1
Number of Congressional Standing Committees (1789–1990)

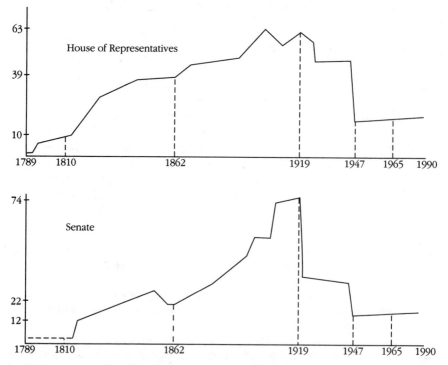

Source: Steven S. Smith and Christopher Deering, *Committees in Congress,* 2nd ed. (Washington: CQ Press, 1990), p. 25.

large part, such stability grew from the reliance on committee-based seniority in determining which veteran legislators would serve on given committees in each new congress, to the extent that "by the turn of the century, [seniority] had become such an 'iron-clad formula' that in both House and Senate party leaders' real discretion in committee assignments was limited primarily to new members."[10]

Although Representative Joseph Cannon (R–Ill.) would challenge the seniority basis for appointment during his speakership (1903–1911), the House's 1910 revolt against him and its decision to reduce the Speaker's powers meant that seniority would prevail on committee assignments; in turn, this meant that both committees and their chairmen would become increasingly powerful over the next fifty years. Davidson and Oleszek explain the workings and impact of a committee-based seniority system:

> The majority party member with the most years of consecutive service on a committee *automatically* became its chairman. *There were no other qualifications,* such as ability or party loyalty. As a result, committee chairmen owed little or nothing to party leaders and much less to presidents. This automatic selection process produced experienced, independent chairmen, but many members chafed under a system that concentrated authority in so few hands . . . [and] promoted the competent and incompetent alike. . . . [Moreover,] the system promoted members from "safe" one-party areas—especially conservative southern Democrats and midwestern Republicans—who could ignore party policies or national sentiments.[11]

Not only did the chambers accept the seniority system, they also steadily consolidated committee jurisdictions during the 1915–1965 period. The Legislative Reorganization Act of 1946 sharply reduced the number of committees in both House and Senate, to nineteen and fifteen, respectively (see Figure 5–1). Thus, most committee jurisdictions expanded tremendously, and the chairmen became even more powerful, leading the Congress into a relatively brief, but important, period of committee government (roughly 1947–1970).[12]

---

[10]Ibid., p. 35.

[11]Roger Davidson and Walter Oleszek, *Congress and Its Members,* 4th ed. (Washington: CQ Press: 1994), p. 207, emphasis added.

[12]See Smith and Deering, op. cit., pp. 38ff. Why, one might ask, did many committee chairs allow their positions to be eliminated, especially in the House? Many chaired panels with modest jurisdictions, and the 1946 act provided benefits to those who were displaced and to those who had anticipated becoming chairs. Committees were granted several staff members, and their powers to oversee the executive branch were enhanced. In practice, committee chairs controlled many of these resources and opportunities, and consolidation of the number of committees worked hand in hand with the rise in resources to empower the chairs as individuals and as a group.

The generally conservative nature of the Congress and the modest goals of the Eisenhower Administration (1953–1961) coexisted smoothly under the decentralized nature of committee government. Committee chairmen, drawn disproportionately from the states of the old Confederacy, generally represented the sentiments of the Southern Democrat–Republican conservative coalition that dominated the Congress. The presence of a pair of legendary congressional party leaders—Speaker Sam Rayburn (D–Tex.) and Senate Majority Leader Lyndon Johnson (D–Tex.)—did little to reduce the committee chairs' dominance. Both Rayburn and Johnson would consult closely with them, but neither pushed a legislative agenda that was unacceptable to the committee barons. Eventually, large numbers of new members, most notably the herd of young, activist Democrats who arrived after the 1958 elections, would begin to restrict the power of committee chairs. But through the 1950s, congressional decision making was dominated by an informal oligarchy of senior party and committee leaders, along with a few other key legislators.

At the very acme of their independent power, committee chairs generally agreed on a modest agenda and an incremental approach to policy making. Within their individual committee domains, they might well be considered masters of their own turf, but in the 1950s most chairmen acted more like brokers, largely content with making minor adjustments to the status quo.[13]

The Squeeze Play: Leaders and Members versus Committee Chairs

The combination of full-committee decentralization and leadership oligarchy served to benefit chairs, like-minded party leaders, and various entrenched interest groups that profited from the predictability of the actions within their areas of concern. For policy activists and impatient rank-and-file legislators, especially majority-party Democrats, government by strong committee was unresponsive and frustrating. Little change came immediately in the wake of the 1958 elections, even though Democratic majorities widened in both chambers.[14]

From 1959 through 1975, committees and their chairs faced dual threats to their independent influence—simultaneous efforts by party leaders to centralize their own authority and by junior members to win power by having

[13]Smith and Deering, op. cit., p. 45. More generally, see William S. White, *Citadel: The Story of the U.S. Senate* (New York: Harper & Row, 1956); Clem Miller, *Member of the House* (New York: Scribner's, 1962); and various articles by Ralph K. Huitt, several contained in Huitt and Robert L. Peabody, eds., *Congress: Two Decades of Analysis* (New York: Harper & Row, 1969).

[14]For a detailed account of the obstacles to shifts in power, see James Sundquist, *Politics and Policy* (Washington: Brookings, 1968).

more responsibilities delegated to subcommittees. By the mid-1970s, these movements had significantly weakened the authority of full committees and their chairs.[15] Nevertheless, the Congress, especially the House, continued to rely on its standing committees as fundamental building blocks for most of its actions.

In the twenty years after 1965, congressional reform reared its head in four special House initiatives, three similar Senate attempts, and two joint efforts.[16] In the House, making committees more responsive was a primary objective. But responsive to whom? Democratic party leaders wanted more control in moving legislation through the House, back bench members of both parties wanted more responsibilities and greater impact on the legislative process, and Republicans sought an effective voice in the legislative process. Between 1971 and 1975, the House acted consistently to reduce the authority and discretion of its full-committee chairs. The initial beneficiaries were clearly the junior Democrats, who gained both as individuals (and potential subcommittee chairs) and as members of the majority-party caucus—which gained substantial authority. Democratic party leaders also obtained a great deal of potential power, which they slowly began to exercise during the late 1970s.

Some key House changes came from reforms passed by the entire chamber, but the most profound developments emerged from the Democratic caucus, which effectively controlled the organization of the body. The two most important elements of reform focused on subcommittee rights and responsibilities and on the selection of committee chairs (and those of Appropriations Committee subcommittees). By 1974, the following limitations had been imposed on full committees and their chairs:

SUBCOMMITTEE REFORMS

Democrats could hold only one legislative subcommittee chair.

Subcommittee chairs could select one professional staff member for their panel.

A "Subcommittee Bill of Rights" guaranteed referral of legislation to subcommittees; bidding for subcommittee seats, which protects junior members; and fixed jurisdictions for subcommittees.

---

[15]For an excellent contemporaneous examination of these changes, see Norman Ornstein, "Causes and Consequences of Congressional Change: Subcommittee Reforms in the House of Representatives, 1970–73," in Ornstein, ed., *Congress in Change,* pp. 88–114.

[16]Smith and Deering, op. cit., p. 47. See also, among others, Roger Davidson and Walter Oleszek, *Congress Against Itself* (Bloomington: Indiana University Press, 1977), and various works by Leroy N. Rieselbach, including, most recently, *Congressional Reform: The Changing Modern Congress* (Washington: CQ Press, 1994), which contains a comprehensive list of congressional reform efforts from 1970–1993.

DEMOCRATIC CAUCUS/LEADERSHIP REFORMS

Automatic secret-ballot caucus votes would be held on the appointment of all committee chairs and Appropriations Committee subcommittee chairs at the beginning of each new congress.

The Steering and Policy Committee was created and given committee appointment powers (stripped from Democratic membership of Ways and Means).

The Speaker would nominate Democratic members of the Rules Committee and also had the right to remove these members.

By the early 1970s, the number of subcommittees had grown sharply, and the number peaked in the mid-1970s. Despite the significant changes of the 1970s in subcommittee powers and authority (at least in the House) and the proliferation of these subunits, decentralization has not continued unabated. Indeed, the number of subcommittees has steadily declined, and both chambers have moved toward consolidation in the 104th Congress (see Table 5–3). Republican consolidation in 1995 followed and strengthened the Democratic movement toward committee consolidation in the previous ten years. In the end, large numbers of subcommittees with highly specialized jurisdictions proved unwieldy for the parent chambers and for party leaders who struggled to provide coherence to legislative decision making.

Although the powers of full committees and their chairs were limited in the 1970s, subcommittees did not become dominant. Rather, particularly in the House, they emerged as important units, whose decisions often set the agenda for subsequent full-committee and floor actions. Subcommittees have proved most significant on relatively routine, low-profile issues, where their specialized knowledge often helps to define problems and prospective legislative solutions. More controversial policies and more highly visible actions, such as health care reform or gun control proposals, move the locus of decision making to the full committee or to the full House and Senate. In addition, chairs of House subcommittees are responsible to the party caucuses of their respective full committees, much as committee chairs must win approval of the party caucus as a whole, so individual chairs remain beholden to their party peers.

TABLE 5–3
Number of House and Senate Subcommittees, Selected Congresses, 1955–1996

	84th (1955–1956)	90th (1967–1968)	94th (1975–1976)	100th (1987–1988)	104th (1995–1996)
House Subcommittees	99	154	172	160	77
Senate Subcommittees	105	126	174	93	70

Source: *Vital Statistics on Congress: 1993-1994, Congressional Quarterly's Players, Politics and Turf of the 104th Congress,* special issue of *Congressional Quarterly,* March 25, 1995.

To an extent, they must follow their colleagues' preferences, in order to lead them.[17]

Republican Reforms in the 104th Congress

When Republicans won control of the House in 1994, the party leadership set its sights on changing various elements of the committee system. Most important has been a major shift in relations between the party and committee leaderships, in which "committee leaders have been put on effective notice that they are expected to be servants of the party."[18] Chairs moved legislation through their committees at breakneck speed during the first 100 days of the 104th Congress in order to meet the schedule set by Gingrich and Majority Leader Dick Armey (R–Tex.). In addition, with his willingness to ignore seniority in choosing three committee chairs (Appropriations, Commerce, and Judiciary), Speaker Gingrich demonstrated that committees and their chairs were to serve the party's agenda, even as they applied their specialized knowledge to writing legislation.

More specifically, the Republican Conference adopted various significant alterations in committee operations:

A one-third reduction in staff.

The control of all staff by the chair.

A three-term limit for committee and subcommittee chairs.

A limit of five subcommittees on most committees, and an overall reduction from 118 in the 103rd Congress to 77 in the 104th.

Abolition of the District of Columbia, Merchant Marine and Fisheries, and Post Office and Civil Service Committees.

Limiting most members to serving on two committees and a total of four subcommittees.

Requiring that all committee votes be published and no proxy voting be allowed.

Requiring that almost all committee meetings be open and allowing coverage by television and radio, if requested.

Speaker may no longer, with modest exceptions, refer bills to multiple committees simultaneously.

Although the limitations on subcommittees and the placement of staff employment at the full-committee level bolster the power of committees and

---

[17]The classic study here is John Manley's analysis of Ways and Means Committee chairman Representative Wilbur Mills (D–Ark.): "Wilbur Mills: A Study of Congressional Influence," *American Political Science Review* 63 (1969): pp. 442–464.

[18]Steven S. Smith, quoted in David S. Cloud, "Shakeup Time," *Congressional Quarterly's Players, Politics, and Turf of the 104th Congress,* March 25, 1995, p. 9.

chairs, most of the other changes have weakened committees. For example, no longer can a chairman dominate committee decisions by controlling the proxy votes of his partisan colleagues, a tactic often employed in the past by Democrats. And term limits for chairs ensure that Republican committee leaders cannot gain undue advantage from extended tenure—either by building up debts or by shaping expectations about future rewards. Without question, the party–committee balance of power has shifted in the House, as Republican leaders have accomplished much of what their Democratic counterparts would have liked to have done. That is, they now exercise greater control over the often autonomous committee units.

Even so, the essential structure of the committee system remains. Different panels offer differing patterns of benefits and opportunities to their members, who eagerly seek (Appropriations) or reluctantly accept (Standards of Official Conduct) their assignments.

DIFFERENT COMMITTEES AND THEIR VALUE TO MEMBERS

In that the bulk of legislative work takes place within committees, obtaining good committee assignments is crucial to most legislators. But what constitutes a "good" assignment? This depends on members' motivations. To be sure, virtually all want to be reelected, so the first thought of many newcomers is to gain a committee slot that will help them win reelection.[19] As we saw with its tobacco subcommittee, the Agriculture Committee has attracted disproportionate numbers of lawmakers with farm or rural interests, and members of the Resources Committee (formerly Natural Resources, and before that, Interior) reflect concerns of the Western states, with their large expanses of federal lands. Such simple geographic relationships are exceptional, however, in that many committees can benefit legislators from virtually any district. The more powerful the committee, the more this is true. The committees that write tax laws and control appropriations certainly contribute to their members' reelection successes, but much more important are their roles in fulfilling two other goals of legislators: to influence policy and obtain power within the House.[20]

Although many veteran legislators who enjoy seniority and key committee positions are able to exercise more internal power and affect a wider range of policies than their less-senior colleagues, most Representatives and senators can use their committee service to pursue multiple goals. Comparing three cohorts of new House members, Smith and Deering (see Table 5–4) found a

---

[19]The classic statement here comes from David Mayhew, *Congress: The Electoral Connection* (Cambridge, MA: Harvard University Press, 1974).

[20]Richard F. Fenno, Jr., *Congressmen in Committees* (Boston: Little Brown, 1973), p. 1.

TABLE 5-4
Committee Preference Motivations Expressed by New Senators (pre-92d, 97th, and 101st Congresses)

Committee	Constituency			Policy			Prestige		
	Pre-92d	97th	101st	Pre-92d	97th	101st	Pre-92d	97th	101st
Policy Committees									
Budget	—	1	1	—	4	6		0	0
Foreign Relations	3	1	0	19	5	2	2	0	0
Governmental Affairs		1	0		3	0	,	0	0
Judiciary		2	0	9	7	2		0	0
Labor	2	3	0	4	4	1		0	0
Mixed Policy/Constituency Committees									
Armed Services	4	4	4	4	6	4		0	0
Banking		2	1		3	6		0	0
Finance	4	8	1	13	9	2		4	1
Small Business	—	4	1	—	4	0		0	0
Constituency Committees									
Agriculture	4	13	8		2	2		0	0
Appropriations	31	6	3	15	3	3	2	2	3
Commerce	13	5	5	5	2	3		0	0
Energy	4	6	3	2	3	2		0	0
Environment	5	5	2	4	1	2		0	0
Unrequested Committees									
Rules and Administration		0	0		0	0		0	0
Veterans' Affairs		2	2	3	0	0		0	0

Source: Steven S. Smith and Christopher Deering, *Committees in Congress,* 2nd ed. (Washington: CQ Press, 1990), p. 101. Pre-92d Congresses, prior to 1970; 97th Congress, 1981–1982; 101st Congress, 1989–1990.

mix of motivations for seeking committee seats, especially on panels offering power and prestige.

Committees in the Senate are not quite as central to the day-to-day behavior of their members as are House panels. Senators have more committee and subcommittee assignments than their House counterparts, and their memberships overlap more. For example, all members of the Senate Appropriations Committee sit on at least two other committees, whereas House members hold exclusive assignments to the Appropriations panel. In both chambers, however, committees generally serve the members' interests. The jurisdictional fragmentation of the committees allows lawmakers, especially Representatives, to find assignments that serve their particular mix of goals.[21]

---

[21]See Smith and Deering, op. cit., p. 110.

Historically, junior members have waited a term or two before moving to the House's "power" committees of Rules, Appropriations, and Ways and Means. In the 104th Congress, however, given the large number of slots that opened up for Republicans, first-termers won six seats on Appropriations, three on Ways and Means, and, most remarkably, one on Rules, where insiders and the leadership dominate.[22] In addition, three first-term Republicans won appointments as subcommittee chairs.

Beyond the motivations of their members, committees also reflect a range of environments such as the visibility of their actions or the partisanship of their decision making. Holding high-profile hearings on health care reform, for example, differs substantially from writing regulations for purchasing military equipment. Various legislators and their committee roles illustrate these differences among committees. Representative John Murtha (D–Pa.), a veteran legislator with a talent for cutting deals and avoiding publicity, is perfectly placed on the low-profile, but very powerful, Appropriations Committee, where he served as a key subcommittee chair. On the other hand, Senator Jesse Helms (R–N.C.), with his continuing desire for the spotlight, has enjoyed his role first as ranking member and then as chairman of the highly visible Foreign Relations Committee. Combining a penchant for publicity and an extensive issue agenda, for sixteen years Representative Henry Waxman (D–Calif.) operated effectively as an Energy and Commerce subcommittee chair, where he successfully pursued a host of initiatives on health and environment issues.

Not only do committees differ but over time they can change, sometimes dramatically. The once-prestigious House Judiciary Committee had a difficult time finding willing members in the 1980s. The obscure, constituency-oriented Interior Committee became an increasingly important battleground for environmentalists and property rights advocates as the Natural Resources Committee in the 1990s. More generally, members of Congress wanted more subcommittees and greater decentralization in the reform era of the 1970s. Twenty years later, both Democratic and Republican members have opted for fewer subcommittees and less fragmentation, although the basic division-of-labor principle continues to structure most lawmakers' work on Capitol Hill.

COMMITTEE POWER IN THE POSTREFORM CONGRESS: REAL, BUT CONTINGENT

Committees are advantaged by their positive capacity, within a large and diverse Congress, to write detailed legislation on hundreds of separate, often complex, topics. Committees possess the tactical advantages of great informa-

---

[22]In the 103rd Congress, in comparison, two Democratic freshmen won Appropriations slots and one was grudgingly accepted by Representative Dan Rostenkowski (D–Ill.) for Ways and Means.

tional resources, the ability to block legislation desired by other lawmakers, and the capacity to shape conference committee agreements at the end of the legislative process.[23] In addition, bringing legislation to the floor, especially in the House, is exceedingly difficult without gaining the approval and cooperation of the relevant committee. Committees are thus powerful, but not all-powerful. They cannot legislate; they cannot require the executive to comply with their wishes; they cannot implement policies once they have been approved.

Even when legislators such as former Ways and Means chairs Wilbur Mills (D–Ark.) and Dan Rostenkowski (D–Ill.) gain a reputation for power, an important element of power in itself, their authority and influence are limited.[24] In the postreform Congress the Democratic Caucus and the Republican Conference alike have chosen to limit the clout of even the strongest, most assertive committee chairs, who must respond to their own committee members, the party leadership, the party caucus, and the wishes of the House as a whole, as expressed through a majority of the 435 members.

What follows are sketches of how two contemporary committee chairs, Representatives John Dingell (D–Mich.) and John Kasich (R–Ohio), have worked to shape legislation within their domains. Although they come from different parties and generations (Dingell was born in 1926, Kasich in 1952), the two representatives share an aggressive, policy-oriented approach to the Congress. Both have used their positions on key committees to set the congressional agenda and to legislate by cutting the best deals available to them. These are strong-minded, strong-tempered individuals who must restrain their own willfulness and act responsively to retain the support of their committees, their fellow partisans, and the House as a whole. In short, they are chairmen for a postreform era.

John Dingell, the Energy and Commerce Committee, and Clean Air

After the sudden death of Representative John Dingell, Sr., in 1955, his son and namesake won the special election for his seat and has served ever since, building seniority on the Energy and Commerce Committee (the Energy label was dropped in 1995) and becoming chairman in 1981 after thirteen terms of service. As chair, Dingell expanded the committee's already extensive

---

[23]For a more extensive discussion of positive and negative power, see Steven S. Smith, *The American Congress* (Boston: St. Martin's, 1995), pp. 211ff.

[24]Mills gave up his Ways and Means chair in 1974 after an ill-fated presidential bid in 1972 and a series of public, alcohol-related embarrassments. He retired from the Congress in 1976. In mid-1994, under indictment on various charges, Representative Rostenkowski stepped down as Ways and Means chair, as prescribed by Democratic Caucus rules. He subsequently lost his reelection bid to a Republican challenger.

jurisdiction, which touched on most important domestic issues.[25] Supported by a large, talented staff that reflected the chair's instinct for the jugular, Dingell influenced governmental approaches to dozens, even hundreds, of issues ranging from health care to university research procedures. At the same time, he protected his basic constituencies in his home Detroit district and within the entire auto industry.[26] This has meant that he has fought relentlessly on its behalf against clean air legislation, remarking unapologetically, "That's what I'm sent here to do."[27]

During the 1980s, Representative Dingell and his committee labored fruitlessly to modify clean air legislation, failing in part because the Energy and Commerce Committee was split over various provisions in an extremely complex bill.[28] In particular, as head of the full committee, Dingell had to contend with Representative Henry Waxman (D–Calif.), who chaired the subcommittee on health and the environment and who represented a Los Angeles district that suffered greatly from auto emissions. The smart and politically savvy Waxman, who challenged a more senior member to win his chairmanship (see chapter 6), has been both a worthy adversary and an often-valuable ally for Dingell throughout his twenty years on the committee.

Even more important than the intracommittee politics of the 1980s was the unqualified opposition of President Ronald Reagan to any new law regulating air quality. Richard Cohen bluntly recounts,

> The end of the Reagan era meant that lawmakers could no longer posture on clean-air legislation. . . . The key change . . . happened at the White House: Nixon and Carter supported clean-air laws and legislation went through. Reagan opposed it so nothing happened. With the [1988] election . . . of George Bush, the self-proclaimed "environmental president," the gridlock of divided government would no longer be an excuse for inaction.[29]

For John Dingell and Henry Waxman, Bush's potential cooperation meant that they could finally legislate, if they could first find common ground between their own positions and then with the president's approach.

Understanding that indefinite delay was no longer possible, and unsure of his ability to control results either within his committee or on the House floor,

---

[25]Republicans substantially cut back the jurisdiction of the Commerce Committee, in part as a rebuke to Dingell's success in expanding it during his fourteen years as chair.

[26]Dingell's wife is employed by General Motors in a government relations position. She does not directly lobby the Congress.

[27]Quoted in Phil Duncan, ed., *Politics in America 1994* (Washington: CQ Press, 1993), p. 802.

[28]This account relies on Richard Cohen, *Washington at Work* (New York: Macmillan, 1992), and Gary C. Bryner, *Blue Skies, Green Politics* (Washington: CQ Press, 1993).

[29]Cohen, op. cit., pp. 43–44.

Dingell sought to forge an alliance with his subcommittee adversary (on clean air legislation, at least). Waxman had begun to rework the Bush Administration's proposed bill in his subcommittee and had made some progress by late 1989, when Dingell joined the discussions. Within a few days, the unlikely duo announced an agreement on the difficult issue of tailpipe emissions, as well as several related items. Dingell had placed his trust in Waxman, and vice versa; these two skilled legislators could then join together to work on behalf of the bill, even as their own constituents expressed reservations about the unexpected alliance.

Although it would take several months for the full committee to agree on a bill and more than a year for clean air legislation to win final congressional approval, the Dingell–Waxman deal held firm; committee member Representative Phil Sharp (D–Ind.) observed that the agreement "allowed the process to go forward dramatically and . . . made it clear that we were going to move forward on a bill."[30] In sum, neither the full-committee chair nor the subcommittee chair felt assured of victory, so they reached a compromise agreement, forged in private, that they hoped would serve as a basis for building an entire bill that could survive intact on the House floor and through the remainder of the legislative process. They more or less succeeded. At least as important for the principals, Waxman won a substantial number of policy points, and Dingell, in the words of one legislator, "prevailed on issues important to him *and he kept control of the committee.*"[31] Even for a strong committee chair like John Dingell, power remained contingent on the support of his committee members and the ability to win majorities on the House floor.

John Kasich, the Budget Committee, and Spending Cuts

As the aftershocks of the 1994 Republican earthquake rumbled through the Congress, the epicenter may well have been in the office of Representative John Kasich, chairman of the House Budget Committee. It is Kasich who must reconcile the Republican promises to cut taxes, cut more than a trillion dollars of spending in seven years, balance the budget, and simultaneously protect the core district interests of his Republican colleagues. If Speaker Gingrich's Contract with America served as Act I of the 104th Congress, Chairman Kasich's budget-cutting proposals would constitute Act II.

As with Gingrich, the Republicans' 1994 victory transformed Kasich from a minority-party "bomb thrower" to a congressional leader with a raft of policy responsibilities, most notably to make good on the promises that he and his party had made to cut overall spending. In the first budget skirmish in the 104th Congress, Kasich succeeded in winning floor approval of his committee's relatively modest $17 billion in proposed 1995 budget rescissions (cuts), but "only

---

[30]Quoted in Cohen, op. cit., p. 77.

[31]Representative Tom Tauke (R–Iowa), quoted in Cohen, Ibid., p. 171.

after snuffing out a rebellion by their own moderates and cutting a deal with conservative Democrats to win their votes."[32] (However, Kasich found himself accused of—and essentially pleading guilty to—double-counting savings from the rescissions package and subsequent cuts to allow for tax reductions.) In addition, he obtained approval from the Budget Committee for $190 billion in spending cuts that included $100 billion in reductions that would effectively cap appropriations for dozens of programs such as the Corporation for Public Broadcasting and a five-year moratorium on the construction of new federal buildings.[33] Already, Kasich has run into jurisdictional battles with Appropriations Committee chairman Robert Livingston (R–La.); nor did his problems stop there. "As he makes his plans clearer, the grousing is getting louder, with some of the bitterest complaints coming from fellow committee chairmen. Snapped one Republican: 'He wants to be secretary of everything.'"[34]

In the end, Kasich, a true believer in spending cuts and smaller government, will see his work amended in the House, compromised in the Senate, fought over in conference committee, and perhaps vetoed by President Clinton. Nonetheless, as chair of the committee that begins the budget-cutting process, he and his colleagues can set the terms for the remainder of the debate. As the optimistic chairman exuded after the first round of cuts in 1995, "you ain't seen nothing yet."[35]

One Last Chance: The Politics of Conference Committees

Whereas Dingell's deal with Waxman probably meant that a clean air bill would eventually pass, Kasich's early victory was merely one necessary, but not determinative, step in a long and winding journey. Kasich and Dingell did each have one more important chance to affect the outcomes of budget and clean air legislation—in the conference committees composed of representatives from both House and Senate that would meet to iron out the differences in the versions of the bills passed by the two chambers. Most, though not all, major legislation requires an ad hoc conference committee, whose composition is determined by party and standing committee leaders. Traditionally, the key committees are well represented in conferences, where the participants must choose how vigorously to defend their chamber's version of the legislation at hand.

The ability of standing committees to influence the outcomes of conference committees has been labeled the "ex post veto" power.[36] By virtue of

---

[32]George Hager, "House GOP Pushes Budget Cuts as Political Stakes Mount," *CQ Weekly Report*, March 18, 1995, p. 794.

[33]Ibid., p. 796.

[34]Karen Tumulty, "Budget, Meet Thy Maker," *Time*, February 27, 1995, p. 19.

[35]Hager, op. cit., p. 794.

[36]See Kenneth Shepsle and Barry Weingast, "The Institutional Foundations of Committee Power," *American Political Science Review* 81 (March 1987), pp. 85–104.

their members' potentially influential participation in conference committee decisions near the end of the legislative process, committees can exercise substantial power, especially when their original proposals are modified on the floor of the House or Senate. The conferees may choose not to lobby hard against such changes; rather, they might choose a version of the legislation closer to the committee's original proposition. The full House or Senate can only vote a conference report up or down; thus, committee members can often have the last word in terms of the shape of a given piece of legislation. Of course, this power is hardly absolute. One of the chambers may reject the conference version, or, on major legislation, there may be conferees from several committees, which negates any advantage a single panel might enjoy.[37]

COMMITTEES AND CHAIRS IN A POSTREFORM HOUSE

What can we learn about the power of committees and their chairs from the Dingell and Kasich experiences on clean air and tax reform? First, chairing a key prestige or policy committee remains one avenue to power within the Congress, especially in the House. Any major legislation within their broad jurisdictions must accommodate the preferences of these chairmen. Second, subcommittees, although important, remain limited in their impact, even with veteran legislators such as Henry Waxman at their helm. Indeed, Kasich's Budget Committee has no subcommittees at all. Third, on important, divisive issues, a committee's partisan majority is the crucial locus of power, at least in the House. For example, in September 1995, Representative Pat Roberts (R–Kans.), chairman of the House Agriculture Committee, found himself unable to hold together a Republican majority of his panel as he sought to reform crop subsidy programs.

Finally, and perhaps most important in terms of assessing their roles in the contemporary House, committee chairs act increasingly either as or with party leaders. The capacity to act effectively in league with the party leadership has grown in significance for prestige committee appointments. In the 1970s and 1980s, both the Rules and Budget committees fell under the domination of the party leadership, and in 1994 the Democratic Caucus chose Representative David Obey (D–Wis.) to chair the Appropriations Committee over the more senior Neal Smith (D–Iowa). Although Smith was well respected and generally supportive of Democratic programs, the Caucus chair noted that the majority Democrats "want[ed] a more activist chairman, someone who is a player, who is aggressive with party initiatives and who takes a larger role in interpreting the work of the committee."[38] With close ties to the Democratic

---

[37]On conferences generally, see Lawrence Longley and Walter Olezsek, *Bicameral Politics* (New Haven, CT: Yale University Press, 1989).

[38]Representative Vic Fazio (D–Calif.), quoted in Richard E. Cohen, "A New Dean in the College of Cardinals," *National Journal*, March 26, 1994, p. 735.

party leadership, a twenty-five-year record of tough-minded liberalism, and strong support from the first-term members in the large class of 1992, Representative Obey was a good chairman for a highly partisan House, where the most significant budget and spending decisions must win approval with little or no minority support. Speaker Gingrich followed a similar tack in naming Representative Livingston, a conservative ally, to head the Appropriations panel in the 104th Congress. Generally, Gingrich dominated the selection of committee chairs more thoroughly than any Speaker since Joseph Cannon (1903–1909).

Committee and party leaders, however, often view the legislative process from different perspectives. Committee chairs desire a degree of autonomy; party leaders want greater control and coordination. It is unlikely that such a fundamental division will be easily bridged, especially in an era of declining resources and difficult, often painful, decisions directed at programs and constituencies (such as ranchers, defense contractors, and the oil industry) that the standing committees have historically protected.

COMMITTEES AND THE SENATE: STRUCTURED INDIVIDUALISM

Most extensive analyses of congressional committees focus the bulk of their attention on the House, where the committee system dominates the members' daily activities. Although Senate committees roughly parallel those in the House, they are less significant—to both the senators and the chamber as a whole—than their counterparts on the other side of the Capitol. As a former House member, Senator Phil Gramm (R–Tex.) expressed surprise at committees' modest significance in the Senate: "Subcommittees are almost meaningless over here. The committees are small enough that all the work is done in full committee. . . . And quite frankly, Senate committees don't do a whole lot. . . . Much of the work is done on the floor."[39] That might come as a surprise to former Armed Services chair Senator Sam Nunn (D–Ga.) or Senate Appropriations chair Mark Hatfield (R–Oreg.), but for most senators, committee assignments are important in affecting their overall ability to act, rather than shaping most of their day-to-day actions. Take, for example, the committee-related shifts of Senator Jesse Helms (R–N.C.) in the past fifteen years.

Helms has concurrently held seats on the Agriculture and Foreign Relations committees, rising by seniority to chair the Agriculture panel when the Republicans controlled the Senate from 1981–1987. Helms could serve North Carolina tobacco interests from this position, and his promise to retain it despite a chance to become chair of Foreign Relations helped him win a tight

---

[39]Quoted in Ross K. Baker, *House and Senate* (New York: Norton, 1989), pp. 59–60.

reelection campaign in 1984. Still, the highly visible Foreign Relations committee offered great possibilities for the conservative Helms, who chose to serve as that panel's ranking minority member in 1987, after the Republicans lost their Senate majority. Senator Richard Lugar (R–Ind.) had served as Foreign Relations chair in 1985–1986, and he challenged the more senior Helms' right to the ranking position. Despite general agreement over Lugar's effectiveness as chairman, Helms won the ranking position on a 24–17 vote. Many moderate Republican senators supported Helms, not because they favored either his conservative or, often, obstructionist brand of politics but because they endorsed the seniority principle.

Helms could thus use his Agriculture chairmanship for reelection purposes and then move to the leadership of Foreign Relations, where he became chairman in 1995, to increase his policy reach on important international policies and appointments during the breakup of the Soviet Union and the search for post–Cold War foreign policies. Even as he practiced the disagreeable politics of delay, to the extent that his own party colleagues reacted strongly against his tactics Helms could use his committee positions to bolster his individual career goals. In the first few years of his Agriculture Committee chairmanship, for example, Helms "virtually abdicated control of the committee . . . , allowing a coalition of Republicans, led by [Finance Committee chair] Bob Dole of Kansas, to take the lead on farm legislation."[40] Subsequently, Helms's "invariable opposition to provisions in committee legislation contributed to the committee's failure to pass foreign aid authorizations in [the early 1990s]."[41]

Helms's choices reflect the Senate's individualism, which shapes its committee system. In general, Senate committees are less important than their House counterparts, and Senate subcommittees are considerably less significant. Most House markups (the actual line-by-line writing of legislation) occur in subcommittee, and House subcommittee chairs ordinarily manage the bills when they move to the chamber's floor. The full committee is the venue for Senate markup activity, and individual senators, serving as sponsors, generally manage individual pieces of legislation on the floor. With talented, long-term staff members, Senate committees are important units, both for the Congress as a whole and as they shape their members' actions. However, committees often bolster the individualism of the Senate, as opposed to the House, where the structure of committees and subcommittees produce fragmentation in that chamber. Once they obtained the majority, some junior Republican Senators pressed for more party control over committees, but Senate party leaders nonetheless remain much less capable of shaping committee actions, in marked contrast to the centralization fashioned by House Republicans in the 104th Congress.

---

[40]Duncan, op. cit., p. 1115.

[41]Ibid.

Six ✑

THE INDIVIDUAL
ENTERPRISE

Before retiring in January 1995, Representative Stephen L. Neal (D–N.C.) had served twenty years in the House of Representatives. The unassuming Neal proved adept at surviving tough election challenges and consistently having a major impact on national banking policy. In only one of ten elections did he obtain more than 60 percent of the vote, and he twice weathered significant redrawing of his district lines (after the 1980 and 1990 censuses). To an extent, Representative Neal played the role of a typical North Carolina Democrat, as he compiled a moderate voting record and opposed tobacco tax increases, but his string of narrow electoral victories resulted from more than just middle-of-the-road voting patterns and careful cultivation of important local interests. Neal created a well-oiled personal organization that linked his official congressional resources with those of his continuing campaign for reelection. More than any vote or financial contribution, this multifaceted enterprise was what helped the congressman survive at home while acting effectively in Washington.

From his earliest days on Capitol Hill (starting in 1975), Neal took advantage of the great capacity of individual legislators to build their own enterprises to serve both their reelection interests and their efforts to affect a wide range of policies. Like many of his peers, Neal combined resources from his own office, his committee positions, and his biennial reelection campaigns to produce a complex personal organization that sustained his individual political career for two decades.

Three major elements made up the Neal enterprise. First were the personal office resources available to every member of the House, which included more than $800,000 in salaries and benefits for Neal and his staff, along with the ability to send franked mail and an allowance of about $150,000 for travel, telephones, computers, and rent on district offices, among other expenses.[1] Added

---

[1]Every member received a base of $122,500 in the 103rd Congress (1993–1994), to which was added a sum for travel and district office–space rent, based on distance from Washington and local rental rates. For these and many other details about congressional offices, see Rick Shapiro, *Setting Course: A Congressional Management Guide,* 5th ed. (Washington: Congressional Management Foundation, 1995).

to this were Neal's staff as a subcommittee chair on the Banking, Finance, and Urban Affairs Committee. These staffers were as much a part of the Neal enterprise as his personal office employees; they owed their positions to Neal as subcommittee chair.

Last, but certainly not least, was Neal's reelection campaign operation. After his bargain-basement ($62,000) upset victory over former major-league pitcher and Republican incumbent Representative Wilmer (Vinegar Bend) Mizell in 1974, Neal's campaign expenditures consistently increased, from $165,000 in the late 1970s to an average of $640,000 between 1988 and 1992. Given a series of hotly contested races, Neal's expenditures were scarcely exceptional. More unusual, however, was Representative Neal's 1986 personal purchase of a $125,000 building to house his campaign organization. Neal paid for the building and numerous improvements by charging his campaign organization rent for its space—rent that happened to be more expensive than that of any other campaign office for a House member.[2]

Making the Neal operation all the more formidable was its overall flexibility, typical for congressional enterprises. Staff could move from the personal office to the committee; personal office workers could spend vacation days and overtime hours working on the campaign; and campaign expenses for a wide variety of political expenses, broadly defined, could allow Neal and his staff wide latitude in keeping the congressman's name before his constituents, all the while operating out of a permanent campaign office in his own building. Over the years, two elements of the enterprise remained clear: (1) Representative Stephen Neal was in charge, a Chief Executive Officer, so to speak; and (2) the organization had one major "product" to push—Representative Stephen Neal as Representative, policy maker, and candidate for reelection. For twenty years, Neal's considerable political skills, supported by a large, sophisticated enterprise, kept him afloat in the turbulent waters of a marginal seat in North Carolina. In 1994, after Neal declined to seek reelection, his seat was captured by a Republican who won 57 percent of the vote.

THE LEGISLATOR AS ENTERPRISE

Nothing captures the fragmentation of congressional politics better or contributes to it more than the husbanding of resources in 535 separate congressional enterprises.[3] The enterprise notion is extremely useful in understanding

---

[2]Sara Fritz and Dwight Morris, *Gold-Plated Politics* (Washington: CQ Press, 1992), pp. 27 and 36.

[3]See Robert Salisbury and Kenneth Shepsle, "U.S. Congressman as Enterprise," *Legislative Studies Quarterly* 6 (November 1981), pp. 559–576; and Burdett A. Loomis, "The Congressional Office as a 'Small (?) Business,'" *Publius* 9 (Summer 1979); and Loomis, *The New American Politician* (New York: Basic, 1988).

the actions of individual legislators within the context of the Congress as a whole. To put it simply, House members and, even more so, senators must allow others to act for them; there is so much to do and so little time. Thus, staffers negotiate agreements, answer letters, feel out allies, return constituents' calls, and perform a thousand other tasks. On occasion, staffers may act on their own, but ordinarily their actions follow the dictates—however general—of their bosses, who historically have had the absolute power to hire and fire their congressional employees.[4]

The idea of an enterprise purposefully blurs the distinction between members of Congress and those who work on their behalf. In the end, the legislators will gain the accolades for the actions of their staffers, whose careers will rise or fall with their bosses' fortunes. Using this idea, we can examine a legislature filled with enterprises—a hallmark of the post-1960 Congress. As Salisbury and Shepsle conclude, "The result of the actions and interactions of 100 senatorial enterprises . . . generates a quite different institution than the one of a century ago, or even a few decades ago, consisting of individual senators acting more or less alone."[5] If enterprises provide more structure to Senate individualism, they exert even more influence on the larger House, where 435 separate legislators have come to possess enough resources to insert themselves into policy making and constituency affairs in dozens of ways.

Since World War II, congressional resources have grown steadily and profoundly (see Figure 6–1). Personal office and committee staff numbers have risen sharply, as have the number of special interest caucuses, the budgets of legislative support agencies,[6] and campaign expenditures. In short, senators and Representatives command adequate resources to pursue multiple, individually defined goals, which range from winning reelection to influencing policy decisions to running for higher office.

Congressional enterprises for veteran legislators often become multimillion-dollar small businesses that must maintain themselves as they seek to promote their members' interests. Despite some variation, most enterprises look roughly like the one depicted in Figure 6–2. At the heart of the miniconglomerate is the

---

[4]An excellent example here is Eric Redman's description of his work on behalf of former Washington Senator Warren Magnuson, who gave Redman and other staff members broad latitude to formulate legislation encouraging doctors to serve in needy areas. See Redman, *The Dance of Legislation* (New York: Touchstone, 1974). In 1995, the Congress adopted the Congressional Accountability Act, which requires it to adhere to almost all federal laws, including those on conditions of employment. This may have some modest effect on the relations between legislators and their staffers, but the essentially personal and political nature of these ties will remain.

[5]Salisbury and Shepsle, op. cit., p. 563.

[6]These include the General Accounting Office, The Office of Technology Assessment, the Congressional Research Service, and the Congressional Budget Office.

FIGURE 6-1
Growth in Congressional Staff, 1891-1991

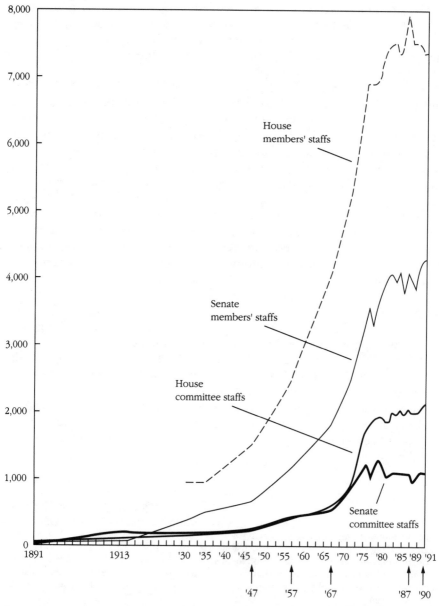

Source: Norman Ornstein, Thomas Mann, and Michael Malbin, eds., *Vital Statistics on Congress,*
1993–1994 (Washington: CQ Press, 1993).

FIGURE 6-2
The Congressional Enterprise

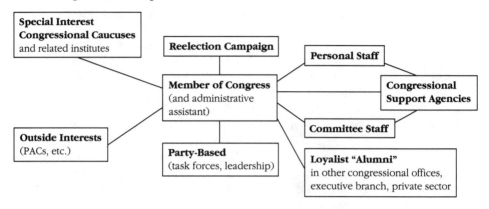

legislator, often in tandem with his or her top aide—usually the administrative assistant. Around this essential nucleus each legislator builds a unique combination of contributing components. Although some senior members may construct their organizations from all the building blocks, most emphasize a few key elements, always including the personal office.

The Personal Office

Except for a handful of lawmakers such as top party leaders or committee chairs, the personal office lies at the heart of each legislator's congressional enterprise. In the House, even the most junior minority-party Representative is entitled to exactly the same personal office allowances as the most senior majority-party member: up to eighteen full-time and four part-time staffers, with an annual salary cap of $557,000.[7] Thus Representative Mike Doyle (D–Pa.), initially elected in 1994, received the same basic personal office resources (staff, travel, communications, computers, etc.) as did his fellow Pennsylvanian Representative William Goodling (R), an eleven-term veteran who chairs the Economic and Educational Opportunities Committee.

Although there is some variation in structure and work assignments, the cast of characters in most congressional offices is roughly the same. It includes an administrative assistant responsible for overseeing the entire operation; several legislative aides, with one often designated as a legislative director; a personal secretary; an office manager; a press secretary; caseworkers (in Washington and in the home district); a top district aide; and other district

---

[7]This is the 1994 figure, benefits not included.

staff.[8] Senate offices are larger and more likely to encourage specialization, but the basic configuration is similar.

Variation also occurs in *what* legislators do with their office staff and other resources—and *where* they do it. Two major generalizations hold true here. First, there are some tasks that virtually all legislators must attend to: answering constituent mail, pursuing "cases" (often regarding bureaucratic snafus) that constituents bring to their attention, seeking new benefits and protecting existing ones for local interests, and maintaining at least minimal knowledge about major legislation under consideration. Much of this work reflects the service and allocation responsiveness that make up a good part of representation.

Beyond these essential tasks and routine office maintenance such as personnel and scheduling, the personal office can be constructed to serve the specific interests of a particular legislator. Thus, the second generalization: Members of Congress have tremendous discretion over how they use their basic resources. A marginal-seat congressman may establish several district offices to deliver the best possible constituency service; he may use substantial amounts of franked mail and send out the maximum number of newsletters each year, all the while making do with a couple of legislative assistants. Conversely, a member who considers herself relatively safe, having consistently won 65 percent of the vote in election contests, might hire six or seven legislative aides to assist her in achieving her own policy goals.

An ambitious House member might well want to hire a top-notch press secretary in anticipation of running for a Senate seat, whereas a junior senator might hope to use a couple of legislative aides to research and write a bill to correct a modest, but real, policy snarl. All House offices receive almost identical resources,[9] but Senate operations vary considerably, given the great differences among state populations.

In sum, the annual personal office resources can be used, within broad limits, to pursue legislators' individual goals. Offices tend to look roughly the same, but this is largely because of a general similarity in members' goals—to win reelection (and perhaps advance to higher office), produce good public policy, and exercise power within the Congress. Their considerable resources allow members a base from which to act effectively as individuals; in particular, they can establish strong constituency ties that make it very difficult for them to be effectively challenged for reelection. Given the resources that allow 535 legislators to play to their constituencies and to operate with such flexibility, the personal office contributes greatly to the centrifugal tendencies

---

[8]Not all offices have all these positions; the best data here come from the private Congressional Management Foundation, which annually surveys congressional offices and reports the changing nature of office organization and salary levels. In particular, see Craig Schultz with Rick Shapiro, *1994 U.S. House of Representatives Employment Practices* (Washington: Congressional Management Foundation, 1994).

[9]House travel funds differ, but only because costs of returning to 435 districts vary greatly.

of the Congress. Along with the control of their individual votes in committee and on the floor, personal office resources represent a key source of individual power for any legislator. These resources can also be used to build coalitions and seek consensus; even the most isolated and iconoclastic members need cooperation from their legislative peers if they are to act effectively in passing legislation.

Committees and Subcommittees

There are strict limits on personal office resources, particularly on the numbers and salaries of staff. Whatever the member's goals might be, if a congressional enterprise is to grow it must lay claim to other assets. Since the 1970s, the Congress has been generous in complementing the resources available to all its members, especially for those in the majority party, who, by dint of their status, chair all committees and subcommittees.

As Figure 6–1 illustrates, committee-based staff in the House tripled in the 1970s, and committee budgets grew even faster. If the committee system of the 1950s and early 1960s had remained intact, this change would simply have meant more resources under the control of a handful of powerful full-committee chairs. As noted in chapter 5, however, subcommittees proliferated in the 1970s, and their chairs came to control substantial resources and power. Not only did total committee staff in the House grow from 461 to 1,600 between 1970 and 1990, but the subcommittee allocation of staff grew from 23.2 percent (107) of total committee staff in 1970 to 45.2 percent (723) twenty years later.[10] In 1970, only one in four subcommittee chairs controlled their own staff, an average of four aides. By 1989, almost half the subcommittee chairs had such control, and their average staff size stood at ten. These figures understate the actual control of staff by subcommittee chairs in the pre-1995 era, however. Although various full-committee chairs may have formally controlled hiring, their subcommittee chairs often named their own choices as aides.

In short, many members of the majority party in the House have greatly expanded their enterprises in the wake of subcommittee changes of the 1970s. Minority staffing on committees and subcommittees has not increased nearly as much as for the majority—a constant irritant for Republicans during the long period of Democratic control. Republicans long requested a third of all committee staff, only to be continually rebuffed.

In the 104th Congress, the majority Republicans moved immediately to bolster the power of full committees by placing the responsibility for hiring staff with committee chairs and by limiting to five the number of subcommittees permitted for most committees. In addition, committee staff numbers were cut by one-third. Overall, the individual enterprises of many members—most

---

[10]Data from Steven S. Smith and Christopher J. Deering, *Committees in Congress,* 2nd ed. (Washington: CQ Press, 1990), p. 152.

notably Democrats and subcommittee chairs—were substantially reduced
while Republican committee chairs have come to control a much greater proportion of available resources. In an admittedly extreme example, former
Energy and Commerce Committee Chair Representative John Dingell (D–Mich.)
was not able to keep Republicans from slashing his committee staff from
almost 100 aides to about 20.[11]

On the Senate side, subcommittee staff have not grown nearly as fast as
in the House; nor are subcommittee aides as important to individual enterprises, given the much larger personal staffs that most senators command. In
addition, more than a fourth of majority-party senators chair full committees
and thus control their considerable resources. Even so, with the relatively
small number of senators, committee staff play major roles in developing policies, and Senate staff are ordinarily much more aggressive in their efforts on
behalf of their bosses.[12] Given senators' larger numbers of committee assignments and attendant responsibilities, it makes sense that staff members take
on greater responsibilities in the Senate. Indeed, many top Senate staff function as entrepreneurs who operate to further the influence of their own
bosses.[13] Such reliance serves to extend the reach of individual senators, as
they designate knowledgeable, skilled, and unelected staffers to act in their
stead.

Special Interest Caucuses

Much as House members have taken advantage of expanding subcommittee resources, so too have they expanded their enterprises by advancing to leadership positions in a host of special interest caucuses. By the mid-1980s, almost
150 such groups had formed, with House organizations outnumbering those in
the Senate by a three-to-one margin (ninety-one in the House to thirty-one in
the Senate; twenty-five more were bicameral groups).[14] For members, especially
junior ones, caucuses have provided opportunities to participate in the policy-
making process in various ways, from constituency service, as with the Auto
Task Force, to building a policy-based coalition such as the Military Reform
Caucus. Resources vary greatly across caucuses, but the strongest groups often
command budgets into the hundreds of thousands of dollars and substantial
numbers of staff. Some of these groups won House designation as officially
sanctioned legislative service organizations (LSOs), which were granted office
space and were allowed to receive financial support from members' accounts.

---

[11]Allen Freedman, "A Survivor Steps Into Minority Role," *CQ Weekly Report,* April 8, 1995, p. 989.

[12]See Michael J. Malbin, *Unelected Representatives* (New York: Basic, 1980).

[13]See David Price, "Professionals and 'Entrepreneurs': Staff Orientations and Policy Making on
Three Senate Committees," *Journal of Politics* 33 (May 1971), pp. 316–336.

[14]Susan Webb Hammond, "Congressional Caucuses in the Policy Process," in Lawrence C. Dodd
and Bruce I. Oppenheimer, eds., *Congress Reconsidered,* 4th ed. (Washington: CQ Press, 1989),
p. 355.

In 1995, the Republican-controlled House denied funding and office space to the twenty-eight groups that qualified as LSOs. This affected most of the major caucuses, but many of these groups obtain much of their funding from outside sources, so the ultimate impact was unclear.

Although caucus leaders have some power to hire and fire, the chief benefit for legislators in being a member of a caucus comes with the ability to employ resources to push favored ideas and to have adequate staff to react to opportunities or challenges as they arise. The variation is great in staff resources among the 150-plus caucuses; some—the Congressional Black Caucus, the Hispanic Caucus, the Northeast–Midwest group, and the Environmental and Energy Study Conference—have established separate institutes outside the Congress, which have served them in good stead in the wake of the 1995 cutbacks. Others have no staff at all and operate out of their chairs' offices, which can amount to a net drain on that legislator's resources.

The benefits for less-senior members, especially in the House, have been clear. Party leaders and committee chairs check with them on policies relevant to their groups, and many command substantial resources early in their careers. For example, Representatives Bob Edgar, a liberal Democrat, and Curt Weldon, a moderate conservative Republican, who have represented Pennsylvania's 7th District since 1974 and 1986, respectively, have demonstrated how junior legislators can profit from caucus leadership. In the late 1970s, Edgar used his positions as head of the Northeast–Midwest Economic Advancement Coalition and the Congressional Clearinghouse on the Future to push for strong environmental policies, especially in the realm of modernizing water infrastructure in older cities—such as his Philadelphia-area district. Although much more liberal than many of his constituents, Edgar used his caucus roles and resources to frame issues that attracted support from his suburban Republican seat.[15]

When Edgar left the House after unsuccessfully seeking a Senate seat in 1986, Weldon won his seat in the House and set new entrepreneurial standards for caucus activity. Weldon's unlikely vehicle has been the Fire Services Caucus, the largest single caucus in the Congress. Not only has this group won some legislative victories, but Weldon, as its founding entrepreneur, incorporated many of its resources into his congressional enterprise (and vice versa, using campaign funds to buy an old fire truck). Given his status as a junior Republican, the caucus leadership role allowed him a wider range of possible actions than those available to his GOP peers. In addition, Weldon's strong ties to the caucus and its resources may well prove a boon to him if he chooses to run for statewide office. In such an effort, he would again follow Edgar's lead; the Democrat had actually incorporated a statewide environmental organization into his campaign operation during his bid for the Senate.

---

[15]For an extended discussion, see Loomis, *The New American Politician*, pp. 152ff.

As of the early 1990s, Representatives belonged to an average of sixteen caucuses, and senators averaged fourteen such memberships, all in addition to their positions on committees, subcommittees, and within their parties. Why would busy legislators want to take on so many obligations?

First, joining most caucuses is a painless task, often requiring little more than agreeing to place one's name on the membership roster; subsequently, a lawmaker can be as active as he or she wants to be. Mere membership in a caucus does have its benefits. Representative Bill Richardson (D–N.M.) observed, "If someone writes me on an arts issue, I can write back and say, 'I'm a member of the Congressional Arts Caucus.'"[16]

Second, some caucuses offer valuable information. This may seem strange, in that Capitol Hill is awash in data, studies, and reports. Caucus-generated information is often different; the best is both easily used and highly reliable. For instance, legislators and staff historically placed great value on the clarity, brevity, and political savvy of Democratic Study Group (DSG) reports and circulars from the Environmental and Energy Conference (EEC). The annual dues for these organizations were not cheap ($4,000 for the DSG), but their large memberships (255 for the DSG and 392 for the EEC in 1993–1994) demonstrated the worth of their publications. In the 104th Congress, both of these groups struggled to maintain their information-providing services in a context in which they were denied official status and access to spending from members' official office accounts. Eventually, both failed to survive as congressional entities, although the DSG publications were purchased by Congressional Quarterly, Inc.

Third, junior members such as Edgar (in the 1970s) and Weldon (in the late 1980s) often found opportunities for action within caucuses that committees or party structures would not have provided them for years. Although many caucuses provide no resources to their leaders, some well-established groups have staffs that complement their leaders' regular enterprises. Despite being denied LSO status in the 104th Congress, groups such as the Congressional Black Caucus and its Hispanic counterpart host expensive fund-raising galas ($500 per seat) to support outside institutes that complement the inside groupings of members. The access to such resources makes these caucus leaders important forces within the House, all the more so as the numbers of African American and Hispanic members have grown sharply in the 1990s.

Finally, there can be some tangible benefits for holding a caucus leadership position, as individual donors and PACs seek out those with apparent influence on their specific issue. For example, in 1990 Representative Bud Schuster (R–Pa.), the cochair of the Congressional Truck Caucus, received

---

[16]Ibid., p. 150.

more than $32,000 in PAC contributions from Ryder, the Teamsters Union, North American Van Lines, and other related groups.[17]

The policy, campaign, and power incentives to join and become active in caucuses are substantial for most legislators, even senators and senior House members like Schuster. The costs of affiliation are often minimal, usually outweighed by the symbolic benefits of membership. For those who invest time and energy in caucus activity, the returns can be great in terms of campaign funds, access to the executive branch, and attention from party leaders. It's no wonder that Curt Weldon founded the Fire Services Caucus in 1987; by providing an attractive, cheap benefit to many of his peers, he could become a force on a narrow, but not insignificant, set of policies. Such an achievement is one basis for influence within the Congress.

Congressional Offices and the Continuing Campaign

In the 1960s and early 1970s, legislators' enterprises grew mainly within the Congress. In 1957, the average House office employed 5.6 staffers; twenty years later, that number had almost tripled, to 15.9. Through the mid-1970s, however, congressional election campaigns remained relatively inexpensive. In 1974, for example, the cost of a typical House campaign stood at $54,000, and incumbents spent less than $57,000 on average (while challengers spent not much less, around $40,000). By 1990, as is shown in Table 6–1, expenditure patterns had changed greatly: Average expenditures had

TABLE 6–1
House Members' Enterprises: Large-Scale Campaign Spending, 1974–1992

Election	$200,000 or more	$500,000 or more
1974	10	0
1976	31	0
1978	128	7
1980	205	28
1982	353	67
1984	354	77
1986	370	105
1988	414	149
1990	430	170
1992	548	252

Source: Norman J. Ornstein, Thomas E. Mann, and Michael J. Malbin, eds., *Vital Statistics on Congress, 1993–1994* (CQ Press, 1993), p. 77.

---

[17]David Segal, "Caucus Crazy," *Washington Monthly* (May 1994), p. 23. Representative Schuster was also the ranking Republican on the Public Works and Transportation Committee, which also made him a target for such contributions. Caucus positions can and do pull together various parts of a member's enterprise—in this instance his committee position and campaign.

risen to $266,000 (incumbents had increased their spending to $390,000, but challengers could muster only an average of $133,000) (see chapter 4 for more details).

Members of Congress obviously had learned to raise and spend vast amounts of funds, to the point that *unopposed* incumbents spent $250,000 on average in the 1989–1990 election cycle. This combination of no opposition and a quarter-million dollars in expenditures means that all funds went to support the political side of the individual enterprise, rather than being siphoned off for advertising, direct mail, or consultants' expenses.[18]

The most important building block of any sitting member's campaign enterprise remains the personal office with its extensive resources and staff. As one close observer of the local arms of congressional enterprises has noted,

> No matter how dazzling a campaign organization a challenger puts together, it will always be an ad hoc group, unfamiliar with the territory and with each other, while the incumbent fields a publicly paid team of experienced veterans to do a task they have succeeded in before . . . and which differs very little from their everyday jobs [such as seeking benefits for constituents as opposed to promising them to voters].[19]

With the congressional staff taking care of routine tasks, the congressional enterprise can exercise great flexibility in expanding its political and electoral dimensions.

Political Expenditures

On top of staff and office resources are piled hundreds of thousands of dollars of political expenditures, which the Congress has defined exceptionally broadly. For example, former Representative (and, as of 1994, convicted felon) Carroll Hubbard (D–Ky.) paid $3,000 in campaign funds for a portrait of his father. Although the exact political purpose of the painting remains unclear, the congressman enjoyed great freedom in defining political expenditures as he saw fit.[20] One intensive study of campaign financing identifies a wide range of so-called political expenditures that systematically contribute to

---

[18]For the breakdown of expenditures in a typical House campaign, see Paul Herrnson, *Congressional Elections: Campaigning at Home and in Washington* (Washington: CQ Press, 1995), p. 74.

[19]John McCartney, "Congressional District Offices: Their Staff and Functions," paper presented at the 1979 meeting of the American Political Science Association, Washington, DC, p. 48.

[20]Fritz and Morris, op. cit., p. 66.

the overall congressional enterprise of many, though not all, incumbents. These include[21]

A well-paid professional campaign staff

Substantial entertainment budgets

Travel expenses (such as auto leases)

Political consultants

Lawyers and accountants

Civic and political donations

A fund-raising apparatus (parties and direct mail)

Investments such as certificates of deposit[22] and Representative Steve Neal's building

Contributions to civic groups and establishment of college scholarships

Although congressional rules formally require expenditures to have a direct political purpose, almost no enforcement has taken place. Indeed, when contemplating a run against an entrenched incumbent, a challenger not only faces the Herculean task of raising funds to match those of the sitting legislator, but also confronts an established enterprise that has often been constructed over years by substantial spending of both federal funds and privately raised political monies.

To be capable of making political expenditures, one must amass substantial campaign resources, and contemporary legislators have proven most adept at raising these funds. Although academics have debated the ultimate impact of incumbents' spending patterns, there is little debate over the rise in costs since the mid-1970s, when the Federal Election Commission was established and began to publish, and make widely available, accurate figures on receipts and expenditures. As we saw in chapter 4, the average Representative's political expenditures have risen from $54,000 in 1974 to $410,000 in 1992, a hefty increase even when taking inflation into account. During the same period, average Senate expenditures have grown from $437,000 to $2,891,000. Crucial here is that many of these funds were expended to perpetuate strong, continuing enterprises—organizations that allow incumbents maximum flexibility in pursuing their individual goals.

In many ways, the enterprises of incumbents in uncontested races and those in the most competitive ones are remarkably similar (see Table 6–2). Both are very

---

[21]Ibid., pp. 29–30.

[22]Investment income in the 1980s was often truly substantial, in that bank CDs paid handsomely. With lower rates of return in the 1990s, this by-product of an enterprise's large cash position has diminished somewhat in importance.

TABLE 6-2
House Campaign Expenditures, 1990

Major Category	Incumbents				Challengers			
	Average	In Hot Races[a]	In Contested Races[b]	Unopposed	Average	In Hot Races[a]	In Contested Races[b]	Open Seats
Overhead								
Office furniture/supplies	$ 9,206	$ 11,238	$ 8,716	$ 7,066	$ 4,117	$ 6,480	$ 2,124	$ 11,843
Rent	6,650	8,902	5,996	4,571	2,662	4,070	1,474	7,960
Salaries	34,898	48,287	30,346	24,306	17,127	28,827	7,258	61,542
Taxes	11,433	14,671	10,462	8,527	2,255	3,722	1,017	10,792
Bank fees	1,003	1,225	973	704	149	206	100	1,241
Lawyers/accountants	8,450	11,587	6,977	7,048	483	800	216	2,974
Telephone	6,593	10,034	5,486	3,703	4,113	6,990	1,686	16,209
Campaign automobile	3,347	4,030	2,420	4,650	363	457	284	1,601
Computers/office equipment	6,733	8,032	6,291	5,707	2,051	3,111	1,157	7,227
Travel	16,247	18,415	15,107	15,603	3,051	4,823	1,556	12,053
Restaurants/food	3,488	3,064	3,455	4,294	243	389	120	810
Total Overhead	**108,049**	**139,485**	**96,229**	**86,179**	**36,614**	**59,876**	**16,992**	**134,255**
Fund-Raising								
Events	49,217	55,514	46,249	46,430	7,895	13,295	3,341	38,529
Direct mail	18,249	25,965	17,582	6,952	3,009	5,634	796	14,549
Telemarketing	1,588	2,450	1,345	771	827	1,807	0	4,192
Total Fund-Raising	**69,053**	**83,928**	**65,176**	**54,154**	**11,732**	**20,736**	**4,136**	**57,269**

Polling	**11,178**	**20,193**	**8,419**	**3,229**	**3,615**	**6,204**	**1,430**	**23,435**
Advertising								
Electronic media	76,109	148,223	55,056	9,860	36,168	67,876	9,421	203,778
Other media	11,594	15,588	11,404	5,332	5,413	7,804	3,396	15,663
Total Advertising	**87,703**	**163,811**	**66,460**	**15,192**	**41,581**	**75,680**	**12,817**	**219,441**
Other Campaign Activity								
Voter contact mail	37,825	65,795	27,546	17,739	18,395	30,119	8,505	64,880
Actual campaigning	28,097	40,712	22,687	21,092	16,472	25,286	9,037	50,061
Staff/volunteers	1,006	995	826	1,501	97	143	58	416
Total Other Campaign Activity	**66,929**	**107,502**	**51,059**	**40,332**	**34,964**	**55,548**	**17,600**	**115,356**
Constituent Gifts/Entertainment	**6,741**	**5,840**	**6,160**	**9,810**	**21**	**36**	**9**	**374**
Donations to								
Candidates from same state	5,226	3,552	6,426	4,875	49	59	41	354
Candidates from other states	4,325	3,060	5,078	4,471	3	6	0	319
Civic organizations	5,490	4,214	6,397	5,245	114	162	73	582
Political parties	11,451	9,726	12,830	10,710	133	152	118	738
Total Donations	**26,492**	**20,552**	**30,731**	**25,301**	**299**	**379**	**232**	**1,993**
Unitemized Expenses	**14,243**	**15,834**	**12,591**	**15,932**	**4,406**	**5,904**	**3,143**	**11,383**
Total Expenditures	**$390,387**	**$557,145**	**$336,825**	**$250,128**	**$133,231**	**$224,363**	**$56,359**	**$563,507**

Note: Totals are for the entire two-year cycle.

a Races where incumbent garners 60% or less of the vote.

b Races where incumbent garners more than 60% of the vote.

Source: Adapted from Sara Fritz and Dwight Morris, *Gold-Plated Politics* (Washington: CQ Press, 1992), pp. 14–15.

different from those of challengers, even those in relatively close electoral contests. Only those candidates who are seeking an open seat regularly put together a campaign that looks much like that of an entrenched incumbent—without, of course, the personal office resources that sitting members traditionally employ.

Most notably, incumbents in tight races spent only modestly more on overhead and fund-raising than did those who were unopposed; the latter spent more on constituents and donations to other races. But candidates who felt their opponents breathing down their necks could ratchet up their spending on polling, advertising, and other campaign activities (such as direct mail). Even when they were engaged in a potentially close race against an incumbent, challengers could not begin to muster the adequate resources to guarantee a strong challenge. They could not match the incumbents' overhead expenditures, which is not surprising. Nor could they come close, even in tight contests, to the figures incumbents could spend on polling, advertising, and other electoral activities—the heart of any campaign. Only open-seat candidates build organizations that resemble an incumbent's enterprise (with no accounting for congressional staff, district offices, communications capacities, and travel expenses). In the end, that is what much of the struggle for open seats is all about—to obtain the resources of incumbency for the future. One measure of the Republicans' 1994 success is that they won twenty-one open seats previously held by House Democrats and six such seats in the Senate.[23]

Additional Enterprise Resources

Legislators' enterprises extend far beyond the structures of personal offices, committees, caucuses, and reelection operations. Many additional resources are available to all, and access to others resides formally or informally with key committee and party leaders.

CONGRESSIONAL SUPPORT AGENCIES   The most democratic resource on Capitol Hill is the Congressional Research Service (CRS), which responds to requests from all members in a reasonably equitable manner. In terms of providing basic information on a wide range of questions (from setting up an office to an economic analysis of the North American Free Trade Agreement), CRS is an invaluable source of timely insights. On more complex questions, which might require extensive staff time (from approximately 800 researchers), CRS is more likely to act quickly and comprehensively on requests from formal leaders within the committee or party hierarchy.

Likewise, the General Accounting Office (GAO), the Office of Technology Assessment (OTA),[24] and the Congressional Budget Office (CBO) provide only

---

[23]Republicans lost four previously held House seats that were open, for a net gain of seventeen. They lost no open Senate seats.

[24]OTA funding was eliminated by the 104th Congress as of October 1, 1995.

modest assistance to legislative backbenchers, even though any member can make requests for studies or information. On the other hand, all members of Congress benefit from the independent information generated by these support agencies through reports and testimony. More than any other legislative body in the world, the Congress has sources of information and analysis that are intentionally separate from the executive branch and the federal bureaucracy. All members can use the volumes of information to help form their own policy positions, explain these positions and related votes to their constituents, and resist the entreaties of party leaders and presidents alike.[25]

LEADERSHIP RESOURCES   During the Democratic postreform era in the House (1981–1994) the joke went that any time one wanted to get the attention of a House Democrat and couldn't remember his name, all one had to do was call out "Mr. Chairman," and the legislator would respond; approximately half the 258 Democrats in the 103rd Congress chaired a committee or subcommittee, and almost all Democratic senators were chairs of some committee or subcommittee. Much the same could be said of the House Democratic leadership in recent Congresses. For example, in the 103rd Congress almost half the 256 House Democrats held some kind of formal party leadership position, including 92 who were considered part of the party's whip system. This inclusive leadership structure helped to define the postreform House, but relatively few resources accompany the vast majority of these positions. Only at the top of the ladder do leadership roles confer many resources, for either political party in either chamber.

For these few Representatives and senators, though, the benefits are substantial. For example, in the 104th Congress, House Whip Tom Delay, the third-ranking Republican leader, controls an office staff of sixteen, and Senate Majority Leader Bob Dole (R–Kans.) has a party leadership staff of twenty, along with four part-time aides. Other top leaders command similar resources. In addition, the four chairs of the respective parties' House and Senate campaign committees enjoy large staffs and travel budgets as they seek and allocate campaign funds and attempt to recruit candidates for upcoming elections. For those legislators who succeed at helping elect (and reelect) their colleagues, the rewards can be great, as former Senate Majority Leader George Mitchell (D–Maine) and presidential aspirant Senator Phil Gramm (R–Tex.) have demonstrated. As a relatively junior senator, Mitchell chaired the Democratic Senate Campaign Committee and took credit for returning the Democrats to majority status with their 1986 election results. When Senator Robert Byrd stepped down from his majority leader position in 1988, Mitchell won the right to succeed him, in part because of his general performance as campaign committee chair and the contributions he had directed to many of

---

[25]At the same time, party and committee leaders can commission studies that will serve to support their own positions. Information can serve both centrifugal and centripetal purposes.

his colleagues. Senator Gramm's ambition has taken a different direction, but many senators are beholden to him for raising and funneling funds to their campaigns as head of the Republican Senate Campaign Committee.

For the most part, party-based resources assist in centralizing the power of leaders, but this is not always the case. In 1993, House Democratic Whip David Bonoir (D–Mich.) emerged as the leading critic of the North American Free Trade Agreement, a pact that Speaker Tom Foley and President Clinton strongly supported. Bonoir pledged not to use the resources of his office to oppose the treaty, but given the integrated nature of the congressional enterprise, it was difficult for him not to use—directly or indirectly—his party resources, even to fight the policy position of his legislative party and his president.[26]

PERSONAL PACS, CAMPAIGN DONATIONS, AND HIGHER-OFFICE CAMPAIGNS　　In 1978, Representative Paul Rogers (D–Fla.), chairman of the important Energy and Commerce Subcommittee on Health and the Environment, retired from the House. The next most senior subcommittee member was the well-respected Representative Richardson Preyer (D–N.C.), and it was widely assumed that the full committee's Democratic caucus would select him to replace Rogers. Representative Henry Waxman (D–Calif.), a talented and aggressive member first elected in 1974, had different ideas, however. Waxman sought the chairmanship, arguing that Preyer's family ties to the pharmaceutical industry and his district's tobacco interests would compromise his leadership of the subcommittee. Ordinarily, a vote among the full committee's Democrats would probably have resulted in a Preyer victory. But Waxman waged an exceptional campaign. Drawing on his fund-raising experience in California, he actively sought the subcommittee position by contributing $24,000 of his own campaign funds to members of the Energy and Commerce Committee.[27] The resulting 15–12 Waxman victory derived at least in part from the contributions, and this action set a precedent for subsequent contests for open committee and leadership positions. Much of Waxman's funding came from health interests, which had specific goals within the legislative process.[28] As a reformer and legislative activist, Waxman was an important target for health interests that desired access to him, regardless of their frequent disagreements with him on the issues.

---

[26]Majority Leader Richard Gephardt (D–Mo.) also opposed the pact, but took a less publicly aggressive stance. He announced that any actions against NAFTA taken by him would emanate from his personal office, but, again, the relationships among various parts of the enterprise make such a commitment difficult to monitor.

[27]This account is drawn in part from Ross K. Baker, *The New Fat Cats* (New York: Priority Press, 1989).

[28]Ibid., p. 50.

By the late 1980s, many races for party leadership slots and key commit-tee chairs employed funds from so-called leadership PACs. Many organized interests see great advantages in supporting potential leaders, who have little trouble in soliciting contributions for their own PACs. The resulting monies provided a great edge to Representative Tony Coelho (D–Calif.), who con-tributed $570,000 to House candidates prior to his election by the Caucus as Democratic Whip, and to Representative William Gray (D–Pa.), who spread around more than $60,000 in his successful 1988 bid to chair the Democratic Caucus.[29]

In the Senate, leadership PACs have proliferated, largely owing to the presidential aspirations of so many senators. For example, Senator Bob Dole has used his Campaign America PAC to support his activities as a presidential candidate, his work as legislative leader, and his general political expenses for frequent trips to support incumbent legislators, governors, and dozens upon dozens of Republican challengers. Well-heeled interests such as agriculture's Archer Daniels Midland corporation get credit from Dole for their contribu-tions to Campaign America, which then distributes some of these funds to other candidates, who, in turn, subsequently credit Dole for their good for-tune.[30] Taking in and disbursing millions of dollars since 1978, Campaign America has become an integral part of the total Dole enterprise, which employs, directly or indirectly, well over 100 individuals at any given time, all of whom owe their positions to the senator.

Leadership PACs do hold some potential for integrating the legislative process. After all, a Waxman or a Dole wants to do more than simply win an important legislative office; such individuals want to have an impact on policy results. However, with more than fifty legislators establishing such organiza-tions, the tendency toward fragmentation dominates.[31] As congressional scholar Ross Baker concludes after his careful study of this trend, the PACs will "magnify the influence of individual members, . . . [who], armed with their own checkbooks, [will make] harder the job of party leaders as they try to manage the delicate balance and often frustrating task of building party majorities."[32] In the House and, especially, the Senate, where every legislator can hope to exer-cise some policy leadership, the additional resource of personal PACs has often served to further fragment an already decentralized institution.

---

[29]Ibid., pp. 35–40.

[30]See Jake Thompson, *Bob Dole* (New York: Donald Fine, 1994). Thompson lists one other large-scale fund-raising component of the Dole enterprise: the Dole Foundation, a nonprofit entity established in 1984 to provide training and education grants to the disabled. Thompson notes that "critics have contended the foundation has been a means for big corporations to earn Dole's favor with large contributions" (p. 229).

[31]Baker, op. cit., Table 2, pp. 78–80.

[32]Ibid., p. 71.

THE CONGRESSIONAL ENTERPRISE: BLESSING AND CURSE

Of all the changes that have affected the United States Congress in the post–World War II era, none has been more striking than the expansion of the individual lawmaker's enterprise. From the moment new members take the oath of office, they each control a million-dollar-per-year operation of staff, communications, travel, and research capacities that allows them to commit substantial resources to reelection efforts, drafting legislation, overseeing the bureaucracy, or seeking higher office. Moreover, if clever at all, they will raise campaign funds that can be spent for broadly defined political purposes. The congressional enterprise helps every lawmaker claim credit for governmental programs, take positions on the issues of the day, and relentlessly advertise their accomplishments. But this is just the minimum enterprise, the stripped-down model that every first-term member gets upon arriving on Capitol Hill (and obtaining the smallest, most distant office from the floor of the House or Senate).

Virtually all senators and many House members enjoy the services of committee staffers, many benefit from caucus positions, and some even create their own PACs to reward their fellow legislators. At the heart of every congressional enterprise stands the individual senator or Representative, to whom each of their respective staff members, campaign consultants, or fund-raisers owes his or her job.[33] And their collective job is to promote the career and interests of their principal—the House member or senator. Party leaders and committee chairs regularly seek their support, but legislators know that, save in extraordinary circumstances, they remain largely unaffected by others' actions. Especially when it comes to reelection, party leaders and committee chairs enjoy no control over the average legislator's enterprise. All House members know that, if reelected, they will retain the core personal staffs of their enterprise, to say nothing of the other campaign, committee, and caucus resources they may have accumulated. In short, party leaders must negotiate with hundreds of Representatives and 100 senators, who control their own electoral destinies and have enough resources to affect the policy process when they so desire. For all the decentralizing forces of subcommittees, committees, and incumbency, the heart of fragmentation and individualism lies in the strength and flexibility of the legislator as enterprise.

---

[33]Even in the 104th Congress, which passed legislation to apply federal laws to congressional operation, legislators retain great powers to hire and fire their staffers.

Seven ❧

PARTIES AND LEADERSHIP: CAPTURING THE CONGRESS

House Republicans are fragmented by interests, institutions, individuals, and ideas. Like any legislative party, the House GOP is split along regional, generational, and economic lines ... compounded by ... the separation of powers, federalism, and bicameralism. Individual ambitions and political ideas also divide the Republicans. These differences of opinion include quarrels over how to win the majority.

William F. Connelly, Jr., and John J. Pitney, Jr.

Writing in mid-1994, Connelly and Pitney[1] could legitimately speculate that Republicans might never regain control of the U.S. House. A few months later, House Republicans did precisely that, ending forty years in the minority and joining their Senate colleagues to organize both chambers for the first time since 1954. The Republican sweep was remarkable, and it set the stage for major changes in the way the House conducts its business. As Speaker Newt Gingrich (R–Ga.) consolidated his power within the body, the Republican party leadership emerged dominant. By agreeing to a series of centralizing reforms, the Gingrich-led Republicans abruptly produced what James Thurber called "a major shift from the balkanized, decentralized subcommittee government we have had."[2] Many specific changes were detailed in chapter 5, but the committee-related provisions discussed there reflect only some of the centralizing reforms. As the 104th Congress began in January 1995, Speaker Gingrich and his Republican majority had, at least temporarily, captured control of the House as no party had since the turn-of-the-century speakerships of Thomas Reed and Joseph Cannon.

At the same time, however, the U.S. Senate, also under newly won Republican leadership, had changed very little in the wake of the 1994 election results. To be sure, Majority Leader Bob Dole (R–Kans.) enjoyed a 54–46

---

[1]William F. Connelly, Jr., and John J. Pitney, Jr., *Congress' Permanent Majority: Republicans in the U.S. House* (Lanham, MD: Littlefield Adams, 1994), p. 153.

[2]James Thurber, quoted in Janet Hook and David S. Cloud, "A Republican Designed House Won't Please All Occupants," *CQ Weekly Report,* December 3, 1994, p. 3430.

Republican margin,[3] but he possessed far fewer leadership resources than Gingrich. Moreover, the Senate's rules and its informal practices, including an unwillingness to rein in individual senators, make any majority leader's job a difficult one. Despite the House Republicans' electoral triumph, their party unity on a series of important votes, and the power accorded Representative Gingrich as Speaker, the structure of a bicameral legislature has limited the impact of the party's centralization of authority within the House.

THE CONGRESSIONAL PARTY: CENTRALIZATION IN CONTEXT

Legislatures, like all institutions, must function with some basic coherence. Political parties provide much of the glue that holds together the disparate ambitions of 535 legislators, buttressed by their enterprises, as well as the fragmented collection of committees, subcommittees, and special interest caucuses. Yet in the United States, political parties have proven much weaker and less capable of producing strong centripetal effects within the legislature than have parties in most other Western-style democracies, and especially those with parliamentary systems.[4]

Assessing the role of parties in the early 1960s, a strong committee era, Richard F. Fenno, Jr., concluded that parties "organize decision-making across committees and across stages [of the legislative process], thereby functioning as a centralizing force in the making of House decisions."[5] Although most members shared emotional attachments to their party and regarded it as one means to exercise power, Fenno noted, "the . . . party label masks a pluralism of geographic, social, ideological, and organizational sources of identification, support, and loyalty. The roots of this pluralism lie outside the chamber, in the disparity of conditions under which the members are elected and in the decentralized organization of the parties nationally."[6] Congressional parties thus grow stronger when partisan divisions within the electorate have increased. In 1994, for example, congressional election results reflected strong partisan forces that helped form the basis for strong party leadership under new Republican Speaker Gingrich. In short, the best opportunities to exercise effective party leadership in the Congress, most notably within the House,

---

[3]Republicans gained seven seats in the 1994 election and added two Democratic defections as Senators Richard Shelby (Ala.) and Ben Nighthorse Campbell (Colo.) switched their affiliation to the GOP.

[4]Parties in most parliamentary systems possess the power to select candidates rather than relying on primary elections to bestow the party label on a candidate.

[5]Richard F. Fenno, Jr., "The Internal Distribution of Influence: The House," in David B. Truman, ed., *Congress and America's Future* (Englewood Cliffs, NJ: Prentice-Hall, 1965), p. 61.

[6]Ibid., pp. 61–62.

have depended on forces largely beyond the control of the leaders, forces that emanate from the society and the electorate.

Not only does the diversity of constituencies weaken the impact of congressional parties, so too does the very resolution of issues that occasionally, but temporarily, divide the country into two broad, party-based factions. Periods of strong, centralized leadership and high levels of partisan voting on Capitol Hill reflect polarization between the parties in the electorate.[7] Circa 1900, Republican Speakers Thomas Reed and Joseph Cannon benefited from electoral results built on clear philosophical differences between two legislative parties that shouldered responsibility for ruling and accountability for their actions. In that era, individual representatives, having won their seats "on the basis of a party's platform," were expected to "support party positions, even against personal convictions or desires."[8] Internal allegiances to a party leader fit neatly into a world in which party machines controlled the candidate selection process.[9] Opposing the party might well mean that a legislator would be denied renomination, and thus reelection, especially in an era before the widespread adoption of primary elections as the means of choosing nominees.

If party machines and a polarized electorate provided the external context for strong direction, the Speaker could act forcefully on party issues within the House.[10] Reed (1889–1891, 1895–1899) and Cannon (1903–1911) each combined their extensive formal prerogatives under the rules with their status as Speaker to carry out their legislative agendas. Moreover, the Speaker was also a party leader who could define those issues appropriate for partisan position taking. As Speaker, Reed or Cannon could bring an issue to the majority Republican caucus, whose collective vote could require its legislators to line up behind the overall party position. Straying from the party might well mean that a dissident would be disciplined by the Speaker through removal from a powerful committee or the rejection of his preferences in fashioning a key piece of legislation, to say nothing of encouraging his local party organization to reject him as a candidate in the next election.

Why should we care much about century-old congressional voting alignments? Whatever the importance of the policies made at the time, this period's practices allow us to assess the actual possibilities for centralization with Congress. Given an external context that produces opposing voting blocs, legislators may opt to strengthen the hand of party leaders by providing them with the tools to lead forcefully, as the Democrats did in the 1980s, with

---

[7]Joseph Cooper and David W. Brady, "Institutional Context and Leadership Style: The House from Cannon to Rayburn," *American Political Science Review* 75 (June 1981), pp. 411–425.

[8]Ibid., p. 413.

[9]Peter Swenson, "The Influence of Recruitment on the Structure of Power in the U.S. House, 1870–1940," *Legislative Studies Quarterly* 7 (February 1982), pp. 7–36.

[10]The following discussion relies in part on Cooper and Brady, op. cit., pp. 412ff.

Republicans following suit after winning control of Congress in 1995. Indeed, the Gingrich speakership has left congressional scholars grasping for parallels in the modern Congress. For example, political scientist Charles Jones observed that the House Republicans' domination of the agenda has no precedent in this century, including during the Cannon speakership.[11]

Nevertheless, if the context of congressional politics can produce strong leadership and intense partisanship, it can also set conditions for relatively weak parties. In fact, from the 1920s through the early 1960s, parties within the Congress often reflected a societal stalemate over the scope of governmental actions and, particularly, the role of federal involvement in matters of race and other domestic matters such as education and health care. If Americans were split by both ideology and region on these issues, so too was the Congress, where three party blocs developed in the wake of the policy initiatives of Franklin Roosevelt's first term (1933–1937) as president: Republicans, Northern Democrats, and Southern Democrats.

Democrats organized both House and Senate for all but two congresses between 1933 and the 1960s.[12] This means they named the Speaker, the majority leader, various other majority-party offices, and all the committee chairs, as well as holding a majority of seats on all legislative committees. But this "procedural majority," which ensured Democratic control in formal terms, often vanished when important, substantive issues came to a vote.[13] Not only was the Congress fragmented among constituencies in ordinary, pluralistic ways but it frequently split sharply along the related lines of region and ideology, as Southern Democrats joined with Republicans to form a "Conservative Coalition" that opposed the liberal initiatives of Democratic presidents and their Northern Democratic allies in the Congress, especially on civil rights and social welfare policies.[14]

As Brady and Bullock point out, "Understanding how the Conservative Coalition works furthers our understanding of the [Congress] as a whole. The voting alliance begun in 1937 between Southern Democrats and Republicans . . . greatly reduced the ability of the majority Democratic party to function as a governing party."[15] Although Republicans and Southern Democrats did consult with

[11]Comment made at American University forum on Congress and the president, April 17, 1995, televised on C-SPAN.

[12]The exceptions were narrow Republican majorities in both houses for the 80th and 83rd Congresses (1947–1949 and 1953–1955, respectively).

[13]David S. Cloud, "Speaker Wants His Platform to Rival the Presidency," *CQ Weekly Report*, February 4, 1995, p. 331.

[14]See John Manley, "The Conservative Coalition in Congress," *American Behavioral Scientist* 17 (1973) pp. 223–247; Mack C. Shelley, *The Permanent Majority: The Conservative Coalition in the United States Congress* (Tuscaloosa: University of Alabama Press, 1983).

[15]David W. Brady and Charles S. Bullock III, "Coalition Politics in the House of Representatives," in Lawrence Dodd and Bruce I. Oppenheimer, eds., *Congress Reconsidered*, 2nd ed. (Washington: CQ Press, 1981), p. 201. According to Brady and Bullock the coalition began to operate in 1937, but the forces that produced this cooperation had existed for some time.

each other, the alliance remained informal; for example, there has never been a Conservative Coalition caucus. Rather, key Republicans such as House Minority Leader Joseph Martin (R–Mass.) or Southern Democrats such as Senator Richard Russell (D–Ga.) would communicate casually, if purposefully, with their allies and encourage the formation of a voting coalition.[16] With Texan Sam Rayburn (a moderate-to-conservative Southerner) at the helm of the House Democratic party for much of the 1940s and 1950s, the Conservative Coalition's ability to defeat liberal legislation was scarcely a great problem. The party and committee leadership, which was heavily weighted with Southerners, ordinarily deferred to the coalition, whose preferences roughly reflected those of the House as a whole.

Rayburn's greatest strengths as Speaker did not derive from his formal powers, which were modest at best. A brief comparison to Reed or Cannon—or Gingrich—demonstrates the personal and policy bases of Rayburn's influence. Speaker Cannon, for example, chaired the Rules Committee and his majority leader headed the Ways and Means panel; these are the two most powerful committees in the chamber. He appointed all committee members and all chairs and could delay making these appointments until well after the Congress had convened. He controlled the legislative schedule with an iron hand and used his power of recognition to reduce opponents' capacity to participate meaningfully in floor debate. Rayburn, in contrast, held relatively few formal powers. He could not control the Rules Committee; it had been captured by the Conservative Coalition during the 1950s under the strong-willed chairmanship of conservative Democrat Howard Smith (D–Va.), who owed his position to his seniority on the committee. More generally, the seniority principle had become so firmly entrenched within the Congress that advancement on committees was virtually automatic, regardless of one's loyalty to the party. Nor did Rayburn control the initial assignments of Democrats to committees.[17] In short, Rayburn possessed few of the leadership tools that Cannon had wielded so effectively to control the agenda and legislative results of the House.[18] Yet legislators almost universally viewed him as a powerful Speaker. How could this be so?

Rayburn did retain significant, if limited, formal powers and the discretion to recognize whom he wanted on the House floor. He also controlled the leadership organization, which kept him well informed on most issues. Rayburn could dominate the final scheduling of legislation, and he often used his position to trade favors with other members—both Republicans and Democrats.[19] Favors such as campaigning for a fellow Democrat, postponing

---

[16]Joseph Martin, *My First Fifty Years in Politics* (New York: McGraw-Hill, 1960), p. 84.

[17]Traditionally, Democratic members of the House Ways and Means Committee had served as the party's "committee on committees." In 1975 this power was transferred to the Steering and Policy Committee, where party leaders possessed much more influence on appointments.

[18]For a brief summary of the tools of powerful leadership, see Robert L. Peabody, *Leadership in Congress* (Boston: Little, Brown, 1976), pp. 41–47.

[19]Ibid., pp. 42–46.

a vote to mollify a freshman Republican, and supporting a new dam for a marginal-seat member allowed the Speaker to build up positive "balances" in his exchanges with legions of Representatives (including those in the minority). As a result of past favors, Rayburn could request assistance on a specific issue from various legislators who would be hard-pressed to rebuff him.[20] In addition, Rayburn's work ethic, his absolute integrity, and his total dedication to the House provided strong foundations for his politicking on given legislative items.

More generally, however, Rayburn was influential because for most of his speakership he reflected the overall moderate-conservative policy leanings of the House during the 1950s. Although he had his differences with President Eisenhower, whom he regarded as a political amateur, Rayburn did not back the activist agenda that growing numbers of Northern Democrats favored. Rather, as a key conduit of information between the White House and the Congress (along with Senate Majority Leader Lyndon Johnson) he operated at the hub of an informal House oligarchy of party leaders and committee chairmen. In the end, however, these tough-minded committee leaders could dominate policy making from their separate, formal power bases. Rayburn had neither the desire nor the authority to move the House very far beyond its comfortably moderate, limited-government course of the 1950s.

The congressional leadership began to undergo significant changes between 1958 and 1961; the fragility of Rayburn's leadership (and that of Lyndon Johnson, in the Senate), which was based on personality and favor trading, came under tremendous pressure with the large Democratic gains in the 1958 congressional elections and the party's 1960 capture of the presidency. In one of his last major actions as Speaker (before his death later in 1961), Rayburn put into motion the twenty-year process of recentralizing leadership powers in the House by wresting control of the Rules Committee from the Conservative Coalition. The committee's four Republicans and two Southern Democrats had been able to thwart the preferences of six regular Democrats, but the Speaker proposed to add three members—two Democrats and one Republican—to the panel; this would allow the leadership to increase its influence on the committee's important decisions as to how the House would structure its consideration of legislation.[21] Building an informal coalition among all 129 Northern Democrats, 30 (of 32) "border-state" Democrats, 36 (of 98) Southern Democrats, and 22 (of 170) Republicans, Rayburn, who

---

[20]These tactics were similar to those used by former Ways and Means Chair Representative Wilbur Mills (D–Ark.), as detailed by John Manley, "Wilbur Mills: A Study in Congressional Influence," *American Political Science Review* 63 (June 1969), pp. 442–464. Mills served as Ways and Means chair from 1958 through 1974.

[21]Ironically, one of the Democrats added to the Rules Committee, an Alabama Representative, did not always support the leadership's positions. But the principle of leadership control of this important committee had been established.

disliked confrontation, won what he called "the worst fight of my life" by the narrow margin of 217–212.[22]

Typical of Rayburn's reverence for the House and his respect for his colleagues, the Speaker opted for a moderate course of reform in which "no member was unseated, nor was party discipline applied. . . . The enlargement resolution, as the Speaker himself said . . . was 'the way to embarrass nobody if they didn't want to be embarrassed.'"[23] Even so, Rayburn understood the stakes at hand; a Democratic president and a Democratic Congress might well be prevented from pushing forward their policies if the Rules Committee remained as an obstacle. Although the expansion of the Rules Committee applied only to the 87th Congress, the obstructionism of this body declined immediately, if not completely, and by the mid-1970s the panel had swung around to serve House leaders in structuring debates and scheduling votes on the floor.[24]

The Conservative Coalition continued to appear with great frequency in congressional voting alignments during the 1960s and 1970s, but the Democratic leadership in the House gradually strengthened itself (this process moved slowly and was frequently obscured by the simultaneous decentralizing trends of stronger individual member enterprises and greater fragmentation within the committee system). However, neither of the two Speakers who followed Rayburn—Representatives John McCormack (D–Mass., 1961–1969) and Carl Albert (D–Okla., 1969–1977)—proved forceful or effective in countering the decentralizing forces that dominated the House in the late 1960s and the 1970s.

Slowly, members of the Democratic Caucus came to see that their leaders needed more authority to run the House. Echoing Woodrow Wilson's 1885 conclusions, political scientist Charles Jones observed that "*somebody must be trusted,* in order that when things go wrong it may be quite plain who should be punished."[25] From their base in the Democratic Study Group (one of the first informal groups on Capitol Hill) from the late 1950s on, liberals continually prodded the Democratic Caucus to reduce the autonomy of full committee chairs and increase the authority of the leadership and the full caucus,

---

[22]Two superb sources detail this important decision: Milton C. Cummings, Jr., and Robert L. Peabody, "The Decision to Enlarge the Committee on Rules: An Analysis of the 1961 Vote," in *New Perspectives on the House of Representatives,* Robert L. Peabody and Nelson W. Polsby, eds. (Chicago: Rand McNally, 1963), pp. 167–194; and D. B. Hardeman and Donald C. Bacon, *Rayburn: A Biography* (Lanham, MD: Madison Books, 1984), pp. 447–466.

[23]Cummings and Peabody, op. cit., p. 193.

[24]Bruce I. Oppenheimer, "The Rules Committee: New Arm of Leadership in a Decentralized House," in Lawrence Dodd and Bruce I. Oppenheimer, eds., *Congress Reconsidered* (New York: Praeger, 1977), pp. 96–116.

[25]Quoted in Charles Jones, "Somebody Must Be Trusted: An Essay on Leadership of the U.S. Congress," in Norman J. Ornstein, *Congress in Change* (New York: Praeger, 1975), p. 266, Wilson's emphasis.

which the Northern Democrats increasingly dominated. More and more, majority-party House Democrats chose to trust themselves, as the caucus, or their leaders, as their direct agents.[26] In particular, the Democratic Caucus gave the Speaker the power to appoint members of the Rules Committee, thus making the committee a loyal "arm of the Leadership."[27] Next, the Caucus moved the committee assignment responsibility to the party leadership–dominated Steering and Policy Committee and thus greatly enhanced the leaders' roles in this process. Finally, to coordinate policy making within the fragmented committee system, the Speaker was granted broad powers to refer bills to multiple committees, often in a well-defined sequence that imposed deadlines on committee action.[28]

During his decade-long tenure as Speaker (1977–1986), Representative Thomas P. (Tip) O'Neill (D–Mass.) and his lieutenants created a new leadership style within a House that had encouraged more individual participation from virtually all members, but especially those of the majority party.[29] In this democratized context leaders became service providers, more than ever, to their colleagues; by offering meaningful support to incumbents, by keeping all the Democratic legislators well informed, and by granting any number of particular favors, the leadership demonstrated its responsiveness. At the same time, the Democratic leaders greatly increased their ability to structure the decision-making process through their formal powers to schedule bills and dominate the Rules Committee. Collectively, congressional Democrats were willing to allow their leadership considerable leeway here, as long as its actions did not conflict with strong membership desires. Finally, the leaders consciously adopted an inclusive strategy, bringing large numbers of members into the leadership during the late 1970s, both in permanent positions (for example, as whips) and in ad hoc capacities (such as those of task force heads and members).

Even as subcommittees proliferated, individual enterprises grew, and new norms encouraged the participation of all members in the late 1970s, party leaders slowly gained more leverage and influence. Underlying the surface fragmentation was a growing acceptance among most Democrats for a strengthened leadership that would allow Jim Wright to become, albeit briefly, one of the House's most powerful Speakers. At the same time, the Republicans grew increasingly united and vocal in their protests against both the Democrats' policy positions and their use of procedures to limit meaningful minority participa-

---

[26]For a good summary of this trend, see Barbara Sinclair, *Majority Leadership in the U.S. House* (Baltimore, MD: Johns Hopkins University Press, 1983), pp. 2ff.

[27]Oppenheimer, op. cit., p. 1977.

[28]See Gary Young and Joseph Cooper, "Multiple Referral and the Transformation of House Decision Making," in Lawrence C. Dodd and Bruce I. Oppenheimer, eds., *Congress Reconsidered,* 5th ed. (Washington: CQ Press, 1995), pp. 211–236.

[29]The following discussion draws on Sinclair, op. cit., pp. 28–29.

tion within the House.[30] By acting as aggressive, effective partisans, the House Democrats simultaneously offered Republicans a model of strong leadership and a clear target for the opposition's efforts to gain control of the House.

Caucus-Based Centralization: The Democratic Model, 1981–1994

The notions of party leadership, partisanship, and party voting overlap within the Congress. Party leaders often structure votes and other decisions to take advantage of party majorities, but they must also take into account the preferences of their followers. Overall, the postreform Congress has become a highly partisan place, particularly the House. In assessing the strength of political parties within the Congress, political scientists frequently analyze changes in two different but related measures of partisanship on roll-call votes.[31] From 1983 on, there is no question that both the proportion of party-based votes and the level of party loyalty on these votes have increased considerably (see Tables 7–1 and 7–2). This increased partisanship has grown in large part because many contemporary Southern Democrats—those who hail from urban areas and districts with high percentages of African American voters—tend to vote a lot like their Northern Democratic colleagues, and voting patterns of the growing number of Southern Republicans closely approximate those of their fellow GOP legislators. As traditionally conservative Southern Democrats have declined in numbers and impact, the Conservative Coalition has become a less active and less powerful force within the House. But the divisions between the parties have increased.

The party-voting scores of Southern Democrats have risen steadily, from an average 53 percent party unity score in the 94th Congress (1975–1976) to an average of 78 percent in the 100th through 103rd Congresses (1987–1994).[32]

---

[30]The Republican position is thoroughly articulated in a paper issued by Representatives Richard T. Armey (R–Tex.), Jennifer Dunn (R–Wash.), and Christopher Shays (R–Conn.), "It's Long Enough: The Decline of Popular Government under Forty Years of Single Party Control of the U.S. House of Representatives" (Washington: House Republican Conference, 1994).

[31]Most, though not all, important votes are recorded. If twenty-five House members or one-fifth of the senators present request a roll-call vote, the chamber goes on the record. This was not always the case; through the 1960s, many key issues were decided on "unrecorded teller" votes, in which Representatives would signify their vote by lining up and walking past vote counters on the "aye" or "nay" side of a given proposal. In the early 1970s, the House ceased this practice and installed an electronic voting system. The number of roll-call votes changed from an average of less than 100 per year in the 1950s to about 175 annually in the 1960s and more than 600 per year in the 1970s. Subsequently, the average declined to about 450 in the 1980s. Virtually all major decisions are still on the record, however. In the Senate, the patterns have been similar, although the rise has been more gradual and the number of roll-call votes has averaged 100–200 fewer per year since the late 1970s.

[32]Figures from Norman Ornstein, Thomas Mann, and Michael Malbin, *Vital Statistics on Congress, 1993–1994* (Washington: CQ Press, 1993), pp. 201–202, and *CQ Weekly Report*, December 31, 1994, p. 3659. See also David W. Rohde, *Parties and Leaders in the Post-Reform House* (Chicago: University of Chicago Press, 1991), p. 57.

TABLE 7-1

Party Unity Average Scores

Average scores for each party in both chambers of Congress					
Year	Democrats	Republicans	Year	Democrats	Republicans
1961	71%	72%	1978	64%	67%
1962	69	68	1979	69	72
1963	71	72	1980	68	70
1964	67	69	1981	69	76
1965	69	70	1982	72	71
1966	61	67	1983	76	74
1967	66	71	1984	74	72
1968	57	63	1985	79	75
1969	62	62	1986	78	71
1970	57	59	1987	81	74
1971	62	66	1988	79	73
1972	57	64	1989	81	73
1973	68	68	1990	81	74
1974	63	62	1991	81	78
1975	69	70	1992	79	79
1976	65	66	1993	85	84
1977	67	70	1994	83	83

Source: *Congressional Quarterly Weekly Report,* December 31, 1994, p. 3658.

Although Southern Democrats remain more conservative than their Northern counterparts, the differences have shrunk considerably, from an approximately 25 percent party-voting divergence in the 90th, 91st, and 92nd Congresses (1967–1972) to a mere 9 percent gap in the 100th Congress. Rohde observes, "in 1971–2, the *average* southern Democrat supported his or her party less than half the time on those votes that divided party majorities. From that point on, southern unity began a gradual increase to almost 80 percent in recent years."[33]

Partisanship in voting does not necessarily flow from a stronger, more centralized party leadership; intense partisanship depends as much on electoral patterns as any set of revised practices within the Democratic Caucus or the House as a whole. In the 1980s, partisanship increased (more party-line votes, more unity on those votes), and party leaders gained more tools for leadership and more experience in employing these instruments (restrictive rules, suspensions of the rules, sequential referrals of legislation to committees). These two developments come together within the Democratic Caucus, where the membership can communicate its wishes to the leadership.[34]

---

[33]Ibid., p. 55, Rohde's emphasis.

[34]For an extended discussion of strong legislative leadership in parties that are relatively weak outside the legislature, see Barbara Sinclair, *Legislators, Leaders, and Lawmaking: The U.S. House of Representatives in the Postreform Era* (Baltimore: Johns Hopkins University Press, 1995), especially pp. 300–306.

TABLE 7-2 Proportion of Partisan Roll Calls

How often a majority of Democrats voted against a majority of Republicans

Year	House	Senate	Year	House	Senate	Year	House	Senate	Year	House	Senate
1954	38%	47%	1964	55%	36%	1974	29%	44%	1984	47%	40%
1955	41	30	1965	52	42	1975	48	48	1985	61	50
1956	44	53	1966	41	50	1976	36	37	1986	57	52
1957	59	36	1967	36	35	1977	42	42	1987	64	41
1958	40	44	1968	35	32	1978	33	45	1988	47	42
1959	55	48	1969	31	36	1979	47	47	1989	55	35
1960	53	37	1970	27	35	1980	38	46	1990	49	54
1961	50	62	1971	38	42	1981	37	48	1991	55	49
1962	46	41	1972	27	36	1982	36	43	1992	64	53
1963	49	47	1973	42	40	1983	56	44	1993	65	67
									1994	62	52

Source: *Congressional Quarterly Weekly Report*, December 31, 1994, p. 3659.

Bearing in mind Fenno's conclusion that we get the kind of Congress that the members give us,[35] we got a postreform Congress in which, from the early 1980s on, the Democratic Caucus empowered its leaders to act aggressively as its agents. This was accomplished in two related ways: (1) through an initial set of decisions at the beginning of each Congress and (2) through continuing conversations between party leaders and the Democratic membership, both in groups and one on one.

At the outset of a new Congress, in January of each odd-numbered year, members of the legislative parties select their respective leaders. In the postreform era, House Democrats elected the Speaker, the majority leader, and chief majority whip[36] and voted to approve all full-committee chairs, as well as each of the thirteen appropriations subcommittee chairs. After 1994, these selections continued, albeit for minority leadership positions and "ranking minority member" slots on committees. In short, the membership has a biennial opportunity to defeat any top party or committee leader who has lost the caucus' confidence. Between 1975 and 1993, Democrats unseated six committee chairs, eased another one out of his position, and, equally important, delivered numerous warnings through negative votes to many other committee heads.[37] For the party and committee leaders, this process is sometimes unnerving, but it is highly valuable in that these figures receive the explicit, formal endorsement of their peers. In an era when party leaders enjoy great formal powers, such as the Speaker's Rules Committee appointments, his chairmanship of the Policy and Steering Committee, and his domination over legislative scheduling, this endorsement by the party's legislators has given Democratic leaders wide latitude in setting agendas and providing specific assistance to individual members. Yet the grant of authority remains—as Speaker Wright discovered in 1989—contingent on the continuing support of a firm caucus majority.

In the Rayburn era, after briefly coming together to select its top leadership, the Democratic Caucus would virtually disappear, meeting only rarely. The caucus within the postreform Congress remains much more active, both formally and informally. Not only are there regularly scheduled meetings but, more important, the caucus exists within the minds of leaders and backbenchers alike as an active force inside the House. In various circumstances leaders or the rank and file may choose to request a caucus meeting to reach a party position on a major issue (for example, calling for Reagan Administration compliance with Strategic Arms Limitation Talks agreement provisions in 1987). More generally,

---

[35]Richard F. Fenno, Jr., "If, as Ralph Nader Says, Congress Is the 'Broken Branch,' How Come We Love Our Congressmen So Much?" in Norman Ornstein, ed., *Congress in Change* (New York: Praeger, 1975), p. 287.

[36]The whip was appointed until a 1985 rules change mandated election by the caucus.

[37]Leroy N. Rieselbach, *Congressional Politics,* 2nd ed. (Boulder, CO: Westview Press, 1995), p. 93.

leaders are continually gauging caucus support for legislative initiatives and procedural maneuvers.

The active Democratic Caucus has both empowered and restrained the party's leaders. By the early 1990s, a fairly large core group of leaders had emerged as the day-to-day directors of House business. The traditional leaders—the Speaker, the majority leader, and the whip—were joined by three chief deputy whips, along with the caucus chair and vice-chair. In addition, congressional scholar Barbara Sinclair notes, "as the leadership has become more central to the legislative process, members' desires for *representation* in the leadership have intensified."[38] Indeed, when Speaker Foley split the chief deputy whip's office into three positions, he appointed a woman (Barbara Kennelly [Conn.]), a Southerner (Butler Derrick [S.C.]), and an African American (John Lewis [Ga.]), and in 1993 he added a fourth slot for Bill Richardson (N.M.), a Latino. Beyond these attempts to include more factions within the party leadership, this trend toward representation is important in that committees have historically served as the principal agents of representation. Given the emphasis on an expanded, inclusive leadership, however, the centrifugal forces of representation have grown stronger within the House's bastion of centralization.

The core leadership, aided by a formidable staff, serves as information source, sounding board, strategic and tactical decision maker, and, under divided government, interbranch negotiator. Nevertheless, given its highly inclusive style of operation, even an expanded core leadership could not maintain adequate communication lines with more than 250 House Democrats, so the Democrats established a much more extended leadership apparatus, which included almost half of the party's 256 legislators in the 103rd Congress. Of special note has been the systematic expansion of the whip system, which acts as a conduit for information between members and leaders and as an organization for mobilizing votes on the House floor.

In the 103rd Congress (1993–1995), the whip system included the majority whip, four deputy whips, a floor whip, an "ex-officio whip" (Representative Joe Moakley, Rules Committee chair), eleven deputy whips, two "whip task force" chairs, fifty-six leadership-appointed at-large whips, and eighteen assistant whips elected by members of regional zones. The whip system alone included ninety-two Democratic members, well over a third of the party's ranks in the House. But the expansion in the ranks of Democratic leaders did not stop with the whip system. Rules Committee members clearly occupied leadership slots, as did the chair of the Budget Committee and a host of ad hoc task force heads appointed by the majority leader to organize party efforts on specific legislative

---

[38]Barbara Sinclair, "House Majority Leadership in an Era of Divided Control," in Dodd and Oppenheimer, *Congress Reconsidered,* 5th ed., p. 243, emphasis added.

initiatives.[39] In addition, the chairmanship of the Democratic Congressional Campaign Committee (DCCC) represented an important leadership position.

Without question, the Democratic Caucus has sanctioned the development of a strong House leadership; in large part, this derives from the increased ideological homogeneity of the Democratic membership. Nonetheless, substantial limitations on leadership have remained in the 1990s; despite consistently high levels of partisan voting and active, inclusive leadership efforts, party-based policies did not flow smoothly from the House, most notably on such significant issues as free trade and health care.

At first with great hesitancy, and later with vigor and conviction, House Democrats acted to strengthen their party leadership, from the 1961 vote on wresting control of the Rules Committee away from the Conservative Coalition to their willingness in 1987–1988 to follow Speaker Jim Wright's lead in refashioning American foreign and military policy in Nicaragua. The Democratic majority came to structure the context of decision making in the House, which meant that the minority Republicans became less and less able to influence outcomes.[40] The trend toward strong party leadership in a weak-party era illustrates the trends toward more ideological cohesiveness among parties in the House, as well as the members' cost–benefit calculations, which increasingly led them to encourage leaders' latitude in structuring decisions.[41] Strong party leadership remained conditional on these calculations by the members and on the ideological divisions between the two parties, however, and Democratic leaders became more and more dependent on manipulating the agenda and structuring floor votes through the aggressive use of the Rules Committee.[42] Many, if not most, Republicans found themselves holding no stake in the institution of the House; with little remorse they would seek to tear down this Democratic institution. In 1994 they succeeded.

Postreform Politics in the Republican Mold

With the stunning results of the 1994 elections, Republicans gained control of the House after forty years as the minority. We shall explore in some detail the strong, centralized leadership adopted by the GOP. First, however, let us examine how the party operated as a minority within the contemporary House.

---

[39]On task forces, see Sinclair, *Majority Leadership,* op. cit.

[40]On the theory of partisan control, see Gary W. Cox and Matthew McCubbins, *Legislative Leviathan* (Berkeley: University of California Press, 1993); for a Republican analysis of Democratic control of the House, see Representatives Armey, Dunn, and Shays, op. cit.

[41]Barbara Sinclair, "The Emergence of Strong Leadership in the 1980s House of Representatives," *Journal of Politics* 54 (August 1992), pp. 657–684.

[42]Rohde, op. cit., p. 174.

THE DILEMMA OF OPPOSITION   With the exception of a modest number of Northeastern Republicans (sometimes called Gypsy Moths), the generally conservative Republicans have maintained reasonably high levels of party voting (see Table 7-1). As members of a long-standing minority in the House, Republicans found themselves holding little authority, which freed them to pursue a variety of strategies in seeking to affect policy outcomes.[43] Simple hard-boiled opposition always served as one alternative, of course, but historically, many Republicans have opted to cooperate with the Democratic majority, hoping to affect policies in committee or by providing key votes on the floor. The Rayburn-era House presented frequent opportunities for committees' ranking minority members to become important forces in shaping congressional policies. For example, in the 1950s and 1960s, Appropriations Committee chair Clarence Cannon (D–Mo.) consulted not just regularly, but almost continuously, with ranking minority member John Taber (R–N.Y.) in reaching agreements on spending bills.[44]

In the 1970s and 1980s, House Republicans found themselves in increasingly difficult straits. First, they often were expected to support the policies of a Republican president, even though their minority status denied them any effective means to implement the executive agendas articulated by Nixon, Reagan, and Bush. Second, Democratic majorities, especially after 1982, acted in highly partisan ways within committees and on the House floor. Republicans could do little in the face of the Rules Committee decisions to structure floor debates and votes, and the Speaker's control of scheduling allowed them little voice in decision making on either policies or procedures. A strong Democratic leadership and an increasingly unified set of Democratic members meant that House Republicans enjoyed few opportunities to influence outcomes.

In step with its generally conservative membership and often in reaction to the strengthened, sometimes arrogant, Democratic leadership, the House minority frequently chose confrontational strategies through the 1980s and into the 1990s. Indeed, the well-publicized actions of Representatives Newt Gingrich (R–Ga.), Robert Walker (R–Pa.), and Richard Armey (R–Texas), among many others, heightened tensions in the increasingly partisan House. Gingrich enlisted other young, activist Representatives to join him in the Conservative Opportunity Society, an informal grouping that functioned simultaneously as in-House think tank and guerilla base in challenging the established powers of both parties.

Two decisions—one imposed by the Democrats, the other taken by the Republican conference—demonstrated the growing strength of the confrontational elements within the GOP. On May 1, 1985, following an extended and highly partisan process, the House opted in a partisan vote to give a

[43]See Jones, op. cit.

[44]Richard F. Fenno, Jr., *The Power of the Purse* (Boston: Little, Brown, 1966).

contested seat to an Indiana Democratic incumbent, even though the state had certified the Republican challenger as the winner of the November election. Every Republican House member marched out of the chamber in protest; even the most moderate, least confrontational Republicans found this decision too much to swallow. Representative Vin Weber (R–Minn.), a Gingrich ally, observed that "it was essential to Newt and his success to drive home the point that after [thirty] years . . . something corrupting had happened to Democratic rule and it was just not in our interest to be in bed with the Democrats."[45]

The second decision came from within the Republican conference four years later. President Bush tapped House Minority Whip Dick Cheney (R–Wyo.) to become secretary of defense. The ensuing leadership contest pitted Gingrich against veteran Representative Edward Madigan (R–Ill.). Buoyed by the early support of some frustrated moderates such as Nancy Johnson (R–Conn.), Gingrich won the whip post by an 89–87 count. By the narrowest of margins, the Republican conference had decided to move in a confrontational direction.

In the early 1990s, Republicans sought to link the unpopularity of the Congress with its Democratic leadership, especially in the House. In a comprehensive broadside, Representatives Richard Armey (R–Tex.), Jennifer Dunn (R–Wash.), and Christopher Shays (R–Conn.) published an extensive attack on an unresponsive and allegedly corrupt Democratic House. They concluded, for example, that "forty years of single party control of the House of Representatives has created a *corrupt institution isolated from public sentiment*. . . . the ruling party has collectively used [its] powers to partisan ends. It has unleashed its investigatory power on enemies in the other party, while turning a blind eye and a deaf ear to equal or worse violations by some of its own. It has used its power over support institutions [such as the House Post Office] to give jobs to its supporters and to cover up scandals within them."[46]

In short, the Republican House minority chose to oppose with increasing aggressiveness and hostility, as they sought to link an unpopular postreform Congress with its Democratic leadership. Given that no Republican incumbent lost his or her seat in the 1994 midterm elections, the conclusion can be drawn that they succeeded.

THE REPUBLICANS ORGANIZE THE HOUSE   In the wake of the 1994 sweep, which gave Republicans a gain of fifty-two seats and a 230–205 margin in the House,[47] the Republican conference approved rules for the party and the

---

[45]Quoted in Dan Balz and Charles R. Babcock, "How Newt Climbed the Hill," *Washington Post National Weekly Edition*, January 9–15, 1995, p. 11.

[46]Armey, Dunn, and Shays, op. cit., p. 131.

[47]Democrats actually won 204 seats, but Bernard Sanders (Ind.–Vt.) caucused with them. By late 1995, the defections of Democratic Representatives raised the Republicans' ranks to 234.

chamber that centralized leadership authority more firmly than at any time since the overthrow of Speaker Cannon. Building on the examples and structures provided by congressional Democrats in the postreform era, the Republican rank and file empowered Speaker Newt Gingrich to dominate the reconfiguration of many House practices and procedures, as well as giving him great power in selecting committee chairs and making committee appointments.

More than any party leader since Cannon, Gingrich received a sweeping grant of authority from his party colleagues. Moreover, the House Republicans demonstrated overwhelming unity throughout the highly publicized first 100 days, in which they passed nine of ten items in their so-called Contract with America. The House cast 302 recorded votes in its first three months, and Republican levels of party unity reached near unanimity on all but a few issues such as term limits. On Contract items, 141 of 230 House Republicans voted with the party 100 percent of the time, and of seventy-three GOP freshmen, fifty-three compiled perfect records and seventy-one voted with the party at least 94 percent of the time.[48] This unity came in part from the momentum of capturing the House and having an agenda that had been developed through polling and focus groups, as well as in long discussions among Republicans over the past decade; but Gingrich was also credited for his skillful handling of both the seventy-three first-term members and the moderate wing of the party within the House. Indeed, "Gingrich has sought to encourage, rather than suppress the activist tendencies of the freshmen" by providing key committee appointments to the Appropriations, Budget, and Ways and Means Committees, as well as meeting with a different group of Republican freshmen every week.[49] Moderate Representative Sherwood Boehlert (R–N.Y.) observed that Gingrich has proven a good listener, as "he challenges the moderates to unite, talk things over and come up with a plan."[50]

Beyond the Contract and a broad policy vision of a smaller national government, Gingrich's strong backing in the conference derives in large part from two perceptions: (1) Many junior members think they owe their elections to him because of financial support, a nationalized election, and, for a lot of them, personal campaign visits, and (2) almost all House Republicans would admit, however grudgingly, that they would not have won control in 1994 save for Gingrich's persistence and majority-building activities over the previous decade.

The strength of Gingrich's party leadership remains conditional, though, on the continuing support of his fellow partisans. As major spending cuts,

---

[48]Donna Cassatta, "Republicans Bask in Success of Rousing Performance," *CQ Weekly Report,* April 8, 1995, p. 990.

[49]Carroll J. Doherty, "Time and Tax Cuts Will Test GOP Freshman Solidarity," *CQ Weekly Report,* April 1, 1995, p. 916.

[50]Cassatta, op. cit., p. 990.

thorny social issues, and reelection considerations move to center stage, the Speaker and his leadership team may well increase the use of the very procedural tactics, such as rules restricting amendments on the floor, that they found highly objectionable when employed by the Democrats against them. Indeed, congressional scholar Barbara Sinclair concludes that in terms of using special rules and procedures to control the legislative process, "the story of the 103rd Congress [with a Democratic majority] and that of the 104th [with a Republican majority] is more one of continuity than of change."[51] In the end, this means that House leaders have been able to legislate, even under the difficult circumstances of slim majorities and divided control of the legislative and executive branches.

The Senate: Leadership Redefined, Not Enhanced

Historically, the Senate has not encouraged strong partisanship or strong party leadership as much as the House. Writing in 1993, political scientist Steven Smith concluded that "although party cohesiveness and polarization ebb and flow, creating variation in the conditions associated with strong party leadership, only for a brief period in the past forty years has a Senate party been so strong that it could win most votes without help from the other party."[52] This assertion rings true, yet the job of Senate party leaders has changed considerably over the years. Unlike their House counterparts, Senate leaders have not seen their positions consistently strengthened in the postreform Congress. When partisanship has become sharply defining, it has most often occurred in a specific context, as with the Republicans' continuing opposition to Democratic proposals on health care and other initiatives in the last few months of 1994; this unity was built largely on the anticipation of capturing the chamber rather than any coherent program that brought individual Republican senators together.

Each Senate party elects a floor leader and a whip, as well as chairs of committees on policy, committee assignments, and campaigns.[53] Although Republicans have historically distributed these jobs more widely than have Democrats, the fact is that, aside from the majority and minority leader positions, no one slot is especially important. Undeniably, Senate leaders possess many fewer weapons than do their House counterparts. Rather than controlling the chamber's schedule, the majority leader endlessly negotiates and renegotiates the order of business. The minority leader serves as his chief

---

[51]Barbara Sinclair, "Change and Continuity in the Legislative Process: The U.S. House and Senate from the 1970s to the 1990s," paper presented at the 1995 American Political Science Association meetings, Chicago, August 31–September 3, 1995, p. 16.

[52]Steven S. Smith, "Forces of Change in Senate Party Leadership and Organization," in Dodd and Oppenheimer, *Congress Reconsidered*, 5th ed., p. 265.

[53]Roger Davidson and Walter Oleszek, *Congress and Its Members*, 4th ed., (Washington: CQ Press, 1994), p. 192.

sparring partner in these sessions,[54] and each leader must represent the interests of his own party's members. Nor do Senate party caucuses provide broad grants of authority to their respective leaders; rather, the fundamental expectation of party leaders is to serve "the _personal_ political needs of party colleagues."[55] Former senator Fred Harris, writing in 1993, argued that party conferences (or caucuses) have grown in strength within the Senate of the 1980s and 1990s, but that these groupings have largely allowed individual senators, all with their own agendas, to influence leaders who continually seek consensus.[56]

Partisan voting levels have risen in the Senate, although not as much as in the House. Comparing the first four years of the Nixon Administration to the four years of the Bush presidency, Senate partisanship, although very similar to the House in the earlier era, did not keep pace (see Table 7–3). Moreover, increasing levels of partisan voting do not necessarily result from strong party leadership. As in the House, the Senate Democratic party has become more homogeneous, as Southern senators act more like their Northern peers and as Republicans win higher proportions of Southern seats. In addition, many of the votes in the Bush era came on fiscal and budgetary matters, which provided the Democrats with very little incentive to help a Republican administration.

Even though their authority is close to nil, their power modest at best, and their influence open to question, contemporary Senate leaders work extraordinarily hard just to keep the chamber from bogging down entirely. Former

TABLE 7-3   Senate and House Party Unity Scores, 1969-1972 and 1989-1992

Chamber and Party	1969-1972 Unity*	1989-1992 Unity*
House Democrats (all)	71%	86%
House Southern Democrats	48%	78%
House Republicans	74%	80%
Senate Democrats (all)	73%	81%
Senate Southern Democrats	51%	72%
Senate Republicans	73%	81%

* Four-year averages. Scores reflect the percentage of occasions that members vote with a majority of their fellow partisans on votes in which most (>50%) Democrats vote against most (>50%) Republicans.

Source: Norman J. Ornstein, Thomas E. Mann, and Michael J. Malbin, eds., _Vital Statistics on Congress, 1993-1994_ (Washington, DC: CQ Press/AEI, 1994), pp. 201–202.

---

[54]A brief period of viewing C-SPAN II's coverage of the Senate will flesh out this brief description. Late each evening, Majority Leader Dole and Minority Leader Tom Daschle (D–S.D.), along with a handful of other interested senators, converse at length about how the schedule will proceed. Nothing is resolved until all actors are satisfied with the arrangements.

[55]Smith, op. cit., p. 262, emphasis added.

[56]Fred R. Harris, _Deadlock or Decision: The U.S. Senate and the Rise of National Politics_ (New York: Oxford University Press, 1993), pp. 184ff.

Majority Leader Robert Byrd has labeled the responsibilities of the floor leader as essentially those of a "slave" to his fellow senators.[57] A leader spends countless hours on the Senate floor seeking to reconcile the interests and egos of 100 separate lords and ladies, each of whom jealously guards his or her own prerogatives. Overall, the contemporary Senate demands of its top leaders at least five overlapping tasks:

1. Managing the affairs of their respective parties

2. Scheduling Senate business in accord with members' wishes

3. Monitoring floor deliberations, including the crafting of unanimous consent agreements that govern debates/votes

4. Serving as conduit between the Senate and the White House (and the House) in managing an increasing number of interbranch/interchamber agreements (e.g., on budgets)

5. Representing the party and the Senate to the media.[58]

Compared with their House counterparts, leaders in the postreform Senate spend much more time on management tasks (1–3 above) and much less on the formulation of policy alternatives. In addition, since the 1950s to 1960s, Senate floor leaders have changed their relationships with presidents and the media in ways that have not enhanced their power.

One of the major tools of floor leaders such as Republican Everett Dirksen (1959–1969) and Democrat Lyndon Johnson (1953–1960) was their regular access to the president, especially through unpublicized contacts by phone or in informal meetings. Dirksen and Johnson both maintained excellent relationships with President Eisenhower, and when Johnson became president in 1963, relations between him and Dirksen, the Minority Leader, reached new levels of intimacy. One senator concluded that Dirksen and Johnson were so close that "they understood, they knew, what was going on in each other's mind."[59] In fact, Dirksen often knew more about Johnson's thinking than did Majority Leader Mike Mansfield. This worked to Dirksen's great advantage in the early years of LBJ's presidency; later, Dirksen remained close to Johnson,

---

[57]Quoted in Roger H. Davidson, "Senate Leaders: Janitors for an Untidy Chamber?" in Lawrence Dodd and Bruce Oppenheimer, eds., *Congress Reconsidered,* 3rd ed. (Washington: CQ Press, 1985), p. 225.

[58]This list comes from Roger H. Davidson, op. cit., p. 236. Steven Smith, writing in 1993, eight years after Davidson's article, depicts leaders' responsibilities in terms of more partisan expectations of the members; although many of these relate to individual reelection campaigns and other personal needs, there exists at least the possibility of substance-oriented leadership. See Smith, op. cit.

[59]Senator Joseph Pearson (R–Kans.), quoted in Burdett A. Loomis, "Everett McKinley Dirksen: The Consummate Minority Leader," in Richard A. Baker and Roger H. Davidson, eds., *First Among Equals* (Washington: CQ Press, 1990), p. 252.

but as their efforts increasingly focused on the Vietnam War, his ties ultimately diminished his authority among his fellow Republicans.

If Dirksen gained strength from his links to a series of presidents, he also demonstrated the value of taking his partisan opposition to the press. Wonderfully quotable and witty, Dirksen understood that he could hold his small (thirty-six or fewer senators from 1959 to 1969) Republican minority together in part by focusing attention on himself. Twenty years later, Senators Robert Dole (R–Kans.) and George Mitchell (D–Maine) won their respective floor leader roles in part because of their communications skills, but neither Dole, Mitchell, nor any of the post-Dirksen leaders benefited from strong, personal ties with any of the post-Johnson presidents. In fact, Dole as Majority Leader maintained a healthy distance from the Reagan White House, and Mitchell (leader between 1989 and 1994) often served as a tough-minded partisan adversary to President Bush. Both these performances came at the behest of their party colleagues in the Senate, who wanted Dole to remain relatively independent and Mitchell to provide a partisan counterpoint to the executive branch.

In the end, regardless of their ties to presidents or the attention accorded them by the media, Senate leaders must operate under rules that do not allow them much control over the pace of floor debate or the content of amendments offered by individual senators.[60] Unlike the House, the Senate is not a majoritarian body. A determined minority of forty-one senators can stop the body in its tracks through the filibuster, and a single member can often hold it hostage by rejecting a request for a unanimous consent agreement that governs the conduct of floor debate on a given issue. Unlike their House peers, Senate leaders cannot easily structure votes or schedules, nor can they routinely set time limits for debate. Rather, leaders must cajole their colleagues, privately and publicly; compromise with them; and provide consideration for 100 different schedules, preferences, and egos. Even within one's own party, a leader has limited power. In 1995, for example, after moderates and conservatives split almost evenly on electing a whip (conservative Trent Lott [R–Miss.] defeated incumbent Alan Simpson [R–Wyo.]), Majority Leader Dole has taken to eating lunch alone each Wednesday, as members of the two wings of the Senate party meet separately. Even when the party is almost completely united, a leader finds it difficult to impose sanctions on a wayward legislator. For example, even though all Republican senators save one voted in favor of the balanced budget constitutional amendment in 1995, the amendment—already passed by the House—failed in the Senate by a single vote, 66–34. When a few, mostly junior, Senate Republicans sought to sanction the lone holdout (Appropriations Committee Chair Mark Hatfield [R–Oreg.]), the

---

[60]See Steven Smith, *The American Congress* (Boston: Houghton Mifflin, 1995), pp. 232ff, for an excellent extended example of the problems inherent in making the Senate move with even moderate speed on a major issue.

party conference, with Dole's blessing, refused even to vote on imposing any penalty.

Even so, Senate leaders can sometimes make a difference—especially when the entire body or the party must be represented in negotiations with the executive (as in budget "summits") or when they stand behind the extended work of their individual colleagues who have taken on a specific policy task such as tax or welfare reform. Either the individualism of the Senate must be overcome (as in negotiating with the executive) or used productively (as in helping policy entrepreneurs build majorities). Rarely can Senate leaders take full credit for making their institution run even passably well. Rather, a functioning Senate, however messy and inefficient, requires that its leaders act more as facilitators than as aggressive commanders. In the final analysis, the notion of Senate leadership remains largely a contradiction in terms within an institution that remains individualistic to a fault.

PARTY AND THE LIMITS OF CENTRALIZATION IN THE POSTREFORM CONGRESS

The very individualism of the Senate provides one clear set of limitations on the potential for strong, centralized leadership within the Congress. In the House, however, party leadership has grown extremely strong, as evidenced by partisan voting levels, the extended whip system, and the formidable powers that leaders possess to control appointments, schedules, and legislative procedures. Although Republicans, in the wake of their forty years in the minority, have granted Speaker Gingrich substantial powers over committee appointments, legislative schedules, and policy agendas, the leadership remains beholden to the party conference, just as Democratic leaders served as agents of their caucus. Moreover, on many issues neither party, in or out of the Congress, can generate well-articulated positions.

In 1993, for example, many House Democrats found it impossible to vote for President Clinton's initial budget, which was actively supported by their leaders. Only grudgingly were enough Democrats rounded up, arms sore from extensive twisting, to pass the budget agreement. In that case, at least, Clinton could rely on Democratic House leaders to act on his behalf in seeking out the 218 Democrats, among them Representative Margolies-Mezvinsky (see chapter 1), essential for the budget package's success.

Conversely, Democratic party leaders found themselves profoundly split over the North American Free Trade Agreement (NAFTA) in 1993, which President Clinton vigorously supported. While Speaker Tom Foley maintained a low profile, Majority Leader Richard Gephardt (D–Mo.) and Chief Whip David Bonior (D–Mich.), who both hail from the industrial "Rust Belt," led the opposition to NAFTA despite the position of their party's first president in more than a decade. Why the split? The answer is straightforward: Democrats in the House were deeply divided, to the point that a majority would vote against the agreement. This opposition stemmed not from internal House politics, but from the profound hostility toward NAFTA among many key party constituencies, none more important than organized labor.

The House Democratic Caucus handled this division by treading gingerly around it, as did the whip organization. Deputy Whip John Lewis (D–Ga.) reported, "In the regular whip meetings, we just don't talk about it."[61] Unlike votes on abortion or the death penalty, where party may take a back seat to moral considerations, the NAFTA debate focused on crucial long-term policy issues of utmost importance to the Democrats. The extent to which the majority party could not follow its own president illustrates the limits to centralized leadership within the contemporary House. Constituency pressures, contributors' concerns, and the entreaties of organized interests demonstrated the continuing power of local forces on House members both as individuals and as a bloc within their caucus. At the same time, partisan divisions on a single, emotional issue such as NAFTA rarely lead to irreconcilable splits. As one House Democrat put it, "I don't think Gephardt or Bonior are suffering any consequences for not supporting it. The Administration needs Gephardt and Bonior for a great many things. Plus, Gephardt and Bonior represent the majority of Democrats in the House [in terms of NAFTA votes]."[62]

Much the same thing occurred among House Republicans during the 1995 debate on term limits. Although almost 80 percent of the GOP House contingent voted in favor of the least restrictive proposal, Representative Henry Hyde (R–Ill.), Judiciary Committee chairman, led the cross-partisan block that vigorously opposed any form of limitation. Neither party's leadership has been able to construct agreement where there was none; not since Speaker Cannon has a leader possessed adequate powers to succeed at such a task, and in the end Cannon's procedural majority fell apart when he pushed too hard on substantive issues that divided the Republican backbenchers. Leadership in the contemporary United States Congress may be stronger than it was in the 1970s or 1930s, but many real constraints remain firmly in place, especially in the highly individualistic Senate (and even more especially for the majority floor leader). In the House, strong centralized leadership is surely possible, and partisanship has risen sharply in the postreform era. Nevertheless, such leadership remains conditionally based on power willingly but not unreservedly granted by an attentive collection of activist members.[63]

---

[61]Quoted in Robin Toner, "Divided Sentiments, Divided Loyalties," *The New York Times*, November 16, 1993, p. A9.

[62]Ibid.

[63]Rohde, op. cit., chap. 6.

Eight ᗰ

PRESIDENTIAL–CONGRESSIONAL RELATIONS: FOCUS, AUTHORITY, AND NEGOTIATION

I n his systematic study of presidential leadership of Congress, political scientist George Edwards concludes that "the president is not the ruler of the American state but a vital centralizing force, providing direction and energy for the nation's policy making."[1] The fragmented, individualistic Congress requires focus and direction. Although in 1995 the Speakership of Newt Gingrich has offered a historic alternative to strong presidential leadership, in twentieth-century American politics it has been the president whose position has provided the best chance of offering a coherent vision of where the nation should be headed. Convincing the Congress to act on this vision is quite another matter, however.

Setting the agenda is only one aspect of the president's ability to direct the actions of a fragmented Congress. Legislators must also work within a policy-making process that has increasingly given broad authority to the Executive Office of the President. With the growth of programs, regulations, and spending since the New Deal, the institution of the presidency has held the responsibility for making sure that prospective legislation, specific appropriations, and budget decisions compose a roughly coherent whole. The centralized authority for making these decisions has become formalized within the Office of Management and Budget (OMB), a part of the Executive Office of the President.[2] In going about its business, Congress must regularly peer over its collective shoulder, beyond Capitol Hill, to the White House. No matter who occupies 1600 Pennsylvania Avenue or which party organizes the proceedings on Capitol Hill, legislative actions are shaped by the

---

[1]George Edwards, *At the Margins* (New Haven, CT: Yale University Press, 1989).

[2]See Richard E. Neustadt, "Presidency and Legislation: The Growth of Central Clearance," *American Political Science Review* 48 (1954), pp. 641ff; John Hart, *The Presidential Branch,* 2nd ed. (Chatham, NJ: Chatham House, 1995).

chief executive's preferences and the authority for program and budget review held by OMB.

Ronald Reagan's performance as president demonstrates the potential for central coordination of the policy-making process. Immediately after winning the presidency in 1980, President Reagan placed a large tax cut on the legislative agenda, and he lobbied consistently for its passage.[3] The Congress had little choice but to act on this initiative, although there was much politicking and position taking on the exact nature of the cut. In the end, the president won much of what he desired even though most legislators did not agree with Reagan's "supply-side" economics assumptions. His large-scale tax cut proposal dominated the agenda, and lawmakers came under withering pressure to pass the legislation. The executive's agenda-setting power can also work to keep items from receiving serious legislative consideration. Along these lines, President Reagan simply refused to consider reauthorization of clean air legislation, which the Congress was scheduled to address in 1982. Given his opposition to this legislation, the Congress kept the 1977 provisions intact through his tenure and waited until 1989–1990 to negotiate with a more receptive Bush Administration on a revised clean air bill.[4]

The results of the 1980 election and Ronald Reagan's unwavering commitment to lower taxes combined to generate major congressional action—the deep 1981 tax cut. Conversely, the White House's steadfast opposition to revised clean air regulations and the president's willingness to veto any meaningful legislation meant that Congress could accomplish little until Reagan left office.

The president's ability to dominate the agenda is scarcely his only weapon in his attempts to control the policy processes and outcomes. Using Ronald Reagan's presidency as an example again, at least as systematic as his agenda efforts were his administration's operations, centralized in the OMB, to oversee the status of legislation and increase control over regulations issued throughout the government. With its power to review all executive-branch regulations and thus ensure their compliance with presidential priorities, the OMB sometimes thwarted the legislative intent of laws, directing executive agencies to carry out specific policies.[5]

In the post–Franklin Roosevelt era of large-scale government, presidents cannot always get their way, but their wishes, as expressed in policy agendas or control of the regulatory process, must still be taken into account.[6]

---

[3]This story is well told in former OMB director David Stockman's *The Triumph of Politics* (New York: Harper & Row, 1986).

[4]See Richard E. Cohen, *Washington at Work* (New York: Macmillan, 1992), chap. 3; Gary C. Bryner, *Blue Skies, Green Politics* (Washington: CQ Press, 1993), pp. 86–93.

[5]James P. Pfiffner, "The President and the Post-Reform Congress," in Roger H. Davidson, ed., *The Postreform Congress* (New York: St. Martin's, 1992), pp. 216–217.

[6]Paul Light, *The President's Agenda*, rev. ed. (Baltimore: Johns Hopkins Press, 1991).

Nonetheless, even as the presidency has consistently grown in size and power, Congress has remained—both constitutionally and politically—central to national policy making. Political scientist Mark Peterson points out, "both presidents and the public must learn to recognize Congress as the executive's legislative partner." As in any partnership, the actors play distinctive roles; Peterson argues that presidents "should exploit the vantage point of their lofty position to bring coherence to policy making by functioning as agenda *focusers*. . . . Ideas for the nation's agenda will have originated in Congress and elsewhere in the nation. . . . Rather than attempting to be the government and the repository of all solutions for all problems, presidents would identify the problems, challenge others to respond, and work with other participants in the process to craft possible policy solutions."[7]

Reagan's determined support of a tax cut and his consistent opposition to renewed clean air legislation illustrate two ways in which the president can focus congressional attention. On the tax cut, his strong emphasis essentially required the Congress to respond to his initial proposal. Both in terms of modifying his proposal and addressing the issue with great speed, the Congress reacted directly to Reagan's focusing efforts. On the other hand, his unwillingness to consider further clean air legislation gave the Congress the freedom to explore potential courses of action during the 1980s. Thus, when President George Bush signaled his willingness to negotiate seriously on clean air in 1989, the Congress could move with reasonable speed toward a productive legislative partnership, in that it had hashed out many disagreements during extensive deliberations over the 1981–1989 period.[8]

When the president focuses attention on a given issue, especially in the form of specific proposals, he ordinarily acts to centralize the legislative process. Party leaders and the press pay special attention to major presidential initiatives, particularly when the White House maintains continuing and well-coordinated pressure. All things being equal, legislators of the president's party would like to support his proposals. In the absence of presidential leadership, senators and Representatives enjoy more latitude, and the congressional fragmentation of constituencies, committees, and interests is more likely to dominate the policy-making process.

In the end, presidents can hope to exercise no more than partial and temporary influence over legislative actions and outcomes. Presidents such as Franklin Roosevelt, Lyndon Johnson, and Ronald Reagan won great victories, but all suffered serious setbacks. Others, such as Dwight Eisenhower, sought to exercise influence largely in private ways. Nonetheless, even the weakest post–World War II president, Republican Gerald Ford, who rose from serving as an unelected vice-president to face a hostile, activist Democratic Congress

---

[7]Mark Peterson, *Legislating Together* (Cambridge, MA: Harvard University Press, 1990), p. 295.
[8]See Cohen, op. cit.; Bryner, op. cit.

in the wake of Richard Nixon's resignation, exercised considerable power. In his 1974–1976 tenure, he set much of the legislative agenda through his budget-writing authority, and he regularly exercised his constitutional weapon of the veto, thereby affecting legislative consideration of controversial matters.

This chapter will emphasize various elements of presidential–congressional relations, ranging from constitutional roles to the centralization of policy making that derives from continuing budget deficits. In addition, the impact of divided government (when the presidency and the Congress are controlled by opposing parties) will be explored, in that this has been the most common political context in the United States since 1969. Finally, we will focus on the temporary nature of any president's capacity to provide focus and direction to the necessarily messy business of writing laws. The president can dominate parts of the process of agenda setting, but many issues emerge without his prompting. The president may win numerous legislative victories and suffer his share of defeats, but many bills pass with little presidential expression of interest. And although the OMB can monitor regulation writing, it has neither the staff nor the authority to control the entire process. In short, the modern presidency, no matter its size and reach, cannot dominate either the policy debate or the outcome of all policy initiatives. As Bill Clinton has discovered in facing an energized Republican majority on Capitol Hill, presidents must confront and negotiate with a Congress that can both originate and pass policies of its own creation, as well as being able to oversee the administration's execution of the laws.

THE PRESIDENT AS CHIEF LEGISLATOR

As a rule, no member of Congress is as important a legislator as is the chief executive, although Speaker Newt Gingrich has surely tested the absolute nature of such a proposition. Whether in setting the congressional agenda, twisting a lawmaker's arm to support a favored measure, or threatening to veto an unsatisfactory bill, the president can affect the legislative process more forcefully, and in more ways, than the most influential senator or Representative. But does this mean that he gets what he wants? Hardly. A generation of research in presidential–congressional relations has demonstrated that neither partner can overwhelm the other. Rather, as Richard Neustadt observed in 1960 and Charles Jones confirmed more than thirty years later, the separate institutions of the Congress and the presidency must both share and compete for power.[9]

The Constitution offers only modest guidance in defining presidential–congressional relations. For example, Article I gives the Congress the power to declare war, but in the post–World War II era, presidents have committed

---

[9]Richard Neustadt, *Presidential Power* (New York: Wiley, 1960); Charles O. Jones, *The Presidency in a Separated System* (Washington: Brookings, 1994).

American troops to three warlike conflicts (in Korea, Vietnam, and the Persian Gulf) without any formal declaration of war. Congress did agree to the actions through legislation and appropriations, but its attempt through the 1973 War Powers Act to wrest effective control from the executive branch of most decisions to commit troops has proved notably unsuccessful.[10] Likewise, the presidential power to veto legislation is a potent formal weapon, but one that is often most effective when it is used sparingly. Gerald Ford, for example, regularly employed the veto during his two-plus years as president, but largely as a defensive tool against the overwhelmingly Democratic 94th Congress.[11] More creative use of the veto power is available to most presidents. By making credible threats to veto unacceptable bills, presidents can enhance their capability to shape legislation, thus turning a negative power into a positive tool to influence congressional policy outcomes.

Regardless of the executive's formal, constitutional powers, much of the president's ability to affect legislation results from the policy-making context, which comprises principally the president's electoral base, his popularity in the country, and the partisan balance within the Congress. A president who is woefully unpopular (such as Truman), who is confronted with large, opposing-party majorities in both houses of Congress (such as Ford), or who is elected with a modest percentage of the vote (as with Clinton's 43 percent) will have a difficult time winning a string of major legislative victories.

Agenda Setting and the Prospects for Presidential Influence

The core of the president's legislative strength lies in his ability to influence the national policy agenda on issues in both ordinary and extraordinary ways. The most consistent and predictable impact of the presidency comes through the centralization of the annual budget and the executive's capacity to monitor and pull together disparate proposals that bubble up within dozens of separate bureaucratic units. Indeed, the governmental agenda is ordinarily full; that is, there are always many issues, initiatives, and problems for presidents and legislators to consider. As Charles Jones observes, "Since it is not possible to treat all issues at once, Members of Congress and others anxiously await the designation of priorities. These presidential choices are typically from a list that is familiar to other policy actors. Nonetheless, a designator is important, even if he is a Republican having to work with a Democratic Congress. As in any organization, there is a need for someone in authority to say: 'Let's start here.'"[12]

Aside from designating certain issues as priorities in the course of normal policy making, almost all presidents offer up some major initiatives that depart

---

[10]Pfiffner, op. cit., p. 233. More generally, see Louis Fisher, *Presidential War Power* (Lawrence: University Press of Kansas, 1995).

[11]Richard Watson, *Presidential Vetoes and Public Policy* (Lawrence: University Press of Kansas, 1993), p. 35.

[12]Jones, op. cit., p. 181.

markedly from past policies. These proposals—Nixon's welfare reforms, Carter's energy plans, Reagan's tax cuts, Clinton's health care proposals—would require large-scale changes in existing policies and would disrupt well-established policy subsystems made up of congressional committees, interest groups, and bureaucratic units.[13] The president can push only a limited number of major items onto the legislative agenda; Presidents Carter and Clinton both found it difficult to move ahead on a wide range of substantial issues, especially when some of those issues, such as the North American Free Trade Agreement for Clinton, were inherited from the preceding administration. Even so, through the annual State of the Union message and other public pronouncements, presidents can consistently orient the discourse within both the Congress and the public at large.[14]

Ordinarily, the president can focus the attention of the press and the public on a few key issues; on occasion, as with Franklin Roosevelt and Lyndon Johnson, the context permits a broad agenda of large-scale changes. But even for these energetic, forceful leaders who enjoyed the favorable circumstances of large Democratic congressional majorities, the windows of opportunity for focusing legislative attention were relatively brief.[15] Regardless of political circumstances, presidents are well advised to set the agenda on major issues early in their terms—either "move it or lose it."[16] Delay is the enemy of change, and as an institution the Congress encourages delay at every turn in a legislative process that requires a succession of majorities—in committees, in both chambers, and often on conference committee reports. Moreover, presidents begin their terms of office with election victories that provide them with substantial amounts of political capital. Rarely do they increase this store of assets; rather, the longer they wait to introduce key pieces of legislation, the lower the chance of passage.[17]

In the end, even Bill Clinton, a president elected with 43 percent of the popular vote in an era of $200-billion annual budget deficits, could move comprehensive health care reform onto the congressional agenda. But he failed to achieve his policy goal. Leading the 535 legislative horses to the trough does not mean that Clinton or any other president can make them drink.

---

[13]See Frank R. Baumgartner and Bryan D. Jones, *Agendas and Instability in American Politics* (Chicago: University of Chicago Press, 1993); Paul R. Schulman, *Large-Side Policy Making* (New York: Elsevier, 1980).

[14]See Jeffery Cohen, "Presidential Rhetoric and the Public Agenda," *American Journal of Political Science* 39 (February 1995), pp. 87–107.

[15]See James L. Sundquist, *Politics and Policy* (Washington: Brookings, 1968); Arthur Schlesinger, Jr., *The Cycles of American History* (Boston: Houghton Mifflin, 1986).

[16]Light, op. cit., p.218.

[17]Paul C. Light, "Passing Nonincremental Policy: Presidential Influence in Congress, Kennedy to Carter," *Congress and the Presidency* 9 (Winter 1981–1982), p. 78.

Legislating and the Contexts of Presidential Influence

No matter how successful a president is in focusing public, media, and congressional attention on a major initiative, he and his aides must continue to participate in the process of lawmaking. The decentralized Congress— whether in its fragmented, contentious mode of the 1970s, its committee-based, conservative mode of the 1950s and early 1960s, or its more partisan mode of the 1980s and 1990s—has imposed great limitations on the ability of the president to achieve his objectives. Indeed, even a renowned "focuser" like Ronald Reagan, who was widely admired for his single-minded emphasis on tax cuts in 1981, subsequently produced a series of budgets that the Congress felt free to ignore, labeling them "dead on arrival" on Capitol Hill.[18]

In the wake of extended scholarly debates over the nature of presidential influence on Congress, a rough consensus has emerged, which paints presidential power within the legislative process as an important force, but subject to many limitations. At a minimum, some restrictions are those of the "pure context" of a separation-of-powers system; such constitutional restraints are magnified by relatively weak political party organizations and electorally independent, well-staffed legislators who need little help from either presidents or parties to remain in office.[19]

No president can change the Senate rules that provide great advantages to those who would delay legislation through extended debate (the filibuster); likewise, informal congressional practices, such as the Senate's reliance on unanimous consent agreements (see chapter 9) to conduct much of its business, are beyond the executive's control. In addition, there are other key elements of the policy-making context that further restrain executive actions. Aside from a second-term president's ineligibility to run for reelection (thus being labeled a "lame duck"), these include the president's margin of victory in his previous election, the partisan balance of congressional seats, and the president's standing with the public.[20] Although they do not determine legislative outcomes, these elements do shape the content and scope of executive initiatives, as well as the strategies the president constructs for winning congressional majorities.

Consider, for example, the range of different circumstances faced by presidents from the 1960s to the 1990s as they worked with their first Congresses (see Table 8–1). Lyndon Johnson's prospects differed dramatically from those of George Bush, for example. With overwhelming Democratic majorities in each house and a backlog of social programs, many of which had been fully

---

[18]Allen Schick, *The Federal Budget* (Washington: Brookings, 1995), p. 58.

[19]Peterson, op. cit., pp. 102ff.

[20]Somewhat strangely, Peterson labels these elements as "malleable" context (ibid., pp. 118ff), but of the three, only the president's popularity can change between elections, and ordinarily not as a direct result of his actions.

TABLE 8-1   Electoral, Partisan, and Popularity Context for Presidents, 1960-1992

President	Year Elected, Percentage of Vote	Initial Party Balance House	Senate	Popularity after First year (%)
Kennedy	1960, 49%	262D–175R[a]	64D–36R	79%
Johnson	1964, 61%	295D–140R	68D–32R	69%
Nixon	1968, 43%	243D–192R	58D–42R	67%
Carter	1976, 50%	292D–143R	61D–39R	59%
Reagan	1980, 51%	243D–192R	46D–54R	49%
Bush	1988, 54%	260D–175R	55D–45R	75%
Clinton	1992, 43%	258D–176R[b]	57D–43R	49%

[a] Includes one extra member for Alaska and Hawaii.

[b] Representative Bernard Sanders (Vt.) elected as Independent.

Sources: *Vital Statistics on American Politics; Vital Statistics on Congress, 1993–1994; The New York Times,* September 18, 1994, pp. 54–55.

aired in the Congress, Lyndon Johnson could seek passage of dozens of significant pieces of legislation in the 89th Congress (1965–1966), literally changing the role of government in society with Medicare, civil rights bills, federal aid to education, and environmental initiatives, along with other elements that made up his Great Society vision.[21] Moreover, Johnson had enough fiscal flexibility that he could actually produce a balanced budget, albeit with a number of gimmicks, during his last year in office.

In contrast, George Bush was hemmed in by Democratic majorities in both House and Senate, a more modest electoral victory, and the prospect of annual $200-billion budget deficits for many years to come. As president, Bush could reach agreement with the Democrats on Capitol Hill on major environmental and deficit reduction legislation, but his role was as a partner to an assertive Congress. Indeed, to address rising deficits, the Democratic-controlled Congress framed a package of legislation that essentially forced Bush to accept a modest tax increase, which broke his "no new taxes" election pledge and split the Republican party.[22]

More generally, Congress's partisan balance and the president's overall political strength shape his capacity to focus legislative attention, both in setting the agenda and in helping to move legislation through the labyrinth of Capitol Hill. Even in difficult circumstances, the president remains a key centralizing force, in that (1) his agenda items require congressional attention (if not agreement) and (2) he alone commands the position from which authoritative negotiations with legislators can take place. Legislating in the decentralized context of the United

---

[21]For a recent perspective by a Johnson loyalist, see Joseph Califano, *The Triumph and Tragedy of Lyndon Johnson* (New York: Simon & Schuster, 1991).

[22]See Jones, op. cit., pp. 266–268; Barbara Sinclair, "Governing Unheroically (and Sometimes Unappetizingly): Bush and the 101st Congress," in Colin Campbell and Bert Rockman, *The Bush Presidency: First Appraisals* (Chatham, NJ: Chatham House, 1991), p. 175.

States Congress necessarily includes focusing attention and deal making, and the president ordinarily serves as both chief focuser and key deal maker.

The initial years of the Carter and Reagan presidencies illustrate the differences in focusing and deal-making skills. Carter sent a large number of proposals to Capitol Hill, 60 percent with accompanying messages that "suggested in each case that they were of the *highest priority* to the administration."[23] If everything is important, nothing is, and the president found himself lacking the political capital (to say nothing of the political skills) to make the deals essential to passing many of his true priorities, most notably comprehensive energy legislation. Conversely, the Reagan Administration's focus on its 1981 tax cut proposals represented a textbook example of direction, only to be followed by a combination of firmness and flexibility in negotiations with members of Congress that outflanked as savvy a legislative veteran as Ways and Means Committee chair Dan Rostenkowski (D–Ill.), even though Democrats retained formal control of the House.

Legislating: Presidential Tools in a Retail Politics Era

My vote cannot be bought, but it can be rented.

Representative John Breaux (D–La.), 1981

I don't have bottom lines. You can't afford them in this business. I mean, we deal with the possible. That's what we have to be guided by: What can we get? What can you do? And as long as it's better than what we have, that's the bottom line.

Senator John Breaux (D–La.), 1994

Despite the rise in congressional partisanship during the 1980s and 1990s, most major legislative initiatives require "cross-partisan" majorities.[24] Although there may not be extensive bipartisan cooperation, some legislators from the opposing party join with the bulk of the president's partisans to forge a temporary majority. Cross-party majorities have long been important; for example, Northern, moderate Republicans would sometimes join liberal Democrats in the 1950s and 1960s to provide the margin of victory for urban initiatives; in 1961, for example, a handful of Republicans gave the Kennedy Administration and Speaker Sam Rayburn their crucial victory in expanding the House Rules Committee, thus wresting control of it from the conservative coalition.

Charles Jones notes that more recent congresses, with increased fragmentation, individualism, and "greater openness in participation [have encouraged] more cross partisanship in lawmaking."[25] Presidents can no longer rely on a handful of party leaders (such as Speaker Sam Rayburn in the 1950s) or

---

[23]Peterson, op. cit., p. 256, emphasis added.

[24]See Jones, op. cit.

[25]Ibid., p. 270.

key committee chairs (such as Ways and Means chair Wilbur Mills in the 1960s) to inform them about what is legislatively possible. Rather, presidents and their agents, including executive-branch liaison staff; congressional leaders, both formal and informal; and even key interest group contacts, must build majorities from the ground up, one vote at a time. It was thus crucial to Ronald Reagan that he could negotiate with Representative John Breaux about Louisiana's oil and gas interests in 1981 as he sought to push through spending cuts. It was not essential that Breaux buy into the entire Reagan program. Rather, the president could "rent" the congressman for a few important votes in return for protecting a handful of key Louisiana interests.

Nevertheless, presidents can neither dictate the final content of legislation nor bargain fecklessly for votes to produce congressional majorities. Often they must attach their support to items already on the legislative agenda, and only when victory is within shouting distance in the Congress can they affect the outcome through bargaining with individual Representatives and senators; presidents possess their greatest advantages on close votes, when they can pressure, bargain with, and cajole fence-sitting lawmakers.

The Presidential Record

Political scientists and pundits have long attempted to measure rates of presidential success in winning congressional support for their proposals. On occasion, as with the outpouring of legislation in 1964–1966 under Lyndon Johnson, the evidence of presidential impact is overwhelming. Most of the time, however, the results are mixed and often depend on how success is measured. Until 1975, *Congressional Quarterly* generated a so-called box score of presidential success, but this measure was flawed and ultimately discontinued.[26] Subsequently, scholars have relied both on other broad measures such as overall success rates and more specific indicators such as the key votes for a given congress. In addition, many scholars have either constructed their own sets of important votes and attempts at presidential influence or relied on historical evidence that indicates those issues on which presidents sought to influence outcomes.[27]

Overall measures of success rates rarely provide much insight into presidential influence. This is illustrated by two examples of *Congressional Quarterly*'s scoring of presidential success rates: In 1981, Ronald Reagan achieved 82 percent support on issues on which he took a position; in 1994, Bill Clinton obtained an 86 percent rating.[28] No sensible analysis of these two presidents and

---

[26]For a discussion of this measure and others, see George Edwards, op. cit., pp. 16ff.

[27]See ibid.; Jones, op. cit., chap. 7; and Peterson, op. cit., especially appendix B, which offers an excellent review of quantitative research.

[28]*CQ Weekly Report*, December 31, 1994, p. 3654.

these two years would have found Clinton to have done better than Reagan. Indeed, Clinton not only lost his major initiative, health care, but found himself stymied by Senate Republicans for much of 1994 in that many major bills were never even brought to a vote.

Perhaps the greatest problem in pinning down presidential influence is the task of disentangling context from presidential impact. The recent Republican presidents that faced Democratic congressional majorities—Nixon, Ford, Reagan, and Bush—won 61.5 percent of the votes on which they took a position; Democrats from Kennedy to Clinton (1993–1994) won 81.5 percent, a margin of 20 percent over the Republicans. Were Democratic presidents more skillful? Hardly, but they did enjoy party control in Congress.

It is more useful to view congressional contexts as offering presidents varying options as they pursue their legislative agendas. Should their lists be long or should they be short, emphasizing only a few key issues? Peterson notes that "large agendas invite problems," yet "as LBJ powerfully demonstrated, extremely ambitious, diverse, and sizable programmatic agendas can be guided through the legislative labyrinth."[29] In the end, a skillful president can offer centralized guidance for a coherent set of proposals, but the congressional context of committees, individual entrepreneurs, and wavering support by some party leaders renders questionable any consistent attempts at strong executive leadership.

BUDGETARY POLITICS: CENTRALIZATION THROUGH CONSTRAINT

When Congress consents to the Executive making the budget it will have surrendered the most important part of a representative government.

Former Speaker of the House Joseph Cannon, 1919

One of the president's most significant powers in setting the national policy agenda has been the capacity to propose an annual budget. Since 1921, the Bureau of the Budget (renamed the Office of Management and Budget [OMB] in 1971) has monitored government spending and produced increasingly large compilations of proposed expenditures. The Congress, of course, retains the power of the purse—the appropriations authority—but the president and his budgetary staff provide both the overarching thrust of proposed spending (for example, by proposing new programs) and the myriad details of where federal monies will be spent.

As federal responsibilities and spending increased from the 1930s through the early 1970s, executive budget officials came to play an important role in

---

[29]Peterson, op. cit., pp. 220–221.

shaping policy initiatives, large and small, old and new.[30] The president and Congress generally agreed on the expansion of executive authority as the scope and complexity of public policy grew steadily. Budget scholar Howard Shuman concludes that "in almost every case the delegation [of congressional authority] resulted in the aggrandizement of the executive at the expense of the Congress, but *this was done willingly, even joyously, and had few narrow or partisan or siege-mentality overtones.*"[31]

By the late 1960s, however, the Congress and the president had begun to engage in budget wars, as spending levels and priorities began to be vigorously contested.[32] Party leaders and increasing numbers of back bench legislators wanted to exercise some control over spending, and Republican President Richard M. Nixon had sought to gain more control over spending levels and priorities through the use of the veto and his willingness to impound funds (refuse to spend them) that the Congress had appropriated. As a Democratically controlled Congress grew frustrated with both an aggressive Republican president and its own incapacity to control overall levels of spending, the stage was set for major reform of the budget process. And, as luck would have it, the Congress confronted a president who had been grievously wounded by the Watergate affair. Indeed, Nixon would resign from office less than two months after the 1974 Congressional Budget and Impoundment Control Act was passed.

Although largely an attack on the executive, the 1974 legislation sought to rationalize budgetary policy making (to control overall expenditures and increase capacities to set priorities) and to strengthen the budget-related capacities of the Congress. By both accident and design, the reforms have paradoxically led to members' greater participation in budgetary politics and, simultaneously, to increased centralization of the ultimate budget decisions.

By setting a supposedly firm timetable for action and by requiring the Congress to address total levels of spending early in the process, the 1974 reforms sought to allow Congress greater control over the levels and composition of federal spending. To accomplish these goals, the Congress needed more resources and some organizational changes; thus, both houses created budget committees, and the nonpartisan Congressional Budget Office (CBO) was established. CBO provides the legislative branch an independent capacity to analyze the mountains of budget-related data and to make the projections for future revenue and spending patterns that are the heart of contemporary fiscal politics. The new committees increased the number of legislators who played a major role in budgetary politics; the well-respected CBO offered leaders, committees, and even individual members the opportunity to pose alter-

---

[30]Lance T. LeLoup, *Budgetary Politics,* 3rd ed. (Brunswick, OH: Kings' Court, 1986), pp. 6ff.

[31]Shuman, op. cit., p. 213, emphasis added.

[32]Allen Schick, *Congress and Money* (Washington: The Urban Institute Press, 1980), chap. 2.

native budget scenarios to those offered by the executive branch's OMB. In a sense, budgetary politics became more open and democratic in the aftermath of the 1974 reforms. Various factions ranging from conservative Republicans to the generally liberal Congressional Black Caucus could propose their own budgetary priorities, even if they had little chance of winning congressional approval.[33]

In fact, the adoption of the budget reforms, especially when combined with the major tax cuts of 1981, conspired to "fiscalize" congressional politics during the 1980s.[34] With annual deficits escalating, budgetary restraints required that key legislators—budget committee members and party leaders, in particular—consider overall patterns of spending. Shepsle concludes, "The most significant consequence of the Budget Act has been that Congress has had little time to consider anything else. . . . The fiscalization of politics has diminished the stature of standing committees, encouraged members to become generalists rather than specialists, ceded political advantage to those in party leadership positions, and put a premium on coordination among policy areas."[35]

The centralization of budgetary politics in the Congress was mirrored by a similar trend in the executive, where the OMB, under former Representative David Stockman, came to dominate policy decisions in the Reagan Administration.[36] Facing the administration and the OMB were top party leaders in Congress, who controlled access to the floor and who could put together comprehensive fiscal packages (including initial budget resolutions, budget reconciliation agreements, and continuing and supplementary appropriations bills). Both the executive and legislative leaders developed a new model of policy making during their successful 1983 efforts to "save" the social security system.[37] In this instance, a nine-member "gang" of executive and legislative leaders (a subset of a larger bipartisan commission) reached agreement on a set of benefit reductions and rate increases; leadership representatives from both legislative parties in both chambers hammered out compromise positions that were offered on an all-or-nothing basis to their respective party members.

Throughout the 1980s, variations on this model dominated budgetary decisions, as leaders annually struggled to produce agreements acceptable

---

[33]Barbara Sinclair, *Legislators, Leaders and Lawmaking: The U.S. House of Representatives in the Postreform Era* (Baltimore: Johns Hopkins University Press, 1995), p. 143.

[34]Kenneth Shepsle uses this term in "The Changing Textbook Congress," in John E. Chubb and Paul E. Peterson, eds., *Can the Government Govern?* (Washington: Brookings, 1989), pp. 259ff.

[35]Ibid., pp. 261–262.

[36]Stockman, op. cit.; William Greider, "The Education of David Stockman," *The Atlantic Monthly*, December 1981.

[37]See Paul Light, *Artful Work* (New York: Random House, 1985); Richard E. Neustadt and Ernest R. May, *Thinking in Time* (New York: Free Press, 1986), chap. 2.

both to the administration and to congressional majorities in each house. Although the memberships of the House and Senate played little role in reaching budget deals, they could—and sometimes did—upset their leaders' applecarts by defeating the entire package. Indeed, as top legislators and presidential envoys met to negotiate, both sides had to bear in mind their constituents. Congressional leaders knew they had to convince majorities of their followers to approve their actions, whereas the president's constituents were the voters whom he would eventually face. Thus, for chief executives and congressional leaders alike, there remain real limits to the exercise of centralized power.

Among legislators, this was forcefully brought home in 1985, when junior Republican senators and conservative Democrats forced the issue of deficit reduction after top-level "budget summitry" broke down. The Congress agreed to a reduction package proposed by Senators Phil Gramm (R–Tex.), Warren Rudman (R–N.H.), and Ernest Hollings (D–S.C.), which they attached to a "must-pass" bill to raise the debt ceiling (without which the federal government would be forced to shut down).[38] To oversimplify a most complicated set of maneuvers, congressional leaders realized that the Gramm–Rudman–Hollings formula of annual, automatic cuts in the absence of real deficit reduction would obtain majority support in both houses. After some modifications, the proposal became law and thus framed subsequent budgetary politics. The centralized powers of congressional leaders had been severely limited by insurgent budget cutters.

Despite some judicial setbacks and legislative modifications, the Gramm–Rudman–Hollings principle of holding down spending through automatic cuts in the absence of legislation remained dominant for several years. Then in 1990, President Bush reluctantly agreed to provisions in the Budget Enforcement Act that contradicted his "no new taxes" pledge of the 1988 campaign. The agreement, hammered out in lengthy, secret negotiations between top administration officials and congressional leaders, also effectively killed the Gramm–Rudman–Hollings experiment in automatic deficit reduction. This ad hoc, highly centralized process required a handful of legislative leaders to represent the entire Congress; neither rank-and-file members, committee chairs, nor Appropriations Committee members were involved. The negotiators did reach a bipartisan agreement with meaningful deficit reductions, but congressional Democrats insisted that a majority of Republicans in each house support it before they would go along. With less than a month before the 1990 congressional elections, legislators found it hard to swallow even modest tax increases and spending reductions that were concentrated in the last years of the five-year plan. House Republicans opposed the package 105–71, and Democrats followed suit, 149–108. The budget summit agreement, cobbled together by top Bush

---

[38]For more extensive discussion, see Shuman, op. cit., pp. 286ff.

Administration officials and most congressional leaders (then–Republican Whip Newt Gingrich was a notable exception), failed overwhelmingly. The legislative troops had taken the only action available to them—opposition to a pact they had no hand in writing.

After more partisan jousting, in which the Bush Administration made further modest concessions on tax increases, the Budget Enforcement Act was passed, only a few days before the elections and with relatively little Republican support. In the House, for example, only 47 of 173 minority members voted for the bill. The highly centralized, highly political negotiations did produce some real deficit reduction, but also resulted in some significant political damage to President Bush. Most members of Congress had little impact on the most important piece of legislation passed during the 101st Congress. When the entire budget became the focus of a policy decision, the fragmentation of the House and the individualism of the Senate necessarily gave way to private negotiations by a handful of top legislative leaders.

POLICY, POWER, AND DIVIDED GOVERNMENT

The politics of the 1990 Budget Enforcement Act provides an apt illustration of decision making under divided government, the dominant pattern over the 1969–1993 period, when Republican presidents (save Carter, 1977–1981) faced Democratic Congressional majorities (save the Senate, 1981–1987). In 1990, a Republican president and a Democratic Congress could, however haltingly, produce a substantial policy change. At the same time, disagreements between the president and GOP legislators and between Democratic congressional leaders and many Democratic backbenchers did not generate great confidence in either the content of the legislation or the process of lawmaking. Moreover, there were few clear lines of accountability as voters sought to reward or penalize those responsible for the legislation. Unfortunately for George Bush, the president offered a clearer target in 1992 than did most senators and Representatives seeking reelection.[39] Nonetheless, Congressional Democrats found themselves in the electorate's sights in 1994.

Political scientist David Mayhew has demonstrated that divided government has not prevented the federal government from enacting major legislation on important public policy topics.[40] Divided government, particularly since the early 1980s, has required congressional negotiation with the White House, whether on budget issues, clean air, or social security reform. Negotiation encourages centralization, in that only a handful of leaders can effectively

---

[39]Congressional turnover, especially with 110 new members in the House, was high in comparison with recent elections, but few defeats could be linked directly to budget positions.

[40]David Mayhew, *Divided We Govern* (New Haven, CT: Yale University Press, 1991).

represent the legislature. More generally, Mayhew has raised systematic questions about the nature of American policy making, a process that has been increasingly viewed as being centered in the presidency.[41] Despite the growth of the so-called imperial presidency in the 1960s and early 1970s, the president remains enmeshed in a system of shared powers, even in foreign and military affairs, where chief executives retain wider latitude.[42] From time to time, certain presidents may take advantage of circumstances (such as party majorities and crises) to extend their influence, but congressional reaction is rarely long in coming, as legislative leaders seek to assert their institutional prerogatives.[43] Although Lyndon Johnson pushed the 89th Congress mercilessly to pass Democratic domestic programs and to support the growing American involvement in Vietnam, he correctly recognized that his window of opportunity for great change would probably close with the 1966 election.[44] Richard Nixon, operating without Republican majorities in either chamber, recognized the need for extraordinary administrative actions, such as impounding huge amounts of appropriated funds, placing key loyalists in departmental slots, and encouraging clandestine operations, that would by-pass normal congressional participation in many policy decisions.

In surveying presidential–congressional relations, Charles Jones concludes that "understanding the production of laws requires analysis of law-making" and that the "system is now, *and always has been,* one of 'separated institutions sharing powers' as Neustadt puts it [originally in 1960]."[45] Indeed, within the context of an extended period of split-party control of government, Jones reformulates Neustadt's observation as "separated institutions competing for shares of power."[46] The 104th Congress, with its Republican majorities, offers renewed support for such a conclusion. Speaker Newt Gingrich clearly succeeded at establishing the policy agenda and, early on, dominated the legislative process. But a bicameral system, with its separation of powers, denies the likelihood of congressional dominance, save for overwhelming majorities. With the veto, the bully pulpit, and the possibility of a successful run for a second term, President Clinton can continue to compete for a substantial share of power. Nevertheless, the Gingrich speakership has built on the continued strengthening of Democratic congressional leadership in particular and

---

[41]See, for example, Arthur M. Schlesinger, Jr., *The Imperial Presidency* (Boston: Houghton Mifflin, 1973).

[42]See Barbara Hinckley, *Less than Meets the Eye* (Chicago: University of Chicago Press, 1995).

[43]John Bader, "Congressional Party Leadership and Policy Priorities under Divided Government," paper presented at the 1994 American Political Science Association meetings, New York, NY.

[44]See Jeff Fishel, *Party and Opposition* (New York: David McKay, 1973); Sundquist, op. cit.

[45]Jones, op. cit., p. 207, emphasis added.

[46]Ibid., p. 207.

of Congress in general since 1973.[47] The 1995–1996 Republican agenda-setting successes have offered a Congress-centered alternative to issue development and legislation. More generally , Congress has reestablished itself as at least a full partner in national policy making.

---

[47]See James Sundquist, *The Decline and Rise of Congress* (Washington: Brookings, 1983), and various works by David Rohde and Barbara Sinclair on party leadership.

Nine ~

THE LEGISLATIVE PROCESS AND THE RULES OF THE GAME

If you let me write procedure and I let you write substance,
I'll screw you every time.

Representative John Dingell (D–Mich.)

F rom universities to corporations to legislative bodies, all institutions operate under parallel sets of expectations, one established by formal rules and structures, the other resulting from informal arrangements that have grown up over an extended period of time. Legislatures rely heavily on the different kinds of order that are imposed by formal procedures and implicit understandings. Watching Congress on C-SPAN, one immediately observes the elaborate courtesies that legislators ordinarily extend to one another, even when they are engaged in fierce battles over a particular bill. Courtesy is one of many important, if informal, rules of the game that most members observe, although perhaps less so in the contemporary Congress than thirty or forty years ago. In addition, procedural and time limitations that characterize the way the House does business appear largely absent in the Senate, where debate meanders forward at a snail's pace as senators speak ad infinitum to an almost empty chamber about a series of often unrelated issues.

The House and the Senate operate under separate sets of formal rules, and each chamber fosters its own legislators' so-called folkways[1]—expectations about behavior that influence actions on Capitol Hill. For example, courtesy and hard work are encouraged, and insolence and sloth are discouraged (if not eliminated). Folkways are especially important in Congress, where all members are technically equal in that they have won elections from similar constituencies and each can cast a single vote. In such an organization, power relationships are often delicate and unstated, expressed through agreed-upon norms rather than in explicit procedures.

---

[1] Donald Matthews first employed the "folkways" notion in his groundbreaking *U.S. Senators and Their World* (New York: Vintage, 1960).

Overall, formal rules play a larger role in the House than the Senate, whereas norms are more important in the Senate. This makes sense, because the larger House must rely on procedures in order to reach decisions in a timely, less-than-chaotic manner. Members of the smaller Senate depend much more on informal agreements reached among all senators.[2]

This chapter will first discuss the ways in which formal rules affect the legislative process and then consider the evolution and impact of congressional folkways. Neither chamber can function effectively without a blend of formal and informal strictures, but the mixes of procedures and norms differ greatly on the different sides of the Capitol.

RULES, PROCEDURE, AND THE LEGISLATIVE PROCESS

Although the Congress is a thoroughly rule-oriented institution, only a few of its important procedures are mandated by the Constitution; these include the requirement that each chamber maintain a journal, that half the membership constitutes a quorum, that tax bills must originate in the House of Representatives, and that the two chambers can override a presidential veto by a two-thirds vote in each body.[3] Beyond these basics and the more expansive constitutional limitations on the entire federal government, the House and Senate have been free to establish their own distinct sets of rules. The published House rules currently run to more than 700 pages, whereas the Senate makes do with about 100 pages.[4]

After being introduced by individual legislators, bills are referred to committees by the Speaker or the Senate's presiding officer, who consult when necessary with the parliamentarians of the respective chambers. As appointees of the majority party, the parliamentarians work closely with the leadership. In the Democratic House of the 1980s and 1990s, a steadily growing number of bills were referred to multiple committees (almost one in five by the 1991–1992 period).[5] In the 104th Congress, majority Republicans refashioned committee jurisdictions, which dramatically reduced the need for such referrals.[6]

No more than one bill in ten eventually becomes law, and the vast majority of bills never make it out of committee. Many proposals are introduced

---

[2] See Ross K. Baker, *House and Senate,* 2nd ed. (New York: Norton, 1995), pp. 71–73.

[3] Steven S. Smith, *The American Congress* (Boston: Houghton Mifflin, 1995), pp. 25–26.

[4] Ibid., p. 43.

[5] Gary Young and Joseph Cooper, "Multiple Referral and the Transformation of House Decision Making," in Lawrence Dodd and Bruce I. Oppenheimer, eds., *Congress Reconsidered,* 5th ed. (Washington: CQ Press, 1993), p. 214.

[6] After a committee finishes with a bill, the Speaker can send it on to a second panel; he can also split a bill and send separate provisions to different committees.

with no hope of passage or are duplicates of other bills. Senators and Representatives may simply want to claim credit for offering a bill, especially when they recognize that constituents or interest groups are keeping tabs on their actions. More generally, the legislative process is one of winnowing desirable or politically popular proposals from those that have little merit or hope of passage. At the same time, the House remains a majoritarian body whose rules encourage dispatch, assuming that consistent voting majorities can be mobilized. The individualistic Senate, however, makes it more difficult for majorities to work their will.

The House

PATHS OF LEGISLATION   All bills are not created equal, nor do they move along the same path toward final passage. Minor bills appear on the House Consent Calendar and are considered on the first and third Mondays of each month; other legislation can take the shortcut of being considered under a suspension-of-the-rules procedure, which requires a two-thirds affirmative House vote and cannot routinely exceed $100 million in expenditures.[7] Within the Democratic postreform House of the 1980s, more than a third of all legislation was essentially symbolic, commemorating events such as Black History Month and National Peach Week.[8] Although these noncontroversial bills were routinely passed, they did consume a growing amount of legislative resources, and the Republicans pledged to eliminate them in the 104th Congress.

Major legislation moves onto the floor from House committees in two ways. Budget and appropriations measures are entitled to a privileged status that allows them to be brought to the floor at almost any time; most other important legislation must go before the Rules Committee to receive a rule to govern debate and amendments. In addition, budget resolutions and large-scale, or omnibus, spending packages also obtain rules that set out constraints on deliberation and waive procedural points of order;[9] otherwise, the politics of delay could dominate and chaos might well reign on the House floor.

In his case studies of Clinton's national service legislation and changes in student loan mechanisms, Steven Waldman summarizes the two paths that the bills took in gaining legislative approval (see Figure 9–1). After being introduced at the behest of the administration, both proposals went to the House Education and Labor Committee, but national service proceeded as a stand-alone bill, whereas student aid policy was incorporated into the overall budget bill. The politics of the two pieces of legislation were not dissimilar,

---

[7] Roger Davidson and Walter Oleszek, *Congress and Its Members,* 4th ed. (Washington: CQ Press, 1994), pp.330–331.

[8] Roger Davidson, "The Emergence of the Postreform Congress," in Roger Davidson, ed., *The Postreform Congress* (New York: St. Martin's, 1992), p. 17.

[9] Allen Schick, *The Federal Budget* (Washington: Brookings, 1995), p. 79.

FIGURE 9-1
Two Paths to Passage: The Legislative Process in the Postreform Congress

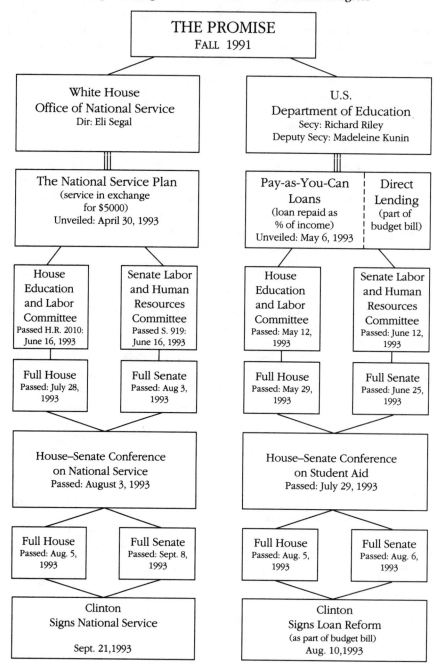

THE PROMISE
FALL 1991

White House
Office of National Service
Dir: Eli Segal

U.S.
Department of Education
Secy: Richard Riley
Deputy Secy: Madeleine Kunin

The National Service Plan
(service in exchange
for $5000)
Unveiled: April 30, 1993

Pay-as-You-Can
Loans
(loan repaid as
% of income)
Unveiled: May 6, 1993

Direct
Lending
(part of
budget bill)

House
Education
and Labor
Committee
Passed H.R. 2010:
June 16, 1993

Senate Labor
and Human
Resources
Committee
Passed S. 919:
June 16, 1993

House
Education
and Labor
Committee
Passed: May 12,
1993

Senate Labor
and Human
Resources
Committee
Passed: June 12,
1993

Full House
Passed: July 28,
1993

Full Senate
Passed: Aug 3,
1993

Full House
Passed: May 29,
1993

Full Senate
Passed: June 25,
1993

House–Senate Conference
on National Service
Passed: August 3, 1993

House–Senate Conference
on Student Aid
Passed: July 29, 1993

Full House
Passed: Aug. 5,
1993

Full Senate
Passed: Sept. 8,
1993

Full House
Passed: Aug. 5,
1993

Full Senate
Passed: Aug. 6,
1993

Clinton
Signs National Service

Sept. 21,1993

Clinton
Signs Loan Reform
(as part of budget bill)
Aug. 10,1993

Source: From THE BILL by Steve Waldman. Copyright © 1995 by Steve Waldman. Used by permission of
Viking Penguin, a division Penguin Books USA Inc.

despite their differing paths. Each proposal could have been defeated on its merits, but the student aid changes could also have been derailed within the highly partisan process that culminated in the August 5, 1993, vote to approve the budget package (see chapter 1).

ORGANIZING HOUSE FLOOR ACTION   Given the ample staff resources of individual members, the proliferation of subcommittees (at least through the 1980s), and the growth of special interest caucuses, Democratic leaders struggled to control legislation that reached the floor of the postreform House. As Barbara Sinclair summarizes,

> The 1970s reformers, most of them liberal Democrats, were motivated by concerns about both policy and participation. The changes they instituted would . . . produce better . . . policy and provide greater opportunities for the rank and file to participate in the legislative process. By the late 1970s many had concluded that unrestrained participation, particularly on the House floor, hindered rather than facilitated . . . good public policy. And in the more hostile political climate of the 1980s [that is, divided government], the policy costs of unrestrained and uncoordinated legislative activism rose further.[10]

Most troubling to party and committee leaders was a sharp increase in amendments offered on the House floor both by members of committees that processed the legislation and by other backbenchers.[11]

Although the House Democratic leaders adopted various tactics to regain control of the floor, including an increased reliance on suspension-of-the-rules votes, the most important procedural changes came in their use of the Rules Committee.[12] This committee dictates both the flow of major, nonprivileged legislation onto the House floor and the procedural limitations that will apply once it gets there. Although the Rules Committee has at times proven to be an obstacle to the Speaker's control of business on the House floor, since the mid-1970s it has become a reliable "arm of the leadership."[13] Given the Speaker's power to appoint (and remove) Rules Committee members, the panel has served the leadership by reporting out rules that structure floor action according to the leadership's wishes. Moreover, it has resolved

---

[10] Barbara Sinclair, "House Majority Leadership in an Era of Legislative Constraint," in Davidson, op. cit., p. 92.

[11] For a detailed analysis, see Steven S. Smith, *Call to Order* (Washington: Brookings, 1989).

[12] Where not otherwise noted, the following discussion is drawn from Walter Oleszek, *Congressional Procedures and the Policy Process*, 3rd ed. (Washington: CQ Press, 1989), pp. 119ff.

[13] See, in particular, Bruce I. Oppenheimer, "The Rules Committee: New Arm of Leadership in a Decentralized House," in Lawrence Dodd and Bruce I. Oppenheimer, eds., *Congress Reconsidered* (New York: Praeger, 1977), pp. 96–116.

disagreements among committees with overlapping jurisdictions as to which bill or combination of bills will be used as the legislation to be considered on the floor.

More importantly, however, the Rules Committee sets time limits for floor debate and establishes which amendments, if any, can be offered. As floor action grew more partisan during the 1980s, Democratic leaders relied heavily on restrictive rules to maintain control of the legislative process, as well as to structure substantive decision making to favor their own policy positions (see Table 9–1). Although some of these rules simply imposed a deadline for amendments, in the 103rd Congress, 45 of 104 rules "barred all amendments [closed rules] or allowed only specific proposals" that the Democratic leadership approved.[14] Only thirty-one rules were open to any amendment from the floor. Some rules even extended the Democrats' procedural control of the House deep into substantive concerns. The Rules Committee employed two specific types of rules that directly affected policy results:

1. The king-of-the-hill rule, first devised in 1982, waived various precedents and procedures in allowing a series of votes on several major policy amendments, each offered as an entire substitute an original proposal. This rule "gave ultimate victory to the last one approved, even if one of the earlier options had gotten more 'yea' votes."[15]

2. The self-executing rule "stipulates a two-for-one procedure: adoption of the rule simultaneously enacts another measure, amendment, or both."[16] Long employed for technical purposes in considering Senate legislation, in the 1980s this ploy was used to enact policies without requiring a direct vote on the issue.

TABLE 9–1   Restrictions on Amendments

Congress	Open Rules	Restrictive Rules	Percent Closed
95th (1977–78)	179	32	15
96th (1979–80)	161	53	25
97th (1981–82)	90	30	25
98th (1983–84)	105	50	32
99th (1985–86)	65	50	43
100th (1987–88)	66	57	46
101st (1989–90)	47	57	55
102nd (1991–92)	37	72	66
103rd (1993–94)	31	73	70

Source: *Congressional Quarterly*, Nov. 19, 1994, p. 3321.

---

[14] Pat Towell, "GOP's Drive for a More Open House . . . Reflects Pragmatism and Resentment," *CQ Weekly Report* (November 19, 1994), p 3321.

[15] Ibid., p. 3320.

[16] Oleszek, op. cit., p. 129.

Through these procedures the Democratic leadership could use the Rules Committee to provide members with the chance to vote in favor of policies they knew would not become law (the initial king-of-the-hill substitutes) and to approve policies without requiring a recorded vote (self-executing rules).

In sum, within a majoritarian institution, the majority-party Democratic members invested in their leadership, the Rules Committee included, the power to structure legislation so that it would have the best chance of winning, often in a highly partisan vote. The only recourse available to Republicans and dissident Democrats was to defeat the rule on the House floor; on occasion this occurred, but ordinarily the Democratic leadership could depend on holding its troops together on the procedural vote to approve the rule. With little effect and growing frustration, the Republican minority of the postreform era argued that the Democratic leadership acted unfairly in constructing rules that restricted the introduction of potentially embarrassing amendments and manipulated the voting process through king-of-the-hill and self-executing procedures.

REPUBLICANS AND RULES: THE 104TH CONGRESS   Among the Republican leadership's strongest pledges in assuming control of the House and promising votes on its Contract with America items was to allow for full, open debate on these and other important issues. At the same time, Speaker Gingrich vowed to bring the ten Contract measures to a floor vote within 100 days. Inevitably, these promises were on a collision course, and Republicans did rely on restrictive rules. They employed self-executing rules, and although they eschewed the discredited king-of-the-hill procedure, they did use a less structured "queen-of-the-hill" rule, which allowed for the substitute amendment receiving the largest number of "aye" votes to win approval. On Contract items, the Republican Rules Committee, by its own count, offered eight open rules of a total of twenty-one rules adopted.[17] Their initial record of 62 percent restrictive, or closed, rules is very similar to recent Democratic Congresses (see Table 9–1).

Generally speaking, the Republican leadership demonstrated how a well-disciplined majority can dominate the House. When push came to shove in the initial 100 days, Speaker Gingrich could call upon his party majority to support him on both procedures and substance (see chapters 7 and 10 for more extended discussions). At the same time, the 100 days' emphasis on speed demonstrated graphically that any benefits of legislative efficiency came accompanied by a set of costs in deliberation.[18] With the partisan shoe on the other

---

[17] Using their own definitions, Democrats figured a bit differently, as they counted seven of twenty-three rules as open. See Mary Jacoby, "Three-Quarters 'Open,' or Two-Thirds 'Closed'? Parties Can't Agree on How to Define Rules," *Roll Call,* April 13, 1995, p. 15.

[18] See James A. Thurber, "Guest Observer," *Roll Call,* March 2, 1995, p. 5; John Aldrich and David Rohde, "Theories of the Party in the Legislature and the Transition to Republican Rule in the House," paper presented at the American Political Science Association meetings, Chicago, August 31–September 3, 1995, p. 13.

foot, Democratic Minority Leader Richard Gephardt (D–Mo.) complained that the Republicans' intense focus on 100 days' accomplishments "caused all of them to jerk stuff through the procedure much faster than it should have been. There hasn't been enough committee consideration or floor consideration."[19] Ultimately, however, the process within a single chamber cannot dominate, and the Senate retained its status as a slower, more leisurely institution that offered both moderate Republicans and Democrats many chances to refashion the House's speedy legislative work (for further details, see chapter 10).

The Senate: Agreeing to Proceed

Although the Senate does have a set of formal rules, most often it operates under unanimous consent procedures that give tremendous leverage to a single senator in negotiating the conditions of debate. In the absence of an informal but binding agreement that structures debate, limits amendments, and imposes time limits, the Senate must labor under its formal rules, which opens the door to delay and gridlock through filibusters.

In many ways unanimous consent agreements resemble House rules, but they are hatched in very different ways. As opposed to the domination of the House process by partisan majorities in the chamber and the Rules Committee, Senate leaders must satisfy all of their interested colleagues from both parties in crafting a set of conditions for debating and amending legislation. Unanimous consent means precisely that: *All* senators must acquiesce to the provisions of the agreement. As with House rules, unanimous consent agreements can be complex, but the complexity tends to serve both the Senate as a whole and specific members rather than advancing the interests of the majority party.

CONGRESSIONAL FOLKWAYS: THE INFORMAL RULES OF THE GAME

Looking back to the 1950s, the "textbook Congress" era seems positively quaint. Speaker Sam Rayburn could sincerely counsel incoming House members to "get along, go along." And Senate Majority Leader Lyndon Johnson would give each new senator a copy of journalist William S. White's *Citadel*, with its glorification of the chamber's "Inner Club," where "Senate types" of legislators informally dominated the institution. To be sure, Rayburn's advice was sound, and White's description accurate. For all the formal leadership and committee structures, both bodies harbored well-accepted sets of norms— informal rules of the game—that governed the behavior of most, if not all, members.

---

[19] Quoted in Donna Cassatta, *CQ Weekly Report*, April 8, 1995, p. 990.

In contrast, the Congress of the 1980s and 1990s has become a thoroughly contentious place. No contemporary Speaker could—or would—deliver Rayburn's fatherly advice, and there is no club of in-group senators that can dominate their chamber. Social ties in both House and Senate have weakened substantially since the 1950s, in part because more and more congressional actions are conducted in public by legislators whose workloads have increased steadily and who have spent rising amounts of time back in their districts. More generally, members of Congress may well reflect the declining levels of trust and civility within the public at large.[20]

The decline of comity scarcely means its elimination. Viewers of C-SPAN can still observe the elaborate formalities and courtesies of the legislative process. But these niceties are often more perfunctory and forced than they were a generation or two ago. The social fabric that holds together congressional life has been frayed, sometimes to the breaking point. And although the U.S. House of Representatives has been affected to a point, the Senate, with its great reliance on individual relations, has suffered far more.

The Senate of the 1950s: The Old Club Ties

In his classic study of the Senate, published in 1960, political scientist Donald Matthews approvingly quoted a senator as observing that each member "of the Senate has as much power as he has the sense to use. For this very reason he has to be careful to use it properly or else he will incur the wrath of his colleagues."[21] Such restraint typified the unspoken limits imposed by the "folkways" that Matthews discovered in his research.

Six general norms governed Senate behavior, according to Matthews:[22]

▶ *Apprenticeship,* which included performing menial tasks (such as presiding over floor debate on routine matters), speaking only occasionally on the floor, and generally deferring to senior senators.

▶ *Legislative work,* which emphasized doing the unglamorous tasks that fill up most days, as opposed to seeking publicity for one's actions and statements.

▶ *Specialization,* which meant focusing virtually all of one's efforts on work within two or three of the ten-plus subcommittees and committees that a member was assigned to.

---

[20] Eric Uslaner, *The Decline of Comity in Congress* (Ann Arbor: University of Michigan Press, 1994), esp. chap. 5.

[21] Quoted in Donald Matthews, op. cit., p. 101. Matthews discusses at length the *men* in the Senate, and this quote makes the assumption of gender. The fact is that the Senate of the 1950s was a white male institution, as it has always been. Senator Margaret Chase Smith (R–Maine) was the single exception in the 1950s.

[22] Ibid, pp. 92ff.

▶ *Courtesy,* which "permitted competitors to cooperate"[23] by discouraging public, personal attacks, especially in floor debate, and encouraging elaborate compliments between senators of all political stripes (for example, "My good friend, the most distinguished senator from _____, has made an excellent point, but I must offer an alternative perspective. . . .").

▶ *Institutional patriotism,* which translated into a willingness to defend the Senate, with a strong emotional commitment to the body and its members.

▶ *Reciprocity,* which was perhaps the single most important folkway, in that the bargaining among senators depended on the unstated premise that no individual would take advantage of the practice of performing mutual favors on a host of issues and procedures.

In the 1950s, most senators played by these informal rules of the game most of the time. There were exceptions, ranging from Senator Joe McCarthy's (R–Wis.) abuse of the investigative process in his hearings on communist penetration of the government to first-term Senator William Proxmire's (D–Wis.) conscious decision not to observe the chamber's norms.[24] But the institution was dominated by veteran legislators, including many Southern Democrats. White's almost reverential description of the "Senate type" captures the essence of respect for the chamber's folkways. Such a loyalist, White writes,

> makes the Institution his home in an almost literal sense, and certainly in a deeply emotional sense. His head swims with its history, its lore and the accounts of past personnel and deeds and purposes. . . . His concern for the preservation is so great that he distrusts anything out of the ordinary, . . . [and] the Senate type knows precisely how to treat his colleagues. . . .
>   Indeed, it may be that [tolerance] is one of the keys to the qualities of the Senate type—tolerance toward his fellows, intolerance toward any who would in any way change the Senate, its customs or way of life.[25]

One effect of general adherence to the Senate's folkways was to reinforce the decentralized power of the committee system, where the norm of seniority, an element of reciprocity, had been elevated to a governing principle for both parties in advancing members toward committee chairmanships. Relying on seniority meant that consecutive service on a committee was virtually the sole criterion for selecting a chair. This encouraged senators to build careers on given panels

---

[23] Ibid., p. 99.

[24] Ralph K. Huitt, "The Outsider in the Senate," *American Political Science Review* (September 1961), pp. 566–575. It may be no coincidence that McCarthy and his successor Proxmire both hailed from Wisconsin. Although the state has elected its share of team players, it did send one of the ultimate nonconformists—Robert LaFollette—to the Senate, and its newest senator, Russ Feingold, based his campaign on his status as an outsider.

[25] William S. White, *Citadel* (New York: Harper & Row, 1956), pp. 85ff.

and defend the related programs and jurisdictions (the turf) against all challenges. At the core of the Senate, according to both supporters (such as White) and critics (such as Senator Joseph Clark [D–Pa.]), was an "Inner Club" of senators who, along with the party leaders, pulled together the committee-based structure that dominated legislative process. This was a tidy state of affairs for a relatively conservative, Southern-dominated Senate that had a limited policy agenda.

Even as Matthews was defining the Senate's folkways and White was celebrating them, the institution and its norms were evolving. Randall Ripley, for example, labels the 1937–1955 Senate as decentralized but sees the 1955–1961 period as one of transition to a more individualistic body, which it was from 1961 on.[26] Given their informality, norms are always susceptible to erosion, and the Senate was beginning to change, however imperceptibly, in the 1950s. Although the large, liberal Democratic "class of 1958" would increase pressure on some of the norms, such as apprenticeship, it was Lyndon Johnson, one of the pillars of the Inner Club, who initiated the slide toward individualism. In a bid to strengthen his own party leadership, as minority leader in 1953, Johnson instituted a committee assignment rule that guaranteed every Democratic senator a seat on at least one major committee. He continued this practice as majority leader (1955–1960), and Republican leaders followed suit. The "Johnson rule" thus enhanced the individual standing of all incoming senators, while simultaneously placing each in the debt of the party leadership. Although this practice did not demolish the apprenticeship norm, it did increase the expectations that every senator had something to contribute, even during their initial months of service.

Norm Change and the Individualistic Senate

In two distinct but related ways, power within the Senate changed dramatically between the late 1950s and the 1970s. First, liberal and mostly non-Southern Democrats rose to occupy key committee positions.[27] Second, the Senate became more thoroughly individualistic as various institutional norms evolved or, in the case of apprenticeship, simply disappeared.

Rohde, Ornstein, and Peabody divided Matthews' six folkways into two separate types:[28]

▶ *General benefit norms* including legislative work, courtesy, reciprocity, and institutional patriotism, which serve all members as well as the Senate as a whole

---

[26] Randall Ripley, *Power in the Senate* (New York: St. Martin's, 1969), pp. 13ff.

[27] See Ibid., David W. Rohde, Norman O. Ornstein, and Robert L. Peabody, "Political Change and the U.S. Senate, 1957–1974," in Glenn Parker, ed., *Studies of Congress* (Washington: CQ Press, 1985), pp 147–188; Barbara Sinclair, *The Transformation of the U.S. Senate* (Baltimore: Johns Hopkins University Press, 1989).

[28] Rohde, Ornstein, and Peabody, op. cit., p. 183.

> ▶ *Limited benefit norms* such as apprenticeship, which serve some senators at the expense of others.

Specialization falls into both categories. They found apprenticeship to have vanished by the early 1970s, while the remainder of the norms remained intact, though somewhat modified.

Even though most folkways were still in place, the demise of apprenticeship, along with a decline in specialization, signaled much greater individualism in the chamber. All 100 senators were expected to participate in the process, and there was little time for learning the ropes through years of committee experience.

By 1984, Rohde and his colleagues noted that "the egalitarian trend that opened up the Senate and shared power more widely among its members still holds sway."[29] Moreover, they observed a decline in the other general benefit norms, as an increasing workload and greater ideological divisions had begun to undermine some of the traditional Senate comity. In particular, they noted Senator Jesse Helms' (R–N.C.) "frequent violations of courtesy and reciprocity."[30] Somewhat perversely, they interpret the public criticisms of Helms by fellow conservative Republican senators such as Arizona's Barry Goldwater and Wyoming's Alan Simpson as indicating that "the behavior of Helms is viewed by colleagues as violations of expectations, which tells us that the norms are still intact."[31]

The juxtaposition of behavior and norms is, of course, one of the problems in assessing the importance of norms. Sooner or later, if there are lots of violations of norms by Helms and others, we are justified in asking if the norms have any effect in restraining behavior. Under the permissive majority leaderships of Senators Mike Mansfield (D–Mont., 1961–1976), Robert Byrd (D–W.Va., 1977–1980 and 1987–1988), and Howard Baker (R–Tenn., 1981–1984) some legislators felt a growing freedom to flout or take advantage of the reciprocity and courtesy norms. Indeed, near the end of his tenure, Baker "wondered aloud whether 'the principal job of the leadership is janitorial.'"[32]

Sooner or later, behavior contradicting the accepted folkways will reformulate the accepted rules of the game. For the Senate, it was sooner; by the late 1980s, Matthews' set of norms, although still generally recognizable, had been so modified that they contributed to a very different institution from that of the 1950s.

---

[29] Ibid., p. 183.

[30] Ibid., p. 183.

[31] Ibid., p. 183.

[32] Quoted in Roger Davidson, "Senate Leaders: Janitors for an Untidy Chamber," in Lawrence Dodd and Bruce I. Oppenheimer, eds., *Congress Reconsidered,* 3rd ed. (Washington: CQ Press, 1985), p. 225.

Obstructionism and the Contemporary Senate

The Senate has always provided great leeway to its members, and its processes have emphasized lengthy deliberation rather than speedy action. Indeed, "extended debate" (the filibuster) is probably the best-known single element of Senate procedure, as much as a result of Jimmy Stewart's performance in *Mr. Smith Goes to Washington* as of the speeches of LaFollette, the record-setting Senator Strom Thurmond (R–S.C.) (more than twenty-four hours straight), or a well-organized group of Southern opponents to civil rights legislation in the 1950s and early 1960s.

In fact, filibusters were rarely undertaken in the decentralized but collegial Senate of the 1950s. They have become much more common in the contemporary chamber, as both individual members and organized factions have used the tactic to bring the chamber's business to a halt over minor issues and even for matters of convenience (such as a scheduling dispute). Despite the procedural importance of filibusters, their frequent use and even more frequent threatened use demonstrate a pernicious side of the increasingly individualistic Senate. In 1982 Senator Russell Long (D–La.), whose service began in 1948, argued as a member in good standing of the Inner Club that "we've given far too much power to the impeders [of action]."[33] Congressional scholar Barbara Sinclair concludes that the Senate has created this situation *"not by changing its rules,* but by being *unwilling and unable* to prevent senators from fully exploiting the power those rules grant to each of them."[34]

Again, we get the kind of Senate that the senators give us. In the 1950s the chamber's individualism was restrained by the general agreement on the folkways that constrained the individual behavior of most senators. Occasional mavericks such as Proxmire or aggressive committee chairman Estes Kefauver (D–Tenn.) could be regarded as lively exceptions to the prevailing norms. As Senator Joseph Biden (D–Del.) observed, "We end up with 100 Proxmires here. One . . . makes a real contribution. All you need is 30 of them to guarantee the place doesn't work."[35]

Given its informality and reliance on cordial, respectful relations among its members, the Senate is fractured by declining reciprocity and courtesy. Tending to the well-being of the entire chamber does not offer many rewards. Rather, as Sinclair bleakly reports, "Asked their prescription for being an effective senator, several staffers (not attached to senators particularly known for pushing their powers to the limit) responded that *the senator who does not*

---

[33] Quoted in Sinclair, *The Transformation of the U.S. Senate,* p. 125.

[34] Ibid., p. 125, emphasis added.

[35] Uslaner, op. cit., pp. 24–25. Uslaner cites Senator Bob Packwood (R–Oreg.) as making a similar estimate of twenty-five or so senators who cannot be trusted to keep their word, thus threatening the key norm of reciprocity.

care if he is liked can be very effective. There is perhaps no better indicator of how much the Senate has changed.[36]

Some observers, such as political scientist Ross Baker, see this interpretation of the Senate as a sort of snapshot in time, taken in the early 1980s and since modified. But given the vitriolic exchanges between senators in the Supreme Court confirmation hearings for Robert Bork (1987) and Clarence Thomas (1991), among other well-publicized disputes, this interpretation seems unduly optimistic. Especially when combined with the frustrations inherent in addressing tough issues within a chamber that is so difficult to lead, it is no wonder that such noted senators as John Danforth (R–Mo.), Warren Rudman (R–N.H.), David Boren (D–Okla.), Bill Bradley (D–N.J.), and Majority Leader Mitchell decided voluntarily to leave the body after 1992.

The House Is Not a Home

Given its size and the related need for organization, informal rules of the game have never been quite as important in the House as the Senate. Nonetheless, norms remain significant in this fragmented body, and all evidence points to a substantial "decline in comity" in the House.[37] The Rayburn-era House (late 1930s–1961) resembled the clubbish Senate in many ways. Apprenticeships were long, specialization expected, and virtually all members assumed that courtesy and reciprocity would govern their relations.

The infusion of new members into the House—especially after the Democratic landslides of 1958, 1964, and 1974 and the widespread Republican victories of 1966, 1978, and 1980—caused a twenty-year reevaluation of legislative folkways.[38] Although the data are sketchy, the trend is clear: Less than half the junior members completely accept the bedrock norms of courtesy and reciprocity. In addition, almost all these legislators reject the notions of apprenticeship and institutional patriotism.

Anecdotal evidence offers solid support for these survey data. Members have scuffled in the House aisles, and others have had to be physically restrained from doing so. The level of verbal attacks has also escalated steadily since the early 1970s. Members who entered the House in the mid-1970s were more attuned to the chamber's folkways as newcomers than they were later as three-term veterans; in 1976, 63 percent of first-termers reported that "personal cordiality" was very important; four years later, only 37 percent of this group agreed.[39]

---

[36] Sinclair, *The Transformation of the U.S. Senate,* p. 204.

[37] See Uslaner, op. cit., chap. 2.

[38] The data here come from Burdett Loomis, *The New American Politician* (New York: Basic, 1988), p. 48; Herbert Asher, "The Learning of Legislative Norms," *American Political Science Review* 67 (June 1973), p. 503.

[39] Loomis, op. cit., p. 48.

In sum, the bonds forged by the informal rules of the game have weakened in the House, much as they have in the Senate. Such a breakdown, both in behavior and reported acceptance of norms, may have fewer obvious consequences in the House, but no one could confuse the 1950s House of Sam Rayburn and Republican leader Joseph Martin with the 1980s chamber of Speaker Jim Wright and Republican leader Newt Gingrich (R–Ga.).[40] There can be little hope that folkways will soon contribute much toward producing a well-integrated, coherent, productive House of Representatives.

RULES, NORMS, AND THE LEGISLATIVE ARENA

The tensions between centralizing and decentralizing elements on Capitol Hill come in many forms; congressional scholars have most often focused their attention on committee and parties as the major elements of such tensions, but the nature of the legislative process—both formal and informal—plays an important role. The postreform Congress has encouraged less comity, more individualism, and behavior that aggressively uses institutional rules for partisan or personal advantage. In the House this has meant the assertion of majority control of the process, whereas the Senate has encouraged almost unfettered individualism. These developments have affected the possibilities for integration and coherence within the Congress in very different ways, with the majoritarian House often facing a Senate that is hard-pressed to act quickly and effectively.

Most obvious, and most important, has been the deterioration of folkways that structured legislative life in the Congress of the 1950s. This is not to say that norms such as apprenticeship made good use of legislators and their skills. Quite the contrary. Junior members' grudging willingness to place their careers on hold for several years as they learned the ropes merely reflected the imposing ability of committee chairs and top party leaders to enforce norms and dominate the legislative process.

Beginning in the late 1950s, an informal grouping of legislators—the Democratic Study Group—brought younger members together to provide a voice for greater distribution of power in the House and an end to apprenticeship. Equally important as a motivating factor for this change was the growing legislative workload that came with the enactment and oversight of the Great Society and Nixon Administration domestic programs. Making and overseeing this raft of new policy virtually required that the Congress make use of all its members, not just a handful of top committee and party leaders.

As a representative institution, Congress reflects the society at large, albeit with some significant distortions. The decline of the key congressional norms

---

[40] See John Barry, *The Ambition and the Power* (New York: Viking, 1989).

of reciprocity, courtesy, and institutional loyalty that together produce comity derives from a parallel erosion of comity in the population as a whole. The very representativeness of Congress is crucial; Uslaner argues that "Congress is first and foremost an institution of interest representation. If the cause of the decline of comity in Congress is a waning of values in the larger society, then neither structural reform nor exhortation can restore the folkways of the 1950s and 1960s."[41]

Well-accepted folkways—reciprocity in particular—could sometimes overcome the representation of narrow interests, especially when compromises could be hammered out behind closed doors. Ironically, reforms that opened up the Congress to public scrutiny (such as more recorded votes, televised sessions, and open committee meetings) provided interests with greatly increased amounts of information as to how they were being treated within the legislative process. Moreover, junior legislators, freed from many of the constraints imposed by the folkways of the Rayburn era, could become much more active as independent operators on Capitol Hill. The "new apprenticeship" of the 1970s and 1980s encouraged members to take on key policy roles in caucuses, party task forces, and subcommittees very early in their careers.[42] Yet John Hibbing demonstrates that of all the components of a legislative career, the only element that changes dramatically over time is significant involvement in the legislative process.[43] It may well take substantial experience to become a major force in lawmaking, regardless of the norms regarding activity. By the mid-1980s, for example, members of the highly active "class of 1974" began after a decade to finally move into the formal positions in parties and committees that would allow them consistent impact on outcomes. [44]

Long careers based on the skillful use of incumbency and its resources may insulate members of Congress from their parties and the president, but many of these same lawmakers do eventually fill formal positions that grant them increased legislative opportunities. To take advantage of these possibilities for influence, however, legislators must move beyond merely representing interests to develop broad, majority-building proposals and strategies. Overall, with its majoritarian rules and structure, as expressed by centralized party leadership control of the Rules Committee, for example, the House has proved capable of harnessing the energy of its junior members to build consistent partisan majorities. On a Capitol Hill that discourages comity and rewards the representation of a series of specific interests, however, generat-

---

[41] Uslaner, op. cit., p. 168.

[42] Christopher J. Deering, "The New Apprenticeship: Strategies of Effectiveness for New Members of the House," paper presented at the 1984 American Political Science Association meetings.

[43] John Hibbing, *Congressional Careers* (Chapel Hill: University of North Carolina Press, 1991), chap. 5.

[44] Loomis, op. cit., chap. 5.

ing the succession of majorities needed to pass important legislation remains a difficult feat, especially given the well-entrenched individualism that is nurtured by the permissive rules and the evolving norms of the Senate.[45]

---

[45] See Fred R. Harris, *Deadlock or Decision* (New York: Oxford University Press, 1993), chap. 4. Harris argues that the nationalization of Senate politics has gone hand in hand with its growing individualism.

Ten ✑

THE CONTEMPORARY CONGRESS: CASES AND CONCLUSIONS

W hat a difference a day makes—in this case, November 8, 1994. Ironically, the unified Democratic control of Congress and the presidency had ended in policy defeat on health care followed by electoral defeat in the House and Senate. Unified Republican opposition to the Clinton health reform package turned to unified Republican support in the House for major changes as expressed in the Contract with America and the acceptance of plans in both houses for balancing the budget in seven years. President Clinton could only assert his relevance in the process by reminding congressional Republicans of his veto power.

Despite a House leadership that grew stronger through the 1970s and 1980s, congressional Democrats, even with fellow partisan Bill Clinton in the White House, found it difficult to pass major pieces of legislation. And on some key policies, most notably the implementation of international trade agreements, the president relied heavily on the support of Republicans in the 103rd Congress (1993–1994). Much of the Democrats' frustration, especially on health care reform, grew from the fragmentation and individualism that often dominate congressional politics, but the potential for strong, centralizing leadership remained. Clinton did push through a tough budget package in 1993, albeit with narrow, reluctant Democratic majorities in both chambers. Even more telling was the Republican unity in opposing many Clinton initiatives as the 1994 midterm elections grew near. Senate Republicans accurately anticipated winning control of their body, and Minority Leader Newt Gingrich proved both seer and architect in building the first GOP House majority in forty years.

Subsequently, members of the Republican Conference rewarded Speaker Gingrich by according great powers to him and his fellow leaders and by supporting his positions, especially on the Contract with America issues, with solid majorities in a series of 300 roll-call votes over the first three months of the 104th Congress. The Republican Senate of 1995, however, looked a lot like the Democratic Senate of 1994; Republicans had overcome the decentralization of the House, but the other body proved more intractable. The fragmentation engineered into our legislature and the entire national government by the Framers continued to structure both the style and substance of policy making.

HEALTH CARE REFORM: A TOO-FRAGILE CONGRESSIONAL FOUNDATION

*There are an enormous number of subplots which
are enormously difficult. When you take on the most
complicated subject ever, expect smooth sailing*—not.

Senator Jay Rockefeller, D–W.Va.

In November 1992 Bill Clinton won the presidency, and Democrats continued to control both chambers of Congress. On a variety of issues, from maternity leave to welfare reform to a voluntary service corps,[1] the Clinton Administration expected a cooperative relationship with Capitol Hill Democrats, with their comfortable, if not overwhelming, majorities of 256–178 in the House and 55–45 in the Senate. Nowhere was this cooperation more eagerly anticipated or more absolutely essential than on Clinton's call for large-scale reform of the health care system.

After months of consultation with a large number of experts, legislative participants, and interest group representatives, President Clinton offered up a comprehensive plan for health care reform, which he announced in a televised prime-time address to a joint session of Congress. The initial response provided a textbook illustration of how the president can set the national agenda: Drawing on tremendous resources within the executive branch and using his capacity to capture public attention through the media, Clinton sought to shape public attitudes and support with his speech and its underlying set of extensive proposals for policy change. In the short run, he succeeded. The morning after his September 23, 1993, speech, "Stanley Greenberg, the president's pollster, crowed that the overnight surveys were winning two-thirds approval. Commentators were saying that no matter how the battle over details might work out, the president had established the right principles."[2]

One year later, the Clinton proposal was dead, buried quietly in the midst of the 1994 midyear election campaigns. Although polling continued to show support for the idea of health care reform, no single plan, whether Clinton's or any of those offered by various legislators, could wend its way through the congressional obstacle course. In the end, reform advocate Paul Starr observed, the opposition to change became increasingly partisan and "Republicans enjoyed a double triumph, killing reform and then watching jurors find the

---

[1] For a brief summary of Clinton's first-term accomplishments, see "Clinton's Good Deeds," *The American Prospect,* Winter 1995, pp. 34–35.

[2] Paul Starr, "What Happened to Health Care Reform?" *The American Prospect,* Winter 1995, p. 20.

president guilty."[3] Moreover, there was no question as to where the corpse was: Body parts were strewn all over Capitol Hill as legislators and lobbyists tore apart the Clinton proposal—along with all the others—limb from limb.

Although congressional fragmentation cannot be blamed for killing health care reform, neither the president nor the Democratic leadership could build the string of consecutive majorities required to pass a major bill. The reasons for this failure illustrate many of the centrifugal forces that often have hindered lawmaking in the postreform Congress.

Health Care in Context: Elections and Interests

In its early months, the election results of 1992 defined much of the context of the 103rd Congress. Their victories in both presidential and congressional election gave Democrats control of both branches for the first time since the Carter Administration (1977–1981). At the same time, President Clinton's 43 percent of the vote, the 19 percent performance of independent Ross Perot, and the huge, 110-member turnover in the House signaled real distrust of Washington politics. Moreover, the forty-five Republicans in the Senate stood ready to filibuster on key items; even if the Democrats stood together, they could not alone produce the sixty votes needed to limit debate, and by the time that President Clinton introduced his health care package in September 1993, he knew that the Democratic leadership could barely muster a majority on a "must-have" presidential priority—the 1995 budget (see chapter 1).

The support of outside interests was no more comforting for the president and congressional Democrats than were the implications of the 1992 elections. Although Clinton came from the business-friendly Democratic Leadership Committee wing of his party, obtained substantial support from well-heeled interests, and had historically compromised to reach moderate policy outcomes, his electoral weakness and early tactical missteps (gays in the military and some executive branch appointments, for example) rendered him suspect among both his friends and potential adversaries. A string of modest legislative victories did little to enhance his status, as his support within the public at large hovered around 50 percent.[4]

---

[3]Ibid., p. 21. This account of health care politics relies on several major sources, including the Starr piece. In addition, the following sections reflect James Fallows, "A Triumph of Misinformation," *The Atlantic,* January 1995, pp. 26–37; John Judis, "Abandoned Surgery," *The American Prospect,* Spring 1995, pp. 65–74; James Pfiffner, "President Clinton and the 103rd Congress: Winning Battles and Losing Wars," Institute of Public Policy paper, George Mason University, 1995; and the continuing reporting by *Congressional Quarterly* reporter Alissa Rubin, whose published work and conversations offered the hope of clarity in the murky waters of health care issues.

[4]For example, Bill Clinton won approval ratings of 41 percent, 50 percent, and 56 percent, respectively, in June, September, and December 1993 surveys conducted by Peter Hart and Robert Teeter for NBC News and *The Wall Street Journal.*

On health care, the president and his Democratic allies did benefit from some important backing. Clinton had made health care reform one of the central issues in the 1992 campaign; coupled with the public's continuing judgment of the health care system as needing repair, the president could legitimately claim a mandate to seek significant reforms. At least as important, most major interests supported some kind of reform. Indeed, as the president made his September 1993 speech, consumers and members of the medical community alike saw the need for change. It was the job of the president and the Congress, of course, to construct a set of proposals that both the public and most interests could agree on, however grudgingly.

President Clinton as Chief Legislator

In his analysis of presidential agenda setting, Paul Light argues that newly elected chief executives should take advantage of their generally high standing in the polls to move legislation early in their administrations, even though that is precisely when they are least knowledgeable as to how to achieve such goals.[5] Rarely has a president faced this "move-it-or-lose-it" dilemma more graphically than did Bill Clinton in 1993. Without question, the president recognized his problem and promised to produce a health care proposal within 100 days of taking office, but internal White House wrangling between his economic team and his health care advisors slowed the formulation of a package, as did the need to address specific budget votes that the administration needed to win. The president's September speech, followed immediately by Hillary Clinton's impressive congressional testimony, did not constitute the introduction of legislation; "the actual text of the bill . . . did not make it to Capitol Hill until 27 October. . . . At the same time the Administration was also fighting the battle over the North American Free Trade Agreement."[6]

The Clinton White House knowingly traded some delays for extensive consultation with a wide range of interests and substantial internal fine-tuning within the administration prior to the plan's presentation. This was not an irrational strategy, but it hurt the president's legislative prospects in two ways. First, it kept health care out of the legislative process until early 1994; thus, "congressional negotiations did not get under way until the midterm elections were within spitting distance."[7] Whatever negotiations occurred, we shall see, became enmeshed in short-term electoral politics. Second, and a very tough call, was the extent to which the Washington press corps was shut out of the administration's considerations. In retrospect, Hillary Clinton admitted that despite the substantial preliminary consultation, "we should [have been] more available to

---

[5]Paul Light, *The President's Agenda* (Baltimore: Johns Hopkins University Press, 1982), pp. 36ff.

[6]Pfiffner, op. cit., p. 10.

[7]Starr, op. cit., p. 22.

chairman.[14] Although the Ways and Means Committee did pass a version of health care reform in June, the package never reached a floor vote. The committee's work under Gibbons did not have the status that it would have had under the control of a politically strong Rostenkowski. As the House looked toward the Senate, no Representative could hold much optimism for passage of major change.

SENATOR MOYNIHAN AND THE POLITICS OF INDIVIDUALISM   As chair of the Senate Finance Committee, Daniel Patrick Moynihan stood as a key figure in constructing any health care reform package that would win Senate approval. Yet Moynihan, with a quick tongue, an acerbic wit, and little reputation as a team player, operated more as an individualistic backbencher than an important committee leader. He reacted to the Clinton plan by labeling its proposed budgetary impact as a "fantasy"; later he admitted that "no one has been more difficult [for the president] at times on health issues than I have. . . . I sometimes wish I hadn't."[15] Finance committee members made some end runs around their chairman in addressing health issues, but Moynihan remained central to any plan that would move through the panel.

In the end, Moynihan had neither the will nor the skill to construct a committee bill; as the 103rd Congress moved into its last few months, the three Senate bills still under consideration were (1) a set of modest changes offered by Minority Leader Robert Dole (R–Kans.), a former Finance Committee chair; (2) Majority Leader George Mitchell's (D–Maine) modified Clinton bill; and (3) a bipartisan effort from moderate Republican John Chaffee (R.I.) and conservative Democrat John Breaux (La.), both members of the Finance Committee. Such a compromise measure, often a staple of Senate policy making, could not overcome the philosophical and partisan obstacles to major change that had solidified by mid-1994.

The Advantages of Opposition: Coalitions of Minorities

From the election campaign of 1992 through the ultimate collapse of legislation efforts in late 1994, large majorities of the American people continued to favor the idea of health care reform. But the legislative process is about turning ideas into policy; no specific proposal succeeded in attracting the string of successive majorities that a bill must attract in order to become a law. Opposition came to the fore both from outside the Congress and from within it. Health care reform brought home the message once again that Congress remains a representative and, ordinarily, responsive institution. One Clinton plan advocate concluded,

---

[14]House Democratic rules require a indicted committee chair to relinquish the position until the charges are resolved. Representative Rostenkowski, who had won a difficult primary challenge in April, subsequently lost his bid for reelection in the November general election.

[15]Quoted in Cohen, op. cit., p. 645.

Despite the comprehensive benefit package and the extras such as pre-scription drug coverage for the elderly, we did not receive passionate support from the groups we were counting on. *We did succeed, how-ever, in mobilizing the opposition.* The scale of the program and its regulatory features also caused sympathetic groups in the business com-munity and opinion leaders in the media to think twice about support for reform.[16]

The loss of support for large-scale reform by major business interests such as the Chamber of Commerce, the Business Roundtable, and the National Association of Manufacturers was damaging. Members of Congress received torrents of communication from small-business groups, who succeeded in mobilizing local interests.[17] Indeed, the National Federation of Independent Business (NFIB), representing 600,000 small businesses, proved crucial in convincing many legislators that support for employer mandates would be politically costly. For example, Representative Slattery "ran into an NFIB 'emergency alert' sent to its 8,000 small business owner members in Kansas."[18]

Not only did coalitions of interests come together to oppose specific bills but the legislative process itself worked to the opponents' advantage. For example, Senate Democrats explored the possibility of incorporating health care reform into the budget reconciliation process, which was exempt from filibusters. A bill would thus need to attract only fifty votes rather than the sixty it would require to invoke cloture and end debate. Senator Robert Byrd (D–W.Va.) foreclosed this possibility; thus, the likelihood of a Senate filibuster, threatened early in the process by Senator Phil Gramm, meant that sixty votes would surely be required. No plan came near to enjoying that level of sup-port. Indeed, by mid-1994, with midterm elections in sight, Republican oppo-sition solidified. After all, the chances for a GOP takeover of the Senate were good, and most analysts predicted substantial gains for the minority in the House. By September, after a year of often hyperbolic debate, the public had lost faith in the Clinton plan even as general support for reform remained high. Republicans could rest assured that they would not suffer if they killed health care reform. To the contrary, as the elections of 1994 demonstrated, they had much to gain.

---

[16]Starr, op. cit., p. 25, emphasis added.

[17]In many instances the small-business lobby, led by the National Federation of Independent Business (NFIB), became a real threat to the U.S. Chamber of Commerce, which represents a wide array of businesses. The Chamber found itself losing membership to the NFIB; this fact helped move the Chamber to reevaluate its health care position.

[18]Dana Priest and Michael Weisskopf, "Death from a Thousand Cuts," *Washington Post National Weekly Edition*, December 17–23, 1994, p. 9.

The Illusion of Party Government

Members of the Congress in the modern era, even members of the President's party, tend to see themselves as soloists. Like prima donnas everywhere, they demand pampering ... [even from] the President personally.

New York Times reporter R. A. Apple

Bill Clinton's election offered hope to those who viewed divided government as promoting gridlock in Washington. No longer, so the argument went, would the president and the Congress each seek partisan advantage in addressing major issues. By some measures, the party government model did affect a good deal of decision making in the 1993–1994 period, in that President Clinton prevailed on more than 80 percent of the votes on which he had taken a position. But on several major issues, most notably health care, the president failed to build either partisan or cross-party majorities that would support his proposals for large-scale change.

Even in an era of enhanced powers for party leaders in Congress, building party-based coalitions on major issues remains a difficult task for both the president and his legislative allies. The basic building blocks of the legislative process—the major committees—could not report out meaningful legislation; nor could the party leadership find agreement within its caucus; nor could the president command adequate attention to protect the core of his own proposal. By responding to scores of specific constituencies and interests, the Congress functioned as a highly representative body in killing health care reform. The House could not even begin to build the series of majorities needed to adopt a bill, and in the individualistic Senate the greatest cohesion came among a growing number of Republicans who opposed any significant changes. Despite the Democratic victories of 1992, the president and the Democratic party leadership could not find adequate public support for any one proposal in 1994 to move health care reform through a fragmented, individualistic, and representative Congress.

THE CONTRACT AND BEYOND: CONGRESSIONAL PARTY GOVERNMENT?

In March 1995, fifty days after Republicans assumed control of the Congress, veteran Capitol Hill reporter Richard Cohen observed that things had changed dramatically, especially in the House:

> Self-styled experts, from lobbyists to think-tank types, are best advised to toss out their old scripts and to start from scratch. The notion of a House that's balkanized into legislative fiefdoms and informal caucuses—realities that, among others, helped to sink President Clinton's health care proposals last year—has become antiquated. Instead, the House is driven by

a Speaker who wields extraordinary power and by rank-and-file Members who are intent on proving to a skeptical public that they can change how Washington works.[19]

That the House passed most of the provisions in the Contract with America (see summary in Figure 10–1) in fewer than 100 days was remarkable. That it did so less than half a year after failing to vote on health care reform was truly amazing. As with the defeat of Clinton's proposal, the basis of the Republicans' Contract success can be found in the core building blocks of the contemporary Congress.

The Changed Context of Congressional Politics

Not only did the 1994 off-year election change the partisan composition of the Congress, at least temporarily it altered the context of congressional decision making. For the first time since Ronald Reagan's election and the Republican cap-

FIGURE 10–1
The Contract with America: House Action

> *Preface: Rules reforms and congressional compliance with all federal laws* (passed, January 4–5, January 17, 1995, respectively)
>
> 1. *Balanced budget constitutional amendment and line-item veto power to the President* (passed January 26, February 6, 1995, respectively)
> 2. Package of *crime bills* (passed by February 10)
> 3. *Family bills* (various) (passed by April 5)
> 4. *Welfare reform* (passed March 24)
> 5. *Middle-class tax cut* (passed April 5)
> 6. *National security reforms,* including reinstatement of missile defense system, prohibition of U.S. troops serving in UN missions under foreign command (passed February 16)
> 7. *Social security:* increased tax on benefits rescinded. (passed April 5)
> 8. *Capital gains tax decreased and unfunded mandates prohibited* (passed in parts by April 4)
> 9. *Civil law and product liability reform* (passed by March 10)
> 10. *Term limits* constitutional amendment (defeated March 29, despite winning 227 votes, 61 short of two-thirds majority)

---

[19]Richard E. Cohen, "The Transformers," *National Journal,* March 4, 1995, pp. 528–529.

ture of the Senate in 1980, electoral forces served to centralize power on Capitol Hill rather than to reinforce the centrifugal pulls of 435 House and 50 Senate constituencies. Signed in September by all but three incoming Republicans, the Contract had little impact on electoral outcomes, but it proved a most effective device for new Speaker Newt Gingrich in tying the electoral triumph to a tangible legislative agenda. "It is fair to say," Gingrich admitted, "that we cleverly picked popular things to do."[20] Nonetheless, moving this agenda through to a series of congressional votes "demonstrat[ed] that campaigns and elections really matter."[21]

Indeed, the 1994 elections mattered in terms of partisan politics and democratic accountability, and the nationalized campaign worked to centralize the power of Speaker Gingrich and the House Republicans. First, Gingrich's ability to funnel funds to challengers and open-seat candidates provided a solid base of backing within the new Republican class of seventy-three conservatives. Second, the returning Republican incumbents almost unanimously gave him credit for building the first House Republican majority in forty years.

In addition, the 1994 elections changed the nature of relations between many interest groups and the Congress. Interests did not suddenly drop their own narrow goals and become altruistic. Especially among the conservative movement and within the business community, many groups were mobilized in support of many Contract items. With the Christian Coalition spending more than $1 million on behalf of Contract items and with many business groups consulting extensively on legislative particulars, House Republican leaders could orchestrate a good deal of outside lobbying to support both the substance and rapid passage of the Contract's bills.

Committees as Agents of the Republican Leadership

[Speaker Gingrich] had committee chairmen ready to fulfill the revolution.

Republican pollster and adviser Frank Luntz

Nowhere were the differences between the Democratic 103rd Congress and the Republican 104th Congress more striking than in the relationships between party leaders and committee chairs. Speaker Gingrich did not have to face entrenched, independently powerful chairmen like John Dingell; rather, grateful Republicans gave him the authority to choose committee leaders, subject to Conference approval. In the end, the Republican chairs were veteran loyalists who almost uniformly worked hand in glove with the party leadership to hurry the Contract items through the legislative process. For example, in January, Judiciary Committee chair Henry Hyde (R–Ill.) cut off debate on a balanced budget plan while Democrats still had amendments to offer, and the

---

[20]Quoted in John F. Stacks, "100 Days of Attitude," *Time,* April 10, 1995, p. 34.

[21]David S. Broder, "Thanks for the 'Contract,'" *Washington Post National Weekly Edition,* April 17–23, 1995, p. 4.

House Government Reform Committee approved unfunded mandates legislation without holding any committee hearings.[22]

In fact, despite heavy workloads, committees largely carried the Republican leadership's water during the 100-day push to enact the Contract. When disagreements surfaced, there was little question of who held the reins of power. After the Government Reform Committee came to a bipartisan agreement on protecting children from intrusive federal surveys, "the leadership jettisoned the compromise" and substituted the original Contract language.[23] Overall, party leaders tended to dominate in their relationships with committee chairs during the consideration of Contract-based legislation in early 1995; the party's self-imposed deadlines denied committees the opportunity to deliberate thoroughly or rally particular interests to support a panel's position. The time constraints of passing the Contract advantaged the party leaders and reduced most committees to supporting roles in the first few months of the 104th Congress.

The House Leadership Ascendant

> *Newt has the contract; I have the schedule.*
>
> House Majority Leader Richard Armey (R–Tex.)

Beyond the extensive powers the Republican Conference granted Newt Gingrich as Speaker (see chapter 7), the Contract with America enhanced the strength of the entire party leadership. The Contract and its 100-day deadline for bringing items to a vote proved an ideal vehicle for channeling the "pent-up demand" of a long-frustrated Republican House minority.[24] At the same time, House Republicans harbored only modest ideological diversity, at least compared with their Democratic counterparts, and Gingrich maintained good relations with his party's moderates in the transition to majority status.

Likewise, Gingrich acknowledged the importance of the seventy-three Republican freshmen, while sometimes reeling in their most aggressive instincts. In considering the balanced budget constitutional amendment, for instance, many freshmen wanted to incorporate language that would require three-fifths of each house to approve any income tax increase; the Speaker argued that adopting this provision would endanger passage of the amendment, and he promised the first-termers a separate vote on the issue.

Even with a unified party, Republican leaders discovered that to remain on schedule they needed to exploit the distinct procedural advantages enjoyed by the House majority. This posed a significant problem for the Republicans, both

---

[22]Janet Hook, "GOP's Race to Move 'Contract' Hits a Few Bumps in Road," *CQ Weekly Report,* January 14, 1995, p. 136.

[23]Donna Cassatta, "Republicans Bask in Success of Rousing Performance," *CQ Weekly Report,* April 8, 1995, p. 988.

[24]Former Representative Bill Frenzel (R–Minn.), quoted in Cassatta, op. cit., p. 986.

politically and philosophically. Among their most bitter complaints against the Democratic leadership were legitimate claims that the Rules Committee systematically denied them the opportunity to offer meaningful amendments. Republican leaders promised that they would not resort to such procedural games to maintain control of floor action. Nevertheless, as time pressures mounted, Speaker Gingrich and Majority Leader Armey sought rules that protected Contract items from attack on the House floor. Representative Christopher Shays (R–Conn.) pointed out that "it just got more and more restrictive as we went along [through the 100 days]. We began to do what we had criticized Democrats for."[25]

In the end, the Republicans' ninety-three-day forced march in passing most of the Contract demonstrated their leadership's clear understanding that the House is a majoritarian body. With only occasional modest lapses, GOP legislators provided consistent backing for a Speaker who acted more like a prime minister than a legislative leader. At least temporarily, the fragmenting elements of committees, caucuses, individual policy entrepreneurs, self-interested incumbents, and particularistic interest groups proved weaker than a legislative party buoyed by long-awaited electoral success and a willingness to invest great power in its leaders.

However, given a bicameral legislature and a divided government, the Contract votes did not reflect an authoritative set of decisions, in that Senate modifications, conference committee negotiations, and presidential vetoes stood between the House Republicans and their agenda of policy change.

In addition, for all the significance of many Contract items, the Republican majorities faced the difficult tasks of actually constructing a balanced budget and making the specific spending cuts to implement the budget plan. Even with centralized House leadership and a set of dedicated freshmen budget cutters, party discipline was scarcely guaranteed. And more problematic by far was the Senate, where legislators simultaneously promised to balance the budget in seven years and fought tooth and nail to save federal programs in their own districts.

Although some senators such as Phil Gramm (R–Tex.) and Alphonse D'Amato (R–N.Y.) have historically called for balanced budgets while funneling every spare federal dollar to their respective states, most of their colleagues have at least sought shared sacrifice. When prospective cuts become real, however, and valuable services may be lost, even the most selfless legislator feels great tension between the pull of national policy requirements and purely local needs. Veteran House member Olympia Snowe (R–Maine) won election to the Senate in the 1994 Republican sweep. She has consistently supported a balanced budget amendment as well as an overall plan that would produce a balanced budget by 2002. "The people of Maine," she stated in

---

[25]Quoted in Jennifer Babson, "Armey Stood Guard over Contract," *CQ Weekly Report,* April 8, 1995, p. 987. For further elaboration of the Republican use of restrictive rules, see chap. 9.

January, "have sent clear and unequivocal signals that we must have the courage and will to balance the Federal budget."[26] At the same time, she has continued to advocate the particular interests of her Maine constituents, fighting to retain federal facilities that range from a Jobs Corps center to a naval shipyard.

Thus, even as she seeks to fulfill a national policy goal and support her party leaders, Senator Snowe remains a fierce advocate for her state and its citizens. The individualistic Senate gives her lots of room to make her case and move to obstruct action if she so desires. What emerges from the Senate reflects Senator Snowe's ultimate choices in resolving the national–local tensions of representation, along with the choices of her ninety-nine colleagues. Without the ability to end debate and force action, nothing comes easily in the U.S. Senate.

THE CONTEMPORARY CONGRESS: ACTION AND DELAY

More than a century ago another Maine legislator, Speaker Thomas Brackett Reed, stood before the House of Representatives and made the revolutionary decision to count as present those members of the Democratic minority who were physically present in the chamber but refused to respond to a quorum call (see chapter 2). This parliamentary decision helped to usher in a period of great centralization in the House and allowed Republicans to dominate the legislative process during the Reed–Cannon era. Eventually, the leadership became overbearing, the members revolted, and the centrifugal forces that had been suppressed became dominant as predictable, seniority-based advancement on committees came to structure congressional life at least until the 1970s. Then, a succession of increasingly strong Democratic Speakers— especially Tip O'Neill and Jim Wright—set the stage for Newt Gingrich's remarkable centralization of authority in the 104th Congress.[27]

As with the Congress circa 1900, the contemporary Congress, for all its centralization of power in the House, retains much of its fragmentation. The extreme individualism of the Senate remains the most notable example of the staying power of centrifugal forces on Capitol Hill. Beyond the Senate, however, the unity of House Republican continues to be tested by divisions on social issues, tax cuts, budget priorities, term limits, and the appropriate role of the federal government.

For example, in 1995 the House leadership strongly backed the efforts of Agriculture Committee chair Pat Roberts (D–Kans.) to revamp the extensive system of farm subsidies. Despite making some concessions to legislators with

---

[26]Quoted in Jane Fritsch, "In Budget Battle, a Different Balancing Act," *The New York Times,* May 20, 1995, p. 8.

[27]Among various analyses of Gingrich's leadership, see Fred Barnes' emphasis on the Speaker's executive skills in "The Executive," *The New Republic,* May 22, 1995.

substantial sugar and peanut interests in their districts, Roberts could not command a majority of his committee to support his so-called Freedom to Farm proposal.[28] In the end, four Republicans who represented districts with substantial cotton interests voted against their chairman and the House leadership, even in the face of potential sanctions from Speaker Gingrich. Hard on the heels of this defeat, the leadership lost two budget votes, results that demonstrated the continuing difficulties of holding the Republican coalition together.[29]

More generally, the very nature of representation demands that tensions among individual legislators eat away at strong, centralized party (or presidential) leadership. In the end, presidents and legislative leaders can do little to affect the fates of the lawmakers they seek to lead. On occasion, as in 1995 (or 1964–1996), members provide the votes and cede the authority that makes for strong leadership. But party leaders and presidents rarely capture the Congress for long, as legislators return to Maine, Kansas, or California to renew their personal contracts with the electorate. The very nature of representation—in Hanna Pitkin's words, "acting in the interest of the represented, in a manner responsive to them"[30]—means that the tensions between action and delay, between centralization and decentralization, will continue to define the nature of the contemporary Congress.

---

[28]David Hosansky, "Cotton Growers Block Republicans," *CQ Weekly Report,* September 23, 1995, p. 2877.

[29]Jerry Gray, "G.O.P. in House Defeats 2 Major Spending Bills," *The New York Times,* September 30, 1995, p. 7.

[30]Hanna F. Pitkin, *The Concept of Representation* (Berkeley: University of California Press, 1967), p. 208.

Index

About the Author ✍️

Burdett A. Loomis earned his PhD at the University of Wisconsin (Madison) and has taught at Indiana University, Knox College, and, since 1979, the University of Kansas. As professor of political science, he offers courses on legislatures, organized interests, and public policy.

Loomis has written and edited several books, most notably *The New American Politician* and *Time, Politics and Policies: A Legislative Year,* and four editions of *Interest Group Politics.* In addition, he directed the Congressional Management Project in 1984, which produced the initial edition of *Setting Course: A Congressional Management Guide.*

In 1975–1976 Loomis served as an American Political Science Association Congressional Fellow, working for then-Representative Paul Simon (D–Ill.). He also coached soccer at Knox College and established a Washington Internship program at the University of Kansas.